RIGHTEOUS
SELF DETERMINATION

THE BLACK SOCIAL WORK
MOVEMENT IN AMERICA

INPRINT EDITIONS
Baltimore

Righteous Self Determination: The Black Social Work Movement in America

Copyright © 2010 Patricia Reid-Merritt
Published 2010 INPRINT EDITIONS. All Rights Reserved.

Library of Congress Control Number: 2010925644

ISBN: 978-1-58073-043-3

Photos courtesy of: Molefi Asante, Jaclene Ashford, Gloria Batiste-Roberts, Shirley Better, Terrence Bradford, Maulana Karenga, Thaddeus Mathis, William Merritt,
The National Association of Black Social Workers, Toni Oliver, Pat Reid-Merritt

Cover design Nathaniel Taintor
Book design by Simona Jones

Printed by BCP Digital Printing, an affiliate company of Black Classic Press, Inc.

To review or purchase Black Classic Press and INPRINT EDITIONS books, visit: **www.blackclassicbooks.com.**

You may also obtain a list of titles by writing to:
Black Classic Press
c/o List
P.O. Box 13414
Baltimore, MD 21203

DEDICATION

To Cenie "Jomo" Williams
A fearless warrior, whose dedication
and commitment
to the struggle for freedom
and liberation for members
of the African American community
embodies the heart,
soul and spirit of the
National Association
of Black Social Workers.

FOREWORD

W hen I began teaching courses at Texas Southern University as an adjunct professor of social work in 2007, I immediately noticed that none of the required textbooks mentioned the National Association of Black Social Workers (NABSW). When discussing professional social work organizations, only the National Association of Social Workers (NASW) and the Council on Social Work Education (CSWE) were recognized. As a long-standing member of NABSW, I asked: "How could this be possible?" Moreover, I was concerned about my ability to convey the history of social work and social work activism in the United States when none of the texts addressed the organizational activities of Black social workers.

With the completion of this book, Dr. Patricia Reid-Merritt has made an important contribution to the social work literature by recounting the history of the Black Social Work Movement and the growth and development of the National Association of Black Social Workers. It is a book I have been waiting for since I began my career as a professor. It offers knowledge and insights about the actions and initiatives of a professional social work organization that has sustained itself for more than 40 years. It highlights the tremendous efforts of

Black social workers, both individually and collectively, to fight for social justice and to advocate for the social well-being of members of the African American community. The knowledge of this movement is vitally important to the next generation of social workers.

This book represents a timely blueprint for the social work profession as it faces the unique challenges of 21st century America, including economic turmoil, increasing income inequality, ethnic and racial conflict, declining employment and limited educational opportunities. The African American community has been especially hit hard by the changing social conditions in the nation. The profession of social work, through the various social agencies, communities and institutions in which it serves, must be prepared to assist individuals, families and communities to negotiate the turbulent social conditions that stand in the way of social progress. Unfortunately, in many cases, the profession continues to have limited understanding, appropriate tools and theoretical perspectives to address the unique challenges and problems that face Black America.

The observations and lessons chronicled here provide considerable guidance for those who have responsibility for the education and training of a new generation of social workers and community activists. What have we learned about the need for service in the Black community? How can we empower and give voice to those who continue the fight for freedom and social equality?

In a time and a place where the Black community's cries for freedom and liberation reverberated throughout the country, the founders of the National Association of Black Social Workers recognized that traditional social work assessments, methodologies and interventions were inadequate to meet the tasks they faced. They sounded the alarm: All was not well within the profession. It was social work's responsibility to seek and ensure the well-being of all members of our society and not merely certain segments. The Black community was underserved; its social needs were not a priority. With courage and little thought for the status they fought so hard to achieve, they set out to explore alternative approaches to social work practice and delivery of service to the Black community. These pioneers were located in a variety of settings, including schools, hospitals, child welfare agencies, public assistance programs and community service organizations. They involved themselves in grassroots organizations, welfare rights organizations, social, civic and professional organizations, and with others who shared their goals and objectives. Many of the activist and community-based strategies NABSW developed and pursued are now a standard part of social agency orientation and the curriculum of socially progressive schools of social work.

The impact of NABSW in the social welfare arena can in part be attributed to the visionary actions of its founders, who were also pioneers in their respective fields. Dr. Shirley Better, Dr. Betty Cleckley, Dr. Mary Davidson, Dr. Douglas Glasgow, Dr. Audreye Johnson, Dr. Georgia Parks, Joan Coleman, George Silcott and Garland Jaggers have left their mark on the profession and on those who followed in their footsteps.

Lastly, Reid-Merritt's discussion of African-centered approaches to social work practice reminds us of how far we have progressed in our search for effective methods of service intervention. Hurricane Katrina illustrated to people of African ancestry, and to the world, that there continues to be a need for African-centered collective advocacy. Without collective and organized advocacy, people are left to fend for themselves. As we read the history of this movement, we are reminded that as social workers our task is to be careful not to ignore or multiply the inequalities of the poor, sick, abused, disabled, abandoned or the oppressed, but to intervene in ways that lessen or remove them from harm.

NABSW has played an important role in shaping my professional career and, I'm certain, the lives of thousands of Black social workers across the nation. Reading this book has helped to strengthen my resolve to continue to work for fair and equitable treatment, social justice and social freedoms for all members of the Black community.

Gloria Batiste-Roberts, Dr.P.H., LMSW-AP
President, National Association of Black Social Workers

Acknowledgements

The writing of any book is a major undertaking. It is, at times, a very difficult, lonely process where one's thoughts, analysis and social commentary struggle to capture the true meaning and significance of the massive volumes of data and information before you. However, the arduous nature of this process is tempered by the freely given assistance of those who support your efforts and encourage you to complete your work.

There are so many individuals, too numerous to mention, who were instrumental in helping me to survive this process. I am grateful for all of their support, especially the members, both past and present, of the National Association of Black Social Workers (NABSW) who so graciously gave their time at focus-group meetings, telephone conversations and e-mail surveys to share their experiences. They were the social activists involved in the Black Social Work Movement. I could not have completed this work without their support. And I am also thankful to my colleagues and the administration at the Richard Stockton College of New Jersey who supported my sabbatical leave to engage in this project.

I owe a special thanks of gratitude to W. Paul Coates, publisher of Black Classic Press, and Natalie Stokes, associate publisher, who expressed enthusiasm from the very beginning of the project about the importance and merits of a book focusing on the organizing of Black social workers during the Black Freedom Movement. In what is known in the industry as a "short turnaround period," both Paul and Natalie worked tirelessly to make certain that this book was completed in time to celebrate at the 42nd annual gathering of NABSW in Philadelphia. I also wish to express my appreciation to Kenyatta Matthews whose copyediting skills are some kind of wonderful!

I am also indebted to NABSW's President Dr. Gloria Batiste-Roberts, who made historical research and publication one of the cornerstones of her administration. It was her persistence that helped to renew my interest in a research project that I began more than 15 years ago with my colleagues from Temple University, Dr. Thaddeus P. Mathis and Dr. Curtis Leonard. As educators, we talked for years about the critical need for books, articles and manuscripts that focused on the Black social work experience. Dr. Mathis, my longtime friend and mentor, remained my trusted reader and confidante throughout this process. His critical review and feedback of each draft chapter helped to clarify my approach and interpretation of the literature, and challenged me to remain balanced and objective as I struggled to detail many of my own personal memories of years of experiences with NABSW.

Two of my colleagues from the National Council for Black Studies (NCBS) also played a key role in helping to shape the direction of the manuscript. Dr. Molefi Asante reviewed earlier drafts of the manuscript and reminded me of the importance of the intellectual giants of the era, who so eloquently articulated the hopes and dreams of the Black community and influenced the philosophy and direction of Black social workers. Dr. Maulana Karenga worked diligently with me during the earlier stages of the writing process. He helped to ensure the accuracy of my work and often reminded me "not to leave any stones unturned." Dr. Karenga's feedback helped me to locate the Black Social Work Movement in its proper historical era, and he frequently discussed the importance of recording missing but historically significant aspects of the multitude of activities that occurred during the Black Freedom Movement.

I owe my sanity, and the high professional quality of the final manuscript, to my daughter, Christina. She was there for me every step of the way and never backed down when insisting that I was mangling the English language. I love you dearly. And to all of my family and friends, especially my husband, Bill, who had to endure another long process of distracted alienation of attention as I completed this process: You remain my heart, my soul and my inspiration.

Patricia Reid-Merritt

PART I

HISTORICAL ANTECEDENTS, ORGANIZATIONAL AND LEADERSHIP PARAMETERS

1

INTRODUCTION

During the height of the Black Power Movement, Black social work professionals, intimately familiar with the social and racial oppression that existed in the Black community, were confronted with a dilemma: continue to press for change within existing professional organizations, or separate themselves and organize a national network of Black social work activists whose primary commitment would be to serve and defend members of the Black community. Such was the case on May 15, 1968, at the 95th annual meeting for the National Conference on Social Welfare (NCSW) in San Francisco, California. The atmosphere was tense. The convention center was cramped with hundreds of professional social workers, mostly white, who were there to consider new approaches to help the "truly disadvantaged." As Black social workers entered the hall, the atmosphere stiffened and the temperature began to rise. Sweat and perspiration stains were visible signs of emotional stress. Roughly ten Black social workers, both male and female, rushed to the front of the auditorium,

1

commandeered the microphones and posted several "guards" near the stage to ensure that their unscheduled presentation was not interrupted. Amid derogatory racial slurs and remarks, Black social workers demanded that the NCSW and social workers in general begin to address the issue of "white racism," which was the leading impediment to social progress in the nation. Their pleas were ignored and a walkout ensued. The movement had started. It marked the beginning of the Black social worker's challenge to the profession of social work. In the coming years, Black social workers would mount an organized assault on social welfare problems that plagued the nation in general and the Black community in particular, challenging public and private agencies that attempted to service the Black community and beginning the process of transformation of Black social service workers from rootless caseworkers and government bureaucrats into culturally conscious advocates for social action, social justice and social change.

A Movement Defined

In the most simplistic and minimalist terms, a movement is defined as "a series of organized activities by people working, concertedly, toward some goal" (Webster, 2008:943). For Black social work professionals, the late 1960s marked the beginning of a series of organized, highly visible activities that eventually gave birth to what can only be described as the Black Social Work Movement (BSWM) in America. It is the author's contention that America did indeed experience such a movement, its ramifications felt by mainstream professional social work, social service agencies and the larger society. This book offers a review of the movement's history; identifies factors that contributed to its development and viability; assesses the movement's magnitude; and provides an analysis of the progress toward the movement's original goals and objectives.

Webster's broad, general definition of a social movement has limited utility for understanding the many parameters that define movement activity. Historians and political scientists offer numerous complex and oftentimes contradictory definitions of what constitutes a social movement. In the classical Marxist (Marx, Engels and Tucker, 1978) tradition, movements were grounded in the struggles of organized labor to overthrow and/or abandon the existing social order. However, contemporary definitions of social movements are more inclusive of the collective struggle of the community in numerous arenas.

Burns (1990:X) posits that social movements are "organized, nongovernmental efforts of large numbers of people to attain significant social and personal change." Evans and Boyte (1986:16) suggest that "social movements are ways in which the dispossessed and powerless have again and again sought simultaneously to revive and remember older notions of democratic participation, on the one hand, and on the other give them new and deeper meanings and applications." Fainstein and Fainstein (1974: XI), who focus on the phenomenon of the urban political movement, define social movements as "an emergent group that proposes to innovate and depends for its success upon the conversion of a social collectivity into action group." According to Schehr (1999:255), social movements emerge when "there is consensual agreement of purpose among group members; group members perceive their efforts as signifying alternatives to prevailing conditions; and group members struggle to re-appropriate dominant culture interpretations of political, economic and cultural phenomena." For Oberschall (1993:1), a pioneer in collective movement theory, social movements are an outgrowth of collective, not individual, action that challenge and threaten established groups with "its potential for being an agent of social change." Finally, Goldberg (1991:2), who provides an in-depth analysis of social movements in 20th century America, argues that a social movement is "a formally organized group that acts consciously and with some continuity to promote or resist change through collective action." Thus, for our purposes, social movements are broad-based expressions of social discontent and involve some form of collective behavior, which attempts to address situations that are viewed as unjust. They represent the collectivity of individuals who are oppressed, dispossessed, disenfranchised and generally "locked-out" of significant forms of participatory democracy and are willing to engage in struggle to bring about change.

There is little disagreement among scholars that the social upheaval that accompanied the modern day struggle for civil rights from the mid-1950s to the mid 1970s constituted the major and perhaps most significant social movement in the United States during the 20th century. This social movement, sometimes described as the Black Freedom Movement (1955-1975), had two main phases: the Civil Rights Movement (1955-1965) and the Black Power Movement (1965–1975). Other identifying terms—the Sit-In Movement, the Freedom Ride Movement, the Student Protest Movement, the Negro Revolution and the Black Liberation Movement—are also used to describe the activities of the era. However, in spite of the various labels attached to it and its varied pursuits, all of these activities were

3

part of a larger effort to secure civil rights, economic justice and social freedoms for African Americans. These many "sub-movements" focused, sometimes exclusively, on different issues ranging from integration of public facilities to the dismantling of legal discrimination. And while each sub-movement developed its own leaders, tactics, identity and direction, they simultaneously contributed to the overall goals and objectives of the larger movement (Franklin & Moss, Jr., 2000; Karenga, 2002; Meyer, 2006).

The organized activities of Black social workers should also be viewed as a sub-movement within the larger context of the Civil Rights and Black Power struggles. Factors that contributed to the organizing of Black social workers included: (1) feelings and experiences of racial oppression, which were shared by most Black Americans; (2) lack of participation, political power and exclusion from decision-making within professional organizations, schools of social work/ welfare and social welfare agencies; (3) direct contact and identification with the poor urban masses; and (4) location within the social welfare system, with the adjoining responsibility of finding ways to alter the distribution as well as the delivery of social welfare resources to members of the Black community.

History

The seeds for an organized movement of Black social work professionals were sown during the turbulence of the Civil Rights Movement and Black Power struggles of the 1950s and 1960s. Following years of formal protest, social agitation and legal maneuvers, the landmark 1954 Supreme Court decision in Brown vs. Board of Education of Topeka, Kansas signaled the beginning of the modern-day Civil Rights Movement in America (Clark, 1963; Franklin & Moss, Jr., 2000; Karenga, 2002). In the decade that followed, millions of Americans were affected as cries for social justice, freedom and equality reverberated throughout the nation and the world.

The persuasive discourse and social consciousness of the Civil Rights Movement spread throughout the nation. In general, and in the Black community in particular, literally hundreds of organized efforts to promote social change, social justice and professional and moral responsibility sprang forth. Among the more notable national efforts were the Southern Christian Leadership Conference (SCLC, 1957), the Student Nonviolent Coordinating Committee (SNCC, 1960), Us (1965) and the Black Panther Party (1966). In addition, already existing organizations were buoyed by the momentum of the Black Consciousness

4

Movement. The National Association for the Advancement of Colored People (NAACP, 1909), the Congress on Racial Equality (CORE, 1942) and the Nation of Islam (1930) enjoyed tremendous membership gains during this period (Malcolm X, 1965; Muhammad, 1965; McKissick, 1969; Bracey, 1970; Brisbane, 1970; Harding, 1970; Franklin & Moss, Jr., 2000).

In an effort to address the unique needs of the Black community and bring forth a Black agenda, Black caucuses emerged within existing professional associations, as "black professionals demanded a focus on their respective interests in the black community" (Sanders, 1970:278). When these caucuses were seen as having little effect upon white-dominated organizations, Black professionals created their own separate entities. Some examples of these include the National Conference of Black Lawyers (1968), the Association of Black Psychologists (1969), the National Black Nurses Association (1970), the Association of Black Political Scientists (1969) and the National Association of Black Social Workers (NABSW, 1968).

NABSW—Precedence, Purpose and Function

The organizing of Black social work professionals gained its initial impetus on the local level. Fed by fervent cries of Black unity, Black solidarity and Black consciousness, groups of Black social work students and professionals, "with little or no communication between them," began to organize in major cities like New York, Philadelphia, Chicago, Detroit and Los Angeles (Sanders, 1970; Johnson, 1988).

Regionally diverse groups of Black social workers began to voice their dissatisfaction with traditional social work at two major national gatherings: First, at the National Association of Social Workers (NASW) Social Action Workshop in Washington, D.C., in April 1968 and second, and most dramatically, at the 95th National Conference on Social Welfare (NCSW) in San Francisco in May 1968.

At the NCSW conference in San Francisco, Black social workers attempted to address, forcefully, the conference's major theme, "An Action Platform for Human Welfare" and its supplemental focus on "The Ghetto and the Politics of Welfare" (NCSW, 1968). Black social workers saw inconsistencies in a conference program that focused primarily on the social welfare needs of members of Black and urban communities but failed to include the voices of those most representative of the population. Moreover, Black social workers were concerned about the profession's long commitment to individualistic, intra-psychic, clinical approaches to social work treatment and social action. Since such approaches ignored structural inequalities in the social welfare system, they suggested that social work professionals, as represented by the NCSW, were not in tune with the pulse of the nation. The social realities and day-to-day problems faced by members of the Black community, including racism, poverty, sub-standard housing and inadequate health care, were not to be resolved with psycho-social, therapeutic treatment or by the socio-political analysis of white liberals who planned programs and policies without the input of the Black community. In addition, Black social workers identified "white racism" as the major impediment to social progress. All social workers, both Black and white, needed to confront this issue.

The actions of the Black social workers were a major challenge to the social work conference, described later by NCSW President Wayne Vasey as a tumultuous week filled with "demonstrations, walkouts, challenging of speakers and picketing" (NCSW, 1968:156). Black social workers were frustrated and disillusioned by the slow pace of change.

However, organized efforts by Black social workers to meet with NCSW officials to air their concerns and grievances at the conference were thwarted. According to Johnson (1978), a "walkout" of Black conferees resulted. Confronted with what was perceived as the continued insensitivity of white social workers in responding to the critical issues faced by members of the Black community, Black social workers joined forces in San Francisco to lay the foundation for NABSW.

Glide Memorial Church, situated across the street from the convention center, opened its doors to the Black social workers and served as a meeting site. As disgruntled conferees discussed their concerns about the insensitivity of NCSW and other social work organizations, the focus of discussion shifted to the need to create a national communication and action network of Black professionals employed within the social welfare system.

Following much debate, a steering committee of 12 Black conferees put forth a ten-point position statement demanding greater social action and advocacy within the formally organized social welfare system. The position statement criticized the NCSW's "white racist administrative and planning structure" for not including members of racial and ethnic minority groups. The statement further demanded that Black people "speak, write, research and evaluate" the Black community; that white social workers and the NCSW attack the problem of white racism as "America's number one mental health problem"; and that there be a public repudiation of "the current welfare system which serves as a tool of oppression of black people as well as the social workers providing the service" (NABSW, 1978). Additionally, Black social workers demanded that NCSW support the National Welfare Rights Organization (NWRO) and mothers and children who were assisted by Aid to Families with Dependent Children (AFDC). Point six of the position statement captured the essence and primary thrust of the emerging movement. It declared:

> *"We, the Black Social Workers of America, will no longer support social welfare systems and/or programs designed to maintain the unequal participation of the black community. Our accountability is to the black communities that we serve" (NABSW, 1978).*

The position statement concluded with the manifesto:

> *"We are committed to the reconstruction of systems to make them relevant to the needs of the Black community and are therefore pledged to do all we can to bring these things about by any means necessary"*
> *(Ibid, 1978).*

Upon their return to the convention site, Black conferees solicited the support and encouragement of their white counterparts, asking that they "sit and stand" with Black social workers to show their support (Ibid, 1978). Under adverse conditions, leaders of the movement again interrupted the morning plenary session and presented their demands to the conferees, but to no avail. Another "walkout" resulted and Black social workers returned to Glide Memorial Church to work toward further developing the vision of a national organization to address the social welfare needs of the Black community.

Thus, the national Black Social Work Movement was officially launched, creating one of the largest Black Nationalist, professional organizations in U.S. history. NABSW would serve as its organizational focal point. The movement was designed to: (1) create a national forum for Black human service professionals to discourse on social welfare issues confronting the Black community; (2) attack racist practices in America's social welfare system; (3) assume an advocacy role and remain accountable to the Black community; (4)

contribute to the transformation of mainstream social work; and (5) provide a foundation for the establishment of a culturally based Black social work practice. Self-determining, defiant and controversial, what lessons can we learn from its 40-year history?

Outline

This book shares the story of that movement by providing an historical analysis of the Black social work activity that occurred from 1968 to the present. It is divided into two main sections. **Part I—*Historical Antecedents, Organizational and Leadership Parameters*—**offers a framework for understanding the movement within the context of America's unique social history. Chapter One provides an introduction and overview, while Chapter Two offers historical background of the social and political activity that launched the movement in the mid-1960s. Chapter Three provides a detailed analysis of the emergence and development of the National Association of Black Social Workers, the focal point for movement activity. It also examines the movement's effort to create an innovative and sufficiently radical approach to social work practice. Chapter Four considers leadership development and implications for the growth and sustainability of a professional Black social work organization dedicated to a social activist agenda. Chapter Five examines the role of presidential leadership and the ongoing responsibility of each administration to maintain the organization and communication networks, thereby creating safe havens for Black social workers to develop professionally as they embraced their racial consciousness, racial identity and commitment to the Black community.

Part II—*Innovative Frameworks for Social Work Practice*—examines the efforts of those involved in the BSWM to create new projects, programs and models conducive to service in the Black community and at the same time provide a forum for the development of new approaches to Black social work practice. Chapter Six examines how developments in the Black intellectual community in areas as diverse as psychology, sociology, political science, economics, cultural nationalism and Africana Studies impacted the success of the movement. Chapter Seven considers how NABSW successfully established a national and international communication network among thousands of Black social workers, human service professionals/paraprofessionals, community organizers and social activists in the nation and the African Diaspora. Chapter Eight looks at critical social issues and major policy initiatives that thrust NABSW in the national spotlight, with a particular focus on family and child welfare policy and licensure of the social work profession. Chapter Nine examines the best models and approaches developed to meet the needs of the Black community through culturally specific models of social work practice. And finally, Chapter Ten provides a review of the success of the BSWM and questions the ongoing relevance of the BSWM, NABSW and Black professional organizations in the 21st century.

References:

Bracey, John H. et. al. (1970). *Black Nationalism in America*, New York: Bobbs-Merrill Company.

Brisbane, Robert H. (1970). The *Black Vanguard: Origins of the Negro Revolution*, 1900-1960, Valley Forge, PA: Judson Press.

Burns, Stewart (1990). *Social Movements of the 1960's: Searching for Democracy*, Boston: Twayne Publishers.

Clark, Kenneth (ed.) (1963). *The Negro Protest*, Boston: Harper Press.

Evans, Sara and Harry C. Boyte (1986). *Free Spaces: The Sources of Democratic Change in America*, Chicago: University of Chicago Press.

Fainstein, Norman and Susan S. Fainstein (1974). *Urban Political Movements: The Search for Power by Minority Groups in American Cities*, Upper Saddle River, NJ: Prentice Hall.

Franklin, John Hope and Alfred Moss, Jr. (2000). *From Slavery to Freedom*, New York: Alfred A. Knopf.

Goldberg, Robert A. (1991). *Grassroots Resistance: Social Movements in Twentieth Century America*, Belmont, CA: Wadsworth Publishing Company.

Harding, Vincent (1970). *Beyond Chaos: Black History and the Search for the New Land (Pamphlet)*, New York: Institute of the Black World.

Johnson, Audreye (1988). *The National Association of Black Social Workers, Inc: A History for the Future*, New York: NABSW.

Karenga, Maulana. (2002). *An Introduction to Black Studies*, Los Angeles: University of Sankore Press.

Malcolm X, (1965). *Autobiography of Malcolm X*, New York: Grove Press.

Marx, Karl, Friedrich Engels and Robert C. Tucker (1978). *The Marx-Engels Reader* (2nd Edition), New York: W.W. Norton & Co.

McKissick, Floyd (1969). *Three-Fifths of a Man*, New York: Macmillan.

Meyer, David (2006). *The Politics of Protest: Social Movements in America*, Oxford University Press, USA.

Muhammad, Elijah (1965). *Message to the Black Man in America*, Chicago: Muhammad's Temple of Islam, No. 2.

National Association of Black Social Workers (1968). Position Statement, New York.

National Conference on Social Welfare (1968). *Conference Proceedings*, Ann Arbor: University of Michigan Library.

Oberschall, Anthony (1993). *Social Movements: Ideologies, Interests, and Identities*, New Brunswick: Transaction Publishers.

Sanders, Charles (1970). "Growth of the Association of Black Social Workers, *Social Casework*," May, pp. 270 – 279.

Schehr, Robert (1999). "Intentional Communities, the Fourth Way: *A Constitutive Integration, in Constitutive Criminology at Work*, Stuart Henry and Dragan Milcvanovic (eds.), New York: State University of New York Press.

Webster, 2008. New World College Dictionary, 4th ed.

2

THE MOOD OF THE NATION

Historians (Franklin and Moss, 2000; Reeves, 2000; Hine, Hine and Harold, 2002; Loewen, 2007) have recorded that 20th century America moved beyond the age of discovery and ushered in a period of unprecedented growth and expansion. In the first half of the century, we took flight from Kitty Hawk, North Carolina, granted women the right to vote, participated in two World Wars and, with the Baby Boom generation, launched a population explosion that would have lasting rippling effects on every aspect of our society. During the second half of the century, we walked on the moon, got wired on the Internet and led the world in the conspicuous consumption of goods and services, proving that there were endless opportunities to supply both useful and frivolous products to a wanton and gluttonous nation. However, it was the social activism of the modern-day Civil Rights and Black Power movements that transformed the nation and gave hope and inspiration to other struggling and oppressed populations throughout the world. And just as the passion and the rhetoric of the movements swept through

African American communities, they also impacted Black professionals who felt the need to respond to the call for social action and social change. A brief historical review offers insight into the major factors that helped to shape the era.

Civil Rights and Social Change

The 1954 Supreme Court Decision in <u>Brown vs. the Board of Education of Topeka, Kansas</u> is often identified as the starting point of the modern-day Civil Rights Movement. America's practice of racial segregation, which was firmly rooted in the Jim Crow laws of the South, was finally struck down when the Supreme Court overruled the long-standing 1896 <u>Plessy vs. Ferguson</u> decision, which sanctioned legal segregation (Higginbotham, 1996). The long battle that led up to the Supreme Court victory resulted from a series of organized efforts by several organizations, including the National Association for the Advancement of Colored People (NAACP), which challenged segregation in the courts; the Congress of Racial Equality (CORE), which tested segregation in interstate bus travel with its use of "Freedom Riders" and launched sit-ins to protest segregation in public accommodations; and the Brotherhood of Sleeping Car Porters (BSCP), which, through union organizing, successfully challenged discriminatory practices in organized labor. These and other social and civil rights groups had been inching forward, challenging and dismantling segregation with small, incremental steps toward social justice. In fact, the success of the Civil Rights and Black Power movements are best viewed through the prism of historical activism that occurred periodically but consistently in the African American community from the period of enslavement to the present, specifically the activities that unfolded during the first half of the 20th century (DuBois, 1969; Berry and Blassingame, 1982; Franklin and Moss, 2000; Karenga, 2002).

There were a number of individuals and organizations that helped to lay the foundation for the modern-day Black Freedom Movement. Mary Church Terrell, Josephine St. Ruffin, Mary McLeod Bethune and other equally determined women were leaders of National Association of Colored Women (NACW), an organization founded in 1896 to uplift the role of Black women, youth and the community through education, civil rights and political advocacy (Giddings, 1984). With more than 300,000 members and local chapters throughout the country, NACW assumed leadership in the Black Women's Movement that gained prominence in the first decade of the 20th century.

14

Founded in 1900 in Boston, Massachusetts, Booker T. Washington's National Negro Business League sought to promote commercial and financial development among members of the Black community. This included small-business owners, private entrepreneurs, lawyers, bankers, real estate developers and others with economic interests (Harlan, 1983). In 1905, W.E.B. DuBois, William Trotter and John Hope were founding contributors to the Niagara Movement, an organization designed to fight racial segregation in all aspects of American life. Composed of Black members only, the group sought an aggressive approach to social change. White activists, hoping to be intimately involved in the struggle for civil rights and political liberties, took note and called for a national conference to discuss strategies for social change. According to Franklin and Moss (2000:319):

> "The young radicals of the Niagara Movement were invited to the conference, and most of them accepted. Among those who did not was Monroe Trotter, who was suspicious of the motives of white people. It was a distinguished gathering of educators, professors, publicists, bishops, judges, and social workers. Among those who participated were Jane Addams, William Dean Howells, Ida B. Wells, John Dewey, John Milholland, DuBois, and Oswald G. Villiard. Plans were made to establish a permanent organization, which came to be known as the National Association for the Advancement of Colored People (NAACP)."

The NAACP would become the leading voice in the civil rights struggle for most of the 20th century (Kellogg, 1967).

Dr. George Edmund Haynes (a social worker) and Mrs. Ruth Standish Baldwin joined forces in 1910 to form the interracial Committee on Urban Conditions Among Negroes. "A year later, the Committee merged with the Committee for the Improvement of Industrial Conditions Among Negroes in New York (founded in New York in 1906), and the National League for the Protection of Colored Women (founded in 1905) to form the National League on Urban Conditions Among Negroes. In 1920, the name was later shortened to the National Urban League" (nul.org/history). The mission of the National Urban League (NUL) was to aid large numbers of Blacks who were fleeing from the oppressive racial conditions in the South, only to discover prejudice and discrimination in the North. The NUL proved instrumental in bringing educational, economic and job opportunities to the new migrants from the South, as well as training Black social workers to work with the new residents (nul.org/history).

In the latter part of the 19th century and well into the 20th, Ida B. Wells-Barnett, with a sharp tongue and even sharper pen, utilized all of her available resources to mount an anti-lynching crusade throughout the North and the South (Karenga, 2002; Giddings, 2008). A founding member of NACW, Wells-Barnett spent a lifetime battling discrimination against Blacks and women. And from 1916 until his imprisonment in 1925, Marcus Garvey successfully organized and led the largest mass movement of African Americans in the United States and in the African Diaspora. The Universal Negro Improvement Association (UNIA), advocated self-determination, economic self-sufficiency and Black pride by refocusing the community's interest on African values and beliefs (Martin, 1976). Terrell, St. Ruffin, Bethune, Washington, DuBois, Trotter, Hope, Haynes, Garvey, Wells-Barnett and thousands of other individuals are representative of the many organized efforts initiated by Black Americans in their quest to gain greater civil rights and social freedoms.

However, considering the milestone events that occurred in the decade following the Brown decision, the modern-day Civil Rights and Black Power movements represented the golden age for the advancement of human and civil rights in 20th century America. And the South proudly laid claim to being the cornerstone of movement activity (McAdam, 1988; Halberstam, 1998).

Rosa Parks' well-known refusal to surrender her seat on a segregated bus in Montgomery, Alabama, sparked the yearlong Montgomery Bus Boycott and catapulted Martin Luther King, Jr., into the role as a prominent civil rights leader. Influenced by the philosophy and social activism of Mahatma Gandhi, Dr. King would serve as the architect for the nonviolent passive resistance movement that would soon engulf the nation (Franklin and Moss, Jr., 2000; King, Jr. and Carson, 2001).

Composed mainly of Black ministers in the South, the Southern Christian Leadership Conference (SCLC) was organized in 1957 following meetings in Atlanta, Georgia, and New Orleans, Louisiana. Dr. King would serve as the organization's first president. SCLC was committed to social activism through nonviolent confrontation. Educational equality and voter registration were key areas of focus (Hornsby, 1975; Garrow, 1986).

Inspired by the courageous acts of defiance by four students at the lunch counter in the Woolworth's Department Store in Greensboro, North Carolina,

Black college students launched sit-in demonstrations at segregated lunch counters throughout the South. The Student Nonviolent Coordinating Committee (SNCC), under the leadership of Ella Baker, was founded in North Carolina in 1960 as a liaison for student initiatives throughout the country (Hornsby, 1975). SNCC successfully orchestrated wide-ranging activities that involved both high school and young college students (Karenga, 2002).

On the 100th anniversary of the Emancipation Proclamation (which freed all those enslaved in the rebellious states of the Confederacy but not those enslaved in the Union states in the North), 250,000 demonstrators gathered for the 1963 "March on Washington for Jobs and Freedom" in the nation's capital. It was here that Dr. King delivered his famous "I Have a Dream" speech as prominent labor leaders, politicians, actors, ministers and lay people from every state in the Union looked on. These combined forms of protest forced the United States Congress to take action, eventually passing the Voting Rights Acts of 1957, 1960 and 1965, and the 1964 Civil Rights Act, some of the most significant civil rights legislation of its time (Franklin and Moss 2000; Karenga, 2002).

The southern initiative would eventually spread to the North and West as concerned citizens, both Black and white, traveled to and from the South to participate in voter registration drives, marches, sit-ins, pray-ins, kneel-ins and other forms of civil disobedience. The same types of protest activities were also taking place in cities like Chicago, Detroit, Los Angeles, Newark, New York and Philadelphia where, following years of the great exodus from the South, Blacks represented sizable population increases in urban metropolitan areas in what came to be known as Black ghettos. In the South, de jure segregation was a clear target; however, the de facto segregation that existed in the northern and western states, like Pennsylvania, New York, New Jersey and California, was equally as effective in limiting opportunities for jobs, housing, quality education and health care for African Americans. Many of these recently arrived migrants felt the need to focus their attention on the racism and social oppression that existed in their new places of residence.

The willingness of Black Americans to engage in the struggle for freedom and liberation began to proliferate around the nation. From a soapbox in Harlem, New York, Malcolm X (1965) rose to prominence as a spokesman for the Nation of Islam (NOI). Unlike the Christian faith, which historically had been home for the overwhelming majority of the Black population, the NOI was "an indigenous African American socio-religious movement that was founded in 1930 by W.D.

Fard in Detroit, Michigan, and developed by Elijah Muhammad" (Botwe-Asamoah, 2005). Its philosophies and practices were viewed as radical by some and mysterious by others. Malcolm X would be NOI's most visible spokesperson, and Muhammad Ali its most visible member.

Fannie Lou Hamer proved that she was "sick and tired of being sick and tired" when she challenged the very principles of participatory democracy at the 1964 Democratic National Convention in Atlantic City, New Jersey. Hamer lashed out at the Rules Committee after its members refused to seat delegates of the Mississippi Freedom Democratic Party (MFDP), which was created as a response to the all-white primary system that existed in the state of Mississippi. Hamer's eloquent stand against the injustices suffered by those in the southern states inspired thousands of poor disenfranchised individuals to join the fight for civil rights. In an atmosphere that spoke of the possibility for change, it heightened the Black community's hopes for progress (Mills, 2007).

In 1960, the youthful idealism of the Kennedy Administration also helped to usher in hopes for governmental actions that would forcefully address the demands for civil rights constitutionally guaranteed to all Americans, regardless of their place of residence. However, if change was going to come, it did not keep pace with rising levels of expectation in the Black community. And the 1963 assassination of the president suggested that there was a deeply imbedded resistance to social change—and the fight for equal rights for African Americans—that permeated the very moral fiber of the nation. The movement for civil and human rights, with its theme of nonviolent passive resistance that began in the South, would give way to more assertive demands for power and social change in the North and West. Ten years following the Supreme Court's affirmation of the 1954 decision by declaring in 1955 (Brown II) that desegregation should occur with "all deliberate speed," the Civil Rights Movement had ended (DuBois, 1969; Berry and Blassingame, 1982; Franklin and Moss, 2000; Karenga, 2002).

Black Nationalism and Black Power

While the Civil Rights Movement sought to convince the nation, through nonviolent passive resistance and moral suasion, that the time was right to grant full citizenship rights to all Americans, and especially those of African descent, the Black Power Movement spoke to the frustrated masses with calls for self-determination, self-defense and demands for "Freedom Now" (Carmichael and Hamilton, 1967; Karenga, 1997). Here, the Civil Rights and Black Power movements are viewed as two separate and distinct entities. While both focused on the need to elevate the rights and freedoms of Black people and other socially oppressed groups, the philosophies, leadership, methods and direction of each movement differed.

Throughout the nation, 1965 proved to be a watershed year for nonviolent social activism. The efforts of civil rights leaders in the South continued to lead to violent attacks on protestors. Police-sanctioned brutality—including beatings, water-hosing and dog attacks—was utilized to deter the activists; the Klu Klux Klan, unfettered by concerns of retribution by local police, juries, courts and justice officials, assaulted civil rights workers under the cover of sheets and darkness. On February 21, 1965 at the Audubon Auditorium in New York City, the articulate and charismatic voice of Malcolm X was silenced by assassin's bullets, but not before his views had profoundly impacted the Black community. (Conspiracy theories abounded as law enforcement struggled to identify those responsible for his death.) And the nation's most deadly social rebellion occurred in the streets of Watts in Los Angeles that August. Within a year, other urban areas would experience similar rebellions as social unrest became a permanent part of America's landscape. When Stokely Carmichael issued the call for "Black Power" at a mass rally in Greenwood, Mississippi, in the summer of 1966, a new movement for social justice surged past the old. The Black community and its leaders began to struggle with the new concept of Black Power (Pinkney, 2000). Its tone was more militant and more threatening to America's social establishment.

According to Karenga (2002:185), the integrationist Civil Rights Movement "was an effort to break down barriers to full participation in U.S. society and remove the penalties and other negative consequences of racial distinctions." However, the Black Power Movement, with its nationalist sentiments, stressed the need "to overcome racist oppression, making a clear distinction between individual acts of discrimination and racism as an institutional arrangement" (Ibid:190).

Hayes and Kiene (1997: 575) describe the Civil Rights Movement as a mainly southern, middle-class-oriented phenomenon, with a nonviolent inte-grationist ideology that eventually became a source "of increasing frustration and disillusionment for a broad segment of the black population in America's northern and western cities." They further argue that: "It was the perceived ineffectiveness of the Civil Rights Movement in the face of an intransigent anti-black power structure that served as a catalyst for the development of the more radical Black Power Movement..." (575).

For Franklin and Moss (2000), the Civil Rights Movement was one of the most significant events of the 20th century, which led to the transformation of America. They also note that the goals and activities of the Black Power Movement differed from those of the Civil Rights Movement that preceded it. They describe the shifting focus of the movements, stating that:

> *"The 1960s was a time of revolution among blacks in the United States. The decade began with high hopes. There was still the belief that the school desegregation decision would somehow bring about a truly democratic educational system in the United States. The sit-in movement, the freedom rides, the marches and demonstrations, and the voter registration drives, supported by untold numbers of whites as well as blacks, suggested that an entirely new and thoroughly effective approach to race relations was in the making. Slowly, then more rapidly, the optimism gave way to pessimism and even cynicism. It was not merely the opposition to equality on the part of the white citizens council or the Northern white mothers who railed against school desegregation or the white construction workers who bitterly opposed the employment of black journeymen and apprentices, but the feeling, bolstered by bitter experience, that justice and equality were not to be extended to blacks under any circumstances that created the gloomy atmosphere out of which the Black Revolution emerged"* *(Ibid:518).*

Stokely Carmichael (1967), Charles Hamilton (1967), Huey P. Newton (1972), Maulana Karenga (2002), Bobby Seale and Eldridge Cleaver (Jones, 1998) were among the young architects of the Black Power Movement. They were among the first to grapple with what Black Power meant in America. Their inspiration came from many sources, including the intellectual works and social activism of heroic Black leaders of the past like Nat Turner, Sojourner Truth, Harriet Tubman, Frederick Douglass, W.E.B. DuBois, Marcus Garvey and Malcolm X, who would become the most influential voice "for the growing consciousness and new militancy of black people" (Lester, 1968:91). In analyzing the views of Malcolm X, Fredrickson (1995) writes:

"Nonviolence without even the sanctioning of self-defense was in his view a betrayal of black manhood and a concession to white ideas of black submissiveness and inferiority. He also regarded integration as a surrender to white supremacy; for its aim of total assimilation into white society implied that blacks had nothing worth preserving. His affirmation of a positive black culture and identity that must be respected, preserved, and given some form of political expression put him in the mainstream of black nationalist thought extending back to Marcus Garvey, Bishop Turner, and Martin Delany—and it was the main source of his growing popularity among African Americans at a time when the dream of integration was beginning to fade" (Ibid: 290-1).

Historian Dorothy C. Salem (1997:370) argues that the Civil Rights Movement "suffered from its own success. Once the goals of legal desegregation had been won, the goals had expanded to include true change in power through the ballot box." Black Power was needed to effect immediate change, a slogan that stirred the passion to act, but one that meant many different things to many people. Fellow historian Tony Martin (1976: 360) suggests that Black Power was the revival of Marcus Garvey's "red, black, and green, his race pride, his self-reliance, his separatism, his anti-imperialism, and his revolutionary nationalism…," and Salem (1997:370) further notes that Dr. King described Black Power as an unfortunate term "because it tends to give the impression of black nationalism.." Christian (2005:144) describes Black Power as "the political, social, cultural, and economic cry for Black self-determination." However, it was Carmichael and Hamilton (1967:3) that captured the essence of the new movement in their well-articulated reading on Black Power, stating that it was "a call for black people in this country to unite, to recognize their heritage, and to build a sense of community."

Social Integrationism and Black Nationalism were two conflicting ideologies that divided the movement. For many, particularly those who had embraced the ideologies and tactics of the Civil Rights Movement, talk of Black Power, self-determination and social independence were difficult concepts to accept. The old, seasoned leadership of the NAACP, SCLC and the Urban League preferred the former; the young, more militant leadership of SNCC, CORE and the newly formed Us and Black Panther Party preferred the latter (Murray, 2005). Some

21

of the same social tensions that divided the integrationists from the nationalists, the young from the old, rural southerners from urban dwellers and the traditional middle-class from the newly empowered eventually led Black professionals to question their roles in mainstream white organizations. It was within this social context that Black professionals struggled to find their voice and set an agenda for professional activism that would address not only their professional needs but the needs of the entire Black community.

Organizing Black Professionals

If the discourse of the Civil Rights Movement—mainstream integration— caused Black professionals to raise questions about their role in professional white organizations, it was the heated passion and militancy of the Black Power Movement that caused them to take action and demand change.

Racism, discrimination, prejudice and poverty had been among the many factors that limited opportunities for Blacks to achieve the education needed to secure highly valued professional positions in the employment sector. At the beginning of the Civil Rights Movement, Blacks were severely underrepresented in every major profession (U.S. Census, 1980). In *Mainstreaming Outsiders* (1981), Blackwell summarizes the obstacles that Blacks faced in the professions, including medicine, dentistry, optometry, pharmacy, veterinary medicine, engineering, architecture, law and social work, from the period of emancipation until the civil rights era. If Blacks desired professional education in the South, the doctrine of separate but equal necessitated building and maintaining all-Black professional schools. This was especially true in the training of health care professionals. According to Blackwell:

> *"...at the turn of the century, a half dozen medical schools were established at historically black institutions. While they existed, they trained almost all black physicians, dentists, nurses, pharmacists and other health care professionals. The implementation of Plessy V. Ferguson's mandate for separate-but-equal assured resegregation, pernicious discrimination, and racial isolation in higher education. Philanthropic contributions declined during the first two decades of the twentieth century. Consequently, such institutions as Shaw University in North Carolina and Virginia Union University, both Church-dominated, were compelled to discontinue their professional*

schools in medicine and law. Negative recommendations from the
Flexner commission resulted in the demise of others. By 1915, Meharry
Medical College (Tennessee) and Howard University in the District of
Columbia remained as the two historically black professional schools
which offered medical and dental degrees" (Ibid:13-14).

Blackwell further explains that in the North, where integration was just a bit more palatable, Blacks gained admission to some of the prestigious white institutions but "confronted quota systems that seriously limited the number of blacks who could be admitted at any given time" (Ibid:14). In addition, Black college students, like women, often had their career choices restricted by prevailing norms and attitudes about the proper roles for those deemed subservient in a white-male-dominated society. Black women were encouraged to be teachers, nurses and social workers (Abel-Smith, 1975). These areas were dominated by women and were among the lowest paying professional occupations. For Black men, education was the leading choice, followed by social work, government, the ministry and mortuary science. However, during the civil rights decade (1960–1970), Blacks made significant gains in educational achievement and employment in the professions. A number of well-documented studies (Farley and Hermalin, 1972; Farley, 1977; Smith and Welch, 1977; Freeman, 1981; Collins, 1983; Hayward and Coverman, 1987; Grubb and Wilson, 1989; Fossett, Galle and Burr, 2001; Conrad, 2005) concluded that Blacks made advances in the attainment of high school diplomas and college and professional degrees, as well as diversifying their employment in various occupations. However, these same studies also point to the continued inequality and gaps in achievement in education and income between Blacks and whites. And in the professions, Reich (1981) has argued that Black professional gains during the civil rights decade occurred mainly in the female-dominated, lowest-paying professions like nursing and social work.

Buttressed by newly passed civil rights legislation, affirmative action policies and ongoing social protests, from 1960 to 1970 Blacks entered institutions of higher education in unprecedented numbers and upon graduation sought jobs in professional areas that had previously limited their opportunities. It was the existence and expansion of this new "critical mass" that provided the impetus for mass organizing among Black professionals.

Black Professional Predecessors

It is important to consider the numerous predecessors to the professional Black organizations that exploded on the scene in the late 1960s and early 1970s. Prior to the modern-day Civil Rights Movement, Black professionals clearly understood the need to form their own professional organizations in a society blatantly segregated by race. And many individuals decided to take up the challenge. For example, in 1895 in Atlanta, Georgia, at the famed Cotton States and International Exposition, a group of medical men met to form the National Negro Medical Association of Physicians, Surgeons, Dentists and Pharmacists (Kenney, 1933). The organization was the precursor to the National Medical Association, a group committed to promoting the collective interests of health professionals of African descent.

The National Bar Association (NBA) was formed by 12 Black lawyers in Des Moines, Iowa, on August 1, 1925, when fewer than 1,000 Black lawyers existed in the United States (nationalbar.org). Dedicated to justice and civil liberties for all, the NBA would focus its fight on the rights of Black and poor people, and would assist its members in developing their roles in the science and practice of jurisprudence.

White America's commitment to the separation of races also included those who were dead. Blacks were treated and died in segregated hospitals, funeralized in Black funeral homes and buried in all-Black cemeteries. Black funeral directors provided a valuable social service. In 1924, Black funeral directors organized under the name of the Independent National Black Funeral Directors Association. Following a merger with the National Colored Undertakers Association in 1940, the group officially was renamed the National Negro Funeral Directors Association and later the National Funeral Directors and Morticians Association, Inc. (nfdma.com).

During the civil rights era, Black professionals, whose numbers had begun to increase as a result of expanding equal education and employment opportunities, were encouraged to join mainstream professional organizations. And nowhere was this more apparent than in the profession of social work (Blackwell, 1981). However, frustrated by the efforts, or lack thereof, of these organizations to address the growing crisis in the Black community, Black professionals began to embrace a philosophy of self-help and self-determination. The time for change was now, and many Black professionals felt a social, if not moral, obligation to use their newly found consciousness and collective strength to fight for social change and social justice in their respective areas. The clarion call for self-determination, coupled with concerns about racism in predominately white organizations, led thousands of Black professionals to pursue a new course of action—the establishment of their own independent professional associations.

Black Professional Self-Determination

There are a number of examples of Black professionals who charted new paths and directions. In April 1968 in San Francisco, the Association of Black Psychologists (ABPsi) was established "to create a psychology of the black experience focused on improving the circumstances of black people." It was their firm belief "that a psychology created mostly by white middle-class men could not explain the situation of people of African descent, and moved to incorporate African philosophy and cultural experience into the creation of a new understanding of black psychology" (abpsi.org). Also in 1968, The National Association of Health Services Executives (NAHSE) organized as a nonprofit association of Black health care executives "for the purpose of promoting the advancement and development of Black health care leaders, and elevating the quality of health care services rendered to minority and underserved communities" (nahse.org). NAHSE was committed to improving the "quality, access and availability to health services and to expand educational opportunities in the field of Health Services Administration" (Ibid).

The National Conference of Black Political Scientists (NCOBPS) was organized in 1969 at Southern University in Baton Rouge, Louisiana. It aimed "to study, enhance, and promote the political aspirations of people of African descent, in the United States and throughout the world" by contributing to the resolution of the many challenges that Black people confront (ncobps.org).

In 1970, Charles D. Moody's invitation to several African American superintendents to attend a meeting at the O'Hare Marriott Hotel in Chicago, Illinois, resulted in the formation of an organization of Black school superintendents. At a follow-up meeting in Miami Beach, Florida, in August 1971, the superintendents formally organized the National Alliance of Black School Superintendents (NABSS). Two years later, the organization "voted to include administrators and other educational personnel in the organization and changed the organization's name to the National Alliance of Black School Educators" (NABSE). Members of NABSE would be committed to servicing school districts with predominantly African American populations (nabse.org).

Finally, following the annual meeting of American Nurses Association Convention in 1971, Black delegates met to express concerns about the status of health care for Blacks in America. It was there that the National Black Nurses Association (NBNA) was born. "The goal of the NBNA was to improve the health status of black people in the United States and to open positions of nursing education and nursing leadership positions for African Americans" (sdblacknurses.org). The mission statement called for "a forum for collective action by black nurses to investigate, define and advocate for the health care needs of African Americans and to implement strategies that ensure access to health care, equal to, or above health care standards of the larger society" (Ibid). The NBNA would establish local chapters throughout the country to help fulfill this goal.

Conclusion

It was in this environment of social turmoil amid conflicting ideologies and philosophies that a sense of social urgency flourished among Black professionals. Black human service workers, deeply involved in the day-to-day struggles of the Black community, may have experienced the greatest need to engage in social action. The Civil Rights Movement was all but dead; Black Power was in full force. The number of Blacks working in the field of social work had swelled by threefold. President Johnson declared a War on Poverty, providing resources to local community action groups in urban areas (Zarefsky, 2005). Black empowerment was viewed as an achievement goal. It was the combination of these forces that provided Black social workers with the strength and vision that was needed to separate themselves from mainstream social work organizations and lay the foundation for the National Association of Black Social Workers. And from that moment on, the profession of social work, and the social agencies in which it operated, would be forever altered by the challenging presence of those who demanded social change, which included input from a new generation of Black social work professionals.

References:

Abel-Smith, Brian (1975). *The History of the Nursing Profession*, Oxford: Heinemann Educational Publishers.

Berry, Mary Frances and John W. Blassingame (1982). *Long Memory: The Black Experience in America*, New York: Oxford University Press.

Blackwell, James E. (1981). *Mainstreaming Outsiders: The Production of Black Professionals*, Bayside, New York: General Hall, Inc.

Botwe-Asamoah, Kwame (2005). "The Nation of Islam," *Encyclopedia of Black Studies*, Molefi Asante and Ama Mazama, (eds.) Thousand Oaks, CA: Sage Publication, pp. 354 – 356.

Carmichael, Stokely and Charles Hamilton (1967). *Black Power*, New York: Vintage Books.

Carson, Clayborne and King, Martin Luther Jr. (2001). *The Autobiography of Martin Luther King, Jr.*, New York; Warner Books.

Christian, Mark (2005). "Black Power Movement," *Encyclopedia of Black Studies*, Molefi Asante and Ama Mazama (eds.), Thousand Oaks, CA: Sage Publication, pp. 144 – 146.

Collins, S. M. (1983). "The Making of the Black Middle Class," *Social Problems*, Vol. 30, pp. 369 – 382.

Conrad, Cecilia A. (2005). "Changes in the Labor Market Status of Black Women, 1960-2000," in *African Americans in the U.S. Economy*, Cecilia Conrad, John Whitehead, Patrick Mason and James Stewart, (Eds.) New York: Rowman & Littlefield Publishers, Inc.

DuBois, W.E.B. (1969). *Souls of Black Folk*, New York: New American Library.

Farley, Reynolds (1977). "Trends in Racial Inequalities: Have the Gains of the 1960s Disappeared in the 1970s?" *American Sociological Review*, Vol. 42, pp. 189 – 208.

Farley, Reynolds and Albert Hermalin (1972). "The 1960s: A Decade of Progress for Blacks?" *Demography*, Vol. 9, pp. 353 – 370.

Fossett, Mark A., Omer R. Galle and Jeffrey A. Burr (2001). "Racial Occupational Inequality, 1940-1980: A Research Note on the Impact of the Changing Regional Distribution of the Black Population," *Social Forces*, Vol. 68:2, December 1989.

Franklin, John Hope and Alfred Moss, Jr. (2000). *From Slavery to Freedom*, New York: Alfred A. Knopf.

Fredrickson, George M. (1995). Black Liberation: *A Comparative History of Black Ideologies in the United States and South Africa,* Oxford: Oxford University Press.

Freeman, R. B. (1981). "Black Economic Progress After 1964: Who Has Gained and Why?" in *Studies in Labor Markets*, Sherwin Rose, ed., Chicago: University of Chicago Press, pp. 247 – 294.

Garrow, David (1986). Burning the Cross: *Martin Luther King and the Southern Christian Leadership Conference*, 1955-1968, New York: Morrow.

Giddings, Paula (1984). *When and Where I Enter: The Impact of Race and Sex in America*, New York: William Morrow and Co.

_____ (2008) Ida: *A Sword Among Lions: Ida B. Wells and the Campaign Against Lynching*, New York: Harper Collins.

Grubb, W. Norton and Robert H. Wilson (1989). "Sources of increasing inequality in wages and salaries, 1960-80," *Monthly Labor Review*, April 1989, pp. 3 – 13.

Halberstam, David (1998). *The Children*, New York: Random House.

Harlan, Louis B. (1983). *Booker T. Washington: The Making of a Black Leader*, New York: Oxford University Press.

Hayes, III Floyd W. and Frances A. Kiene (1997). "The Black Panther Party", in *A Turbulent Voyage: Readings in African American Studie*s, Floyd W. Haynes, III, ed., San Diego: Collegiate Press.

Hayward, Mark D. and Shelley Coverman (1987). "Change in the Racial Composition of Occupations, 1960-1970: How Much Progress for Blacks?" *Sociological Perspectives*, Vol. 30, No. 2. April 1987, pp. 115 – 142.

Higginbotham, Leon (1996). *Shades of Freedom: Racial Politics and Presumptions of the American Legal Process Race and the American Legal Process*, Volume II, Oxford: Oxford University Press.

Hine, Darlene Clark, William C. Hine and Stanley Harold (2002). *The African American Odyssey*, 2nd ed., Upper Saddle River, NJ: Prenctice Hall.

Hornsby, Alton, Jr. (1975). *The Black Almanac*, Woodbury: Barron's Educational Series.

Jones, Charles (ed.) (1998). *The Black Panther Party Reconsidered*, Baltimore: Black Classic Press.

Karenga, Maulana (2002). *An Introduction to Black Studies*, Los Angeles: University of Sankore Press.

_____.(1997). *Kawaida: A Communitarian African Philosophy*, Los Angeles: Sankore Press.

Kellogg, Charles Flint (1967). *NAACP: A History of the National Association for the Advancement of Colored People*, Baltimore: John Hopkins Press.

Kenney, John A. (1933). "Some Notes on the History of the National Medical Association," *Journal of the National Medical Association*, August (25) 3, pp. 97 –105.

Lester, Julius (1968). *Look Out Whitey! Black Power Gon' Get your Mama*, New York: The Dial Press.

Loewen, James W. (2007). *Lies My Teacher Told Me: Everything Your American Textbook Got Wrong*, New York: Touchstone.

Martin, Tony (1976). *Race First*, Westport: Greenwood Press.

McAdam, Doug (1988). *Freedom Summer*, New York: Oxford University Press.

Mills, Kay (2007). *This Little Light of Mine: The Life of Fannie Lou Hamer Civil Rights and the Struggle for Black Equality in the Twentieth Century*, Lexington: University of Kentucky Press.

Murray, Christopher (2005). "The Black Panther Party for Self-Defense", *Encyclopedia of Black Studies*, Molefi Asante and Ama Mazama, (Eds.) Thousand Oaks, CA: Sage Publication, pp. 135 – 137.

Newton, Huey (1972). *To Die for the People*, New York: Random House.

Pinkney, Alphonso (2000). *Black Americans*, 5th ed., Upper Saddle River, NJ: Prentice Hall.

Reeves, Thomas C. (2000). *Twentieth Century America: A Brief History*, Oxford: Oxford University Press.

Reich, Michael (1981). *Racial Inequality: A Political-Economic Analysis*, Princeton: University Press.

Salem, Dorothy C. (1997). *The Journey: A History of the African American Experience*, Dubuque, Iowa: Kendall/Hunt Publishing.

Smith, James P. and Finis R. Welch (1977). *Closing the Gap: Forty Years of Economic Progress for Blacks*, Rand Publishing.

U.S. Census Bureau (1980). *Statistical Abstract of the United States*: Black Americans, www.census.gov/prod/2007pubs/08abstract/vitstat.pdf.

Zarefsky, David (2005). *President Johnson's War on Poverty: Rhetoric and History*, Tuscaloosa, AL: University of Alabama Press.

Websites

www.abps.org

www.nabse.org

www.nahse.org

www.nationalbar.org

www.ncobps.org

www.nfma.org

www.nul.org

www.sdblacknurses.org

3

THE NATIONAL ASSOCIATION OF BLACK SOCIAL WORKERS: THE MOVEMENT'S FOUNDATION

As introduced earlier, the National Association of Black Social Workers (NABSW) was founded in May 1968 in San Francisco. Prior to the closure of the National Conference on Social Welfare (NCSW), Black social workers decided to separate themselves from the mainstream professional organization and began work on the establishment of NABSW. This task was made easier by organized efforts of Black welfare, government and private agency workers in various cities who, as a result of both the Civil Rights and Black Power movements, began to question their roles as agents of social change or social control. Unique to their own individual setting, these initiatives shared common themes and goals, as each area focused on the organizing of Black social workers.

Local Initiatives

In *That Rare Moment in History,* Garland Jaggers (2003) describes the experience that he and other Black social workers were having in Detroit, just one year prior to the San Francisco walkout:

> *"It was on a Friday night in March 1967 at Louis Bates' home on Pinehurst Street in northwest Detroit when he and I had a conversation. We bemoaned the fact that there were very few Negroes in key positions here in Detroit's social welfare systems. A white fellow graduate from Wayne State University's School of Social Work became a director of an agency upon graduation from school. Louis Bates and I struggled to get promoted to supervisor and still struggled to be aware of promotional opportunities. Was it because we were Negro that promotions came so slowly and promotional opportunities were hush-hush in most agencies?*

> *Whatever the reason Louis Bates and I spoke of our belief in a need to organize the Negro male Social Workers in Detroit (sic). With this focus, we had several meetings at my home on Cheyenne with a small group of Negro male Social Workers. With the aid of this group we compiled a larger list of Negro male Social Workers in Metro-Detroit and set a time and place for our first open meeting. Seventy-five invitations were mailed. The organizing of Black Social Workers had begun" (2003:13-14).*

Concerned about the lack of Black involvement in supervisory and management positions in New York City's Welfare Department, Black social welfare workers organized a group called CHARMA (an acronym that, after 40 years, no one recalls the meaning) as a forum to discuss issues related to working conditions. In addition to concerns about their employment status, Black workers sought greater participation in decision-making as it related to client service. Their concerns were not simply limited to issues inside of the Department of Welfare. The status of Black workers, families and the community was of grave concern as well. And the inability of social work to be at the forefront of social change activities caused many to voice their dissatisfaction with the helping profession.

At the 1966 National Association of Social Workers (NASW) conference held in New York City at the Hilton Hotel, representatives from CHARMA approached keynote speaker Whitney Young, a social worker, and inquired why he would agree to speak at a gathering of white social workers that denied leadership positions to Blacks, and for an organization that had refused to take a stronger stance on civil rights issues. According to one participant (who wishes to remain anonymous), "A group of male workers from CHARMA confronted Young at the conference and prohibited him from taking the stage until he responded to our concerns." While many of the city's Black welfare caseworkers were college graduates without professional social work degrees, those with master's level training had also begun to organize themselves to protest covert forms of racial discrimination that restricted opportunities for workers and the communities they were trying to serve. On September 5, 1967, the *New York Times* reported:

> *"Negro social workers have formed their own association to combat the discrimination they charge exists in 'a subtle yet significant fashion' throughout the New York social work community.*

> *The organization, known as the Association of Black Social Workers, was formed late in June. It says it has already recruited more than 400 members, all professional social workers with master's degrees."*

Black social workers in New York City were the first group in the nation to use the title Association of Black Social Workers. T. George Silcott assumed leadership of the new organization. Silcott had recently been appointed as an associate professor at the New York University Graduate School of Social Work. In addition to his activism in New York, he would also assume a major leadership role in the national movement.

According to the *Times* article, Black social workers in New York City expressed concerns about the social work profession's lack of social activism; the limited number of Blacks enrolled in graduate schools of social work; the lack of an inclusive curriculum that addressed the special needs and concerns of Black people; social agencies' neglect of the Black community; and the inability of Black professionals to obtain leadership roles in private social service organizations. These issues would be echoed in other major cities and later magnified on the national level.

The mood in Chicago was similar to that in Detroit and New York City. James Craigen was a founding member of the Concerned Youth Welfare Workers, which later would become part of the Black Catalysts, an organization of professionals primarily employed by the Chicago Commission on Youth Welfare. Craigen, an MSW graduate who had received his degree from Atlanta University in 1962, was employed as a supervisor in the Near-North Unit. Like many of his colleagues, Craigen was one of a growing group of Black professionals hired by the city to work almost exclusively in Black neighborhoods. In early January 1968, Mayor Richard J. Daley (often referred to as the "last of the big city bosses") required a daily report from the Division of Community Services (Royko, 1988; Cohen and Taylor, 2001). These reports kept Daley informed on what was going on in the Black community. Troubled by the constant surveillance tactics, Black supervisors questioned if these practices were being utilized to "spy" on the Black community. According to Craigen (2009):

> *"We started to talk to one another about the Mayor's daily reports. As supervisors, we were college and masters' educated workers. We were very intelligent people who wanted to work toward the empowerment of Black people. We started meetings to discuss our concerns. The group, mostly males because the city was very chauvinistic in its hiring and didn't want females in the supervisory positions, started writing the White Papers to reflect on Black issues and concerns. These White Papers were a statement of core values and explored what we believed to be programming needs in the Black community.*

> *As our movement grew, we expanded to include other workers. We set up a taskforce to determine the actions we would take. This all culminated in a very tense meeting at the Vinzant Restaurant with the city's director of the Youth Commission. Following his derogatory remarks about Martin Luther King, Jr., who had been assassinated*

in April, we were in no mood to be apologetic or conciliatory. We decided to adopt a strategy of advocacy, committed to a tactic of 'all for one and one for all.' Specifically if one were fired, we would all resign. When Taylor Griffin, the systems analyst, was fired, it provided a catalyst for change in Chicago. We all submitted our resignations."

Chicago was just one of many urban cities in the nation confronted with civil unrest and social turmoil generated by the Black Freedom Movement (Franklin and Moss, 1994; Karenga, 2002). Finding ways of "keeping the lid on" poor Black communities in the summer heat was a major concern. The Black supervisory personnel at the Youth Commission were desperately needed. Craigen (2009) further noted:

"We wanted to make the agency more effective in servicing the Black community. We put our demands on the table and made it clear that we would only negotiate with Mayor Daley to rehire all who resigned, fire the director, and remove the spy role from our agency."

By mid July, all had been rehired. It was a sweet victory for the youth welfare workers who successfully achieved all of their demands and continued their social organizing activities in the city in conjunction with other Black organizations. By the time the campaign was over, the 13 supervisors had been joined by more than 200 additional workers, part-time and full-time, and the Concerned Youth Welfare Workers would become part of the Black Catalysts. In fact, it was the Association of Black Catalysts that held the first national gathering of Black social workers prior to the first official conference of NABSW. Jaggers (2003:32) notes:

"...the name N.A.B.S.W. was not yet adopted as a permanent title, rather the group was sometimes referred to as the Association of Black Catalysts, a name suggested in Washington, D.C., by the group which planned the confrontation in San Francisco in May. The conference held in Chicago from August 30 to September 1 was hosted by the Black Catalysts of Chicago yet organized by the steering committee of T. George Silcott, William Robertson, Creige Beverly, Audreye Johnson, Charles D. Hamilton, John Franks and Garland Jaggers."

Within a year, the group had fully connected with the national movement and changed its name to the Chicago Association of Black Social Workers. James Craigen, Karim Childs, Barbara Bacon, Jerome Steverson and Audreye Johnson were among the founding members. All would play significant leadership roles in the years to come. The *White Papers*, which had been developed to guide the actions of Black social welfare workers in Chicago, would also be used as a framework to shape the direction of NABSW.

In Philadelphia, Black social workers organized the Alliance of Black Social Workers under the leadership of William Meeks, Laverne McCummings and Audrey Russell. Meeks and McCummings travelled to Chicago in July 1968 to meet with the newly organized group of Black social workers and offered Philadelphia as the first national conference site (Johnson, 1991). Russell organized chapter members around child welfare issues, specifically the placement and adoption of Black children. The focus on child and family welfare would become a central driving issue for the organization, undergirding the basic values of family preservation. Improving the quality of life for children and families was a dominant theme in social work and drew many to the profession.

Black social workers in southern cities were also engaged in organizing. Lou Beasley was a community activist in Little Rock, Arkansas, and Little Rock was no stranger to social activism. The city, the battleground for the fight to desegregate Central High School, played a key role in the Civil Rights and Black Power movements (Kirk, 2007). Prior to the San Francisco meeting, they, too, had organized themselves into an activist professional association as more and more workers expressed concern about their roles as service providers in the city.

The Association of Black Social Workers of Greater Los Angeles held its first meeting in March 1968. Shirley Better was one of its original founders, as well as a founder of the national organization. Better was an experienced clinical social worker and administrator. She had received her MSW from the University of Michigan, where she specialized in psychiatric social work. Within a few years, Better relocated to Los Angeles because she wanted to take a more active role in the civil rights struggle. When an offer was made to accept a position as director of social services at the Westminster Neighborhood Community Center, she embraced the opportunity to work in one of the most troubled areas of the city. Work at the settlement house was good, but the pace of progress was slow. According to Better (2009):

"Everything was happening. We had no knowledge of other Black social workers organizing around the country. We were in Watts. We had made it past the riots, but we were feeling frustrated. We witnessed all the problems that people were experiencing on the streets. Police brutality was a problem, unemployment was a problem, and housing was a problem. It was difficult to meet people's needs. And the social work profession was not helping the way we felt it should. We felt very disillusioned and felt compelled to do something. Five of us got together and held a meeting: Horace Austin, Georgia Parks, Leonard Mackrel, Barbara Williams and me. And that's when we declared ourselves as the Association of Black Social Workers of Greater Los Angeles. We were educated professionals. We all had MSWs. We knew what we were up against."

Black professional social workers (MSW) were members of a very select class. They had made the decision early in their careers to become social workers and had benefited from the opportunities offered to Blacks in college and at some graduate schools of social work, including Howard and Atlanta universities, which produced the largest numbers of Blacks trained in the profession (Blackwell, 1981). And, due to the very nature of the profession, most social workers were employed, rather exclusively, in nonprofit and governmental agencies. Government work on the local, state and federal levels had gained favor with Blacks following Roosevelt's Executive Order 8802 in 1941 to end employment discrimination in federal hiring (Franklin and Moss, 2000). In the two decades that followed, Blacks came to regard government work, as well as work in the nonprofit sector, as prime places of employment. However, they were still acutely aware of the existence of racism and discrimination by individuals, institutions and society.

Race and Racism

Feelings of and experiences with racism and discrimination were common themes in the Black community. Racism, defined as the inherent belief in the superiority of one group over another (Rogers and Kitano, 1970) was rampant in the United States, affecting every social and economic stratum. America's racist history is extremely well documented and includes: efforts to classify all African Americans as subhuman; denial of basic human and civil rights to people of African descent; destruction of African and African American culture, families and communities; restriction of social, economic and political opportunities; and a host of other devastating actions (Franklin and Moss, 2000; Karenga, 2002; Asante, 2003; Better, 2007). While Blacks made significant social, educational, political and economic gains during the brief period identified as Reconstruction (DuBois, 1968), the historical burden of enslavement, Jim Crow, de facto segregation and social oppression remained formidable obstacles to overcome for every Black American. From the later part of the 19th century and well into the 20th, social progress in the Black community moved forward at a snail's pace. The Black community made numerous attempts, both individually and organizationally, to push for the elimination of racist and discriminatory practices in U.S. society.

Education, however, was viewed as a major means to social and economic mobility and a primary tool in the fight against racism. Black families dreamed of sending their children to high school and college as a way of avoiding poverty and discrimination. Blacks with high school diplomas and college degrees saw their lives improve over their brothers and sisters in the local community but witnessed discriminatory practices in their places of employment. Black high school graduates earned less than their white counterparts. College graduates earned the equivalent of white males with high school diplomas (Sitkoff and Franklin, 2008). And for those in professional fields, opportunities for promotion and advancement were limited. Many workers became frustrated, and rightfully so. As the Civil Rights and Black Power movements spawned activities in small and large cities, and in rural communities as well, signs of restlessness and agitation emerged simultaneously across the nation. Blacks who had successfully maneuvered themselves through the system of higher education were seeking professional careers. Social work appeared ideally suited for those wishing to establish themselves in a career as a paid social advocate. Given their location, advanced levels of educational achievement and the general mood of the nation, it is not surprising that Black professional social workers and government and welfare workers were among the first to voice their dissatisfaction with the system and to begin organizing for social action.

The Call to Social Work

One could easily argue that the initiators of the BSWM were among the most dedicated to the values, philosophy and mission of the social work profession. Indeed, based on various written and verbal accounts, Black social workers took the oath of the profession very seriously.

The social work profession emerged as a 20th century phenomenon, born out of a complex set of social and human needs resulting from the forces of immigration and urbanization (Ambrosino, Heffernan, Shuttlesworth and Ambrosino, 2007; Kirst-Ashman, 2009; Zastrow, 2009). The first professional social work class was offered at Columbia University, New York, in 1898 (NASW, 1977). From the very beginning, the profession appealed to those with idealistic visions of a society that responded to very basic and necessary social and human needs.

Social work's professional values hold strong appeal to those who believe in creating freedom and equality for all in a socially just society (Miley, O'Melia and Dubois, 2009). These value statements are introduced and later reinforced in classes in the schools of social work on the graduate and undergraduate levels and include:

- Inherent rights and dignity of all people
- Right to self-determination
- Societal responsibility to provide resources
- Commitment to social change and social justice

It was the social work profession that pledged itself to work on behalf of children and families; to fight societal abuses that led to social disadvantages; to help uplift the poor; and to seek proper treatment and remedies for those in need. Whether one attended one of the two historically black colleges' School of Social Work or a mainstream institution, the message of the profession was clear: Social work would lead the fight for a socially just society (NASW, 2008). In addition to the well-known historical figures and advocates of the profession like Mary Richards, Jane Addams and Frances Perkins, civil rights advocates Whitney Young, Dorothy Height and Shirley Chisholm also claimed membership in the profession. Young, socially conscious Black students were intrigued by the possibilities that existed within the profession of social work.

NABSW: Formative Years

In the first year of existence, NABSW, gathering strength from individuals and loosely formed organizations throughout the nation, experienced a meteoric rise in the social welfare community. Their members, potential members and those wishing to be associated with the Movement, emerged as some of the most militant voices in their local communities.

Following a series of organizational meetings to plan and develop a national structure, the first "National Conference of Black Social Workers: The Black Family" was held in Philadelphia, less than one year after the NCSW walkout. The conference was hosted by one of the original local affiliates, the Philadelphia Alliance of Black Social Workers (NCBSW, 1969). Philadelphia, founded by statesman William Penn, was not simply the nation's first capital and home to the Liberty Bell. It was a city with an activist spirit, from the organized efforts of Quakers in the Abolitionist Movement to the First Annual Planners Conference for Black Liberation, which was held at the University of Pennsylvania in March 1968 (NCBSW, 1969; Chandler and Mason, 2004; Slaughter, 2008). An impressive array of Black scholars and leaders in the social work profession were invited as presenters, including Janice Porter, William K. Wolfe, Edward W. Robinson, Fay Stevenson, James M. Garnes, Bob Taylor, Solomon Gethers, Lawrence E. Gary, Jessie McClure, Jaggers, Silcott and Walter Palmer. Prominent sociologist Dr. Andrew Billingsley and psychiatrist Dr. Alvin Poussaint delivered keynote addresses.

Over a three-day period, conferees struggled to clarify the purpose and goals of the new association and examine the major issues confronting Black America. They continued to develop the organization's infrastructure and jockeyed for leadership positions. Jaggers was designated the national coordinator, with a host of other local leaders serving as regional representatives, including Norman Johnson, Shirley Jones, Milton Robinson, Robert Williams, Arthur Herman, Horace Alston and Betty Cleckley. It is interesting to note that in the first roster listing 50 regional representatives, at least 20 were women (Jaggers, 2003). In the years to come, questions surrounding leadership, gender and regional representation would be key areas of struggle for the organization.

A series of workshops were held, categorized under the following seven topics: Separation; Impediments; Strengths; Economical and Political Responsibilities; Existing Resources; New Resources; and Toward a New Social Work Theory.

Porter encouraged conferees to "respect and accept our differences and come to love our uniqueness about being black, which is a fortifying and unifying process to overcome the process of separation" (NCBSW, 1969:11). Wolfe explored the mounting divide between middle-class Black professionals and the less fortunate and much poorer working class. Robinson deplored the racist training received by Blacks in the public schools and in schools of social work, and advocated for schools "controlled by us, manned by us, with textbooks written by us, in our places protected by us" (Ibid:13). Stevenson spoke to the state of dependency in the Black community that had been created and maintained by social control agents in support of the white power structure, including policemen, politicians, teachers and social workers.

For Garnes, too many Black social workers had been mesmerized by the new social work notion of "strengths." He warned that such a concept was a mere

> *"value judgment that gives no frame of reference for understanding the black family" (Ibid:26). Taylor utilized the newly formed Welfare Rights Organization to describe how poor Black mothers, with less than a high school degree, have learned how to "wheel and deal with the welfare department in such a way that would make us envious" (Ibid:33). And he further questioned: Is that not strength?*

Gethers understood the need for Blacks to control the resources in their community, particularly those surrounding the social welfare agencies. However, he stressed that:

> *"The building of the black community in the final analysis means more than black people assuming control of political, economic, and social institutions as they presently exist. It means restructuring, reordering, and redirecting these institutions in accordance with values that will make it possible to build a more humane society" (Ibid: 45).*

Attempts by Black social workers to address the economic and political responsibilities for Black professionals committed to the goals of freedom and liberation for all members of the Black community were early indicators that the BSWM would not limit itself to practice issues. For the Movement's members, the social oppression and discrimination that they witnessed in the Black community through their work with clients were inextricably linked to America's broader social structures. Black social workers were interested in attacking a broad array of social problems and issues, leaving some to question whether the newly formed group was attempting to be a professional association or a Civil Rights/Black Power organization. Sanders (1970), in an early assessment of the growth of the New York Association of Black Social Workers (ABSW), identified several "constraints" that were potential impediments to the development and maintenance of a national base. He specifically questioned whether social workers could organize on the basis of "blackness" and whether such attempts would produce a national group that would be goal-specific and financially sound.

Based on an early analysis of the New York City experience, Sanders (1970) concluded that by attempting to address all the problems within the social welfare system, the organization had undertaken a Herculean task. He noted that the issue of "blackness" and how best to represent the Black experience was emotionally charged, producing both cohesion and conflict. Moreover, the association's desire to remain connected with the masses produced a broad-based policy of inclusion rather than exclusion, diluting the organization's ability to target a specific population for recruitment purposes. Furthermore, discontinuity, that is, the inability of members to follow through on assigned tasks and responsibilities, appeared to be an early sign of organizational disintegration. Finally, the lack of sufficient resources, specifically greater mobilization of voluntary support and funding sources, hindered the growth of the association, and innovative approaches to resource development remained unexplored. Sanders warned that ABSW needed conceptual clarity on goals and objectives and a clear analysis of the possibilities of success and failure. Moreover, the organization needed to prioritize its activities and develop a deliberate strategy to attack institutional racism. Sanders' assessment of the New York City experience was cautiously foreboding, and the national organizers were aware of the many obstacles that stood in the way of success.

The preparation of racially and social conscious Black social workers was also a major concern at the first national gathering. The need for educational and training programs relevant to the needs of Black students and the community was the focus of a workshop led by Gary and McClure. Social work students were demanding a change in the "content, the structure, and philosophy of social work education" (NCBSW, 1969:50). While some variations in curriculum were under way to include course content on Black history, culture, families, etc., Gary and McClure concluded that a "major modification within the system" would be needed to alter the current course. Workshop participants called for additional funding for Black students; graduate school admission based on experience; faculty appointments for Black people with "relevant" experience; a Black curriculum developed by Blacks; the inclusion of Black people on university governing boards; and the creation of a Black social work journal.

Perhaps the highlight of the first gathering was the call for a brand-new approach to the practice of social work in the Black community. As summarized in the first volume of the Association's Conference Proceedings, the conferees collective efforts were "dedicated toward the development of a new social work theory based on liberation rather than adjustment" (Ibid: I). Jaggers, T. Silcott and Palmer discussed the need for developing new theoretical approaches to social work practice. They sought to develop a new set of values to guide Black social workers in their practice and committed themselves to build a solid foundation for the new association. Using the language of liberation, Laverne McCummings, Chairman of the Philadelphia Alliance, proclaimed:

> *"If it is clear that the practice of social work by blacks for blacks must operate from a new theory, then this theory of liberation must be fully and unquestionably developed to its fullest by those blacks. This new social theory must not be arrived at by outside sources who would distort the true meaning of liberation. Further, the projection of new values must have as a necessary component, a clear definition of what those values propose to be. Again, it would be chaotic for blacks to begin to talk of a new set of values and to then allow whites to define those values for us" (NCBSW, 1969:iv).*

Self-determination was the operative word. The need for self-examination within the confines of a racially conscious Black community was evident. Separate, and, if necessary, socially defiant actions were merely prerequisite components of what Cross (1971) describes as a much needed Negro to Black conversion experience. The militancy and self-affirming stance that was part of the larger Black Consciousness Movement was present in the BSWM as well. Following the much publicized lead of the NOI, SNCC, CORE, the newly formed organization Us and Black Panther Party (Franklin and Moss, 2000; Karenga,

2002; Joseph, 2006), the founders of NABSW proclaimed that the organization's priority and commitment would be to people of African descent. To help ensure that the organization would achieve its goals, membership would be restricted to Blacks only. And determining who in the Black community was eligible to be part of the organization was a key factor in shaping the future and direction of the organization.

A Radical Orientation to the Social Work Profession

Within two short years, the concerns of individual Black social workers had been elevated to a public outcry. Through their actions on both the local and national levels, those involved in the BSWM had demonstrated their strength and fortitude as they rallied against the many social injustices they witnessed in their communities, as well as their places of employment. Many were fully cognizant of the failures in the system and in the social work profession. But what were the best alternatives to the existing set of values, beliefs and knowledge of social work practice? Were there any practices in traditional social work that were worth preserving? And how do you build a new theory of social work practice based on liberation rather than adjustment? It was necessary for Black social workers to move beyond criticism and develop a more radical, if not racially conscious, approach to social work practice.

Understanding Existing Social Work Organizations

Black social workers needed to continue their focus on building a national organizational base. Many of those who helped to organize the BSWM and wanted to contribute to the development of the new organization had previous experience in the nation's premier social work organizations. They included NCSW, NASW and CSWE.

The National Conference on Social Welfare had a long and rich history. The conferences began in 1874 at a meeting of the American Social Science Association in New York City, where the first Conference of Boards of Public Charities was held (*New York Times,* 1874). Boards of Charities were an aspect of America's early social welfare system. Existing separately and independently in each state, these boards determined the level of support that would be granted to those in need and those institutionalized by the state. In 1880 the name was changed to the Conference of Charities, changed again in 1882 to the Conference of Charities and Correction and in 1917 to the National Conference of Charities and Correction. As the social work profession began to establish its roots in the early 20[th]century, its practitioners gained credibility as working professionals. In 1917, the name was changed to the National Conference of Social Work and lastly in 1957 to the National Conference on Social Welfare (lib.umich.edu). Prior to the establishment of NABSW, Black social workers attended these national conferences hoping to gain insights into new approaches to social work and the delivery of social services. It was at these gatherings that social workers had the opportunities to present papers and workshops on the latest innovations in professional practice.

The National Association of Social Workers (NASW) was established in 1955, just as the nation began struggling with modern-day civil rights issues. It was the consolidation of seven professional social work organizations, including the American Association of Social Workers (AASW), the American Association of Psychiatric Social Workers (AAPSW), the American Association of Group Workers (AAGW), the Association for the Study of Community Organization (ASCO), the American Association of Medical Social Workers (AAMSW), the National Association of School Social Workers (NASSW) and the Social Work Research Group (SWRG). NASW describes as its primary functions the promotion of "the professional development of its members, establishing and maintaining professional standards of practice, advancing sound social policies, and providing services that protect its members and enhance their professional status" (NASW. org). NASW developed hundreds of chapters throughout the United States and in the international community. It also holds annual conferences and professional workshops to facilitate the growth and development of its members. NASW focuses its attention on the well-being of its members, and has a carefully articulated Code of Ethics that guides the professional conduct of its members (NASW, 1977).

The Council on Social Work Education (CSWE) was founded in 1952 as the educational organization for schools of social work. It serves as the nation's accrediting body for institutions of higher education that offer graduate and undergraduate degrees in social work. CSWE "aims to promote and strengthen the quality of social work education through preparation of competent social work professionals by providing national leadership and a forum for collective action" (CSWE.org). The organization establishes and maintains policy and program standards, promotes research and faculty development and, with its annual conference, provides a forum for social work educators to present workshops, papers and their latest research findings. As social work continued to expand during the second half of the 20th century, CSWE took on an important role in advocating for more opportunities for students to prepare to enter the profession. They played a critical role in the establishment of baccalaureate programs which did not exist during the first half of the century.

In the mid-1960s, there were limited opportunities for Blacks to fully participate in any of the professional social work organizations. With all of their great intentions, NCSW, NASW and CSWE were part of the American social system, which provided greater privileges for its white citizens. The racism and discrimination that was part and parcel of the fabric of America also led to segregation and inequality in social service organizations, in the delivery of social welfare services and by those responsible for program development and implementation. Social services were restricted by race; resources were restricted by race; employment opportunities were restricted by race; and participation in policy and decision-making was also restricted by race. As the Civil Rights and Black Power movements unfolded, social work organizations were challenged by the demands for rapid social change within their own professional groups. However, much to its credit, social work was first among the major professions to begin to address questions about Black inequities. According to Blackwell (1981:266):

> *"Unlike other major professions, social work began to take steps to correct the racial inequities in its profession in the same year that the Brown decision was pronounced by the U.S. Supreme Court. In 1954, the Commission on Accreditation for Schools of Social Work 'adopted a mandatory standard' which required assurance of non-discriminatory practices be assured in all schools of social work. According to this policy change, all schools of social work were to conduct their programs without any form of discrimination based upon race, ethnic origin, creed or color. This policy had universal applicability in that it covered selection and admission of students, and conduct in the classroom and in-field practice assignments as*

well as the organization of a school's program. This fundamental principle of non-discrimination in social work has been national policy since 1954."

Blackwell (1981) argues further that social work was in a prime position to move forward, creating opportunities for students, faculty and practitioners to be part of an inclusive, diverse profession. Unfortunately, social work did not rise to the level of expectation created by its own rhetoric. Again, Blackwell (Ibid: 267) states:

> *"As the civil rights movement picked up momentum, social work practitioners, educators, and policy makers vocalized the urgency of producing more black social workers. In principle, social work had always embraced the idea of inclusion and openness for those persons who wished to be trained in the technology of human services and in the methodology of helping others to realize their greatest potential. But principles and practices are sometimes inconsistent and strangely contradictory."*

Finally, he asserts that the profession "suffered from a credibility gap, which centered upon its image with black and other minority groups" (Ibid; 267). Black social workers and members of the Black community were aware of the profession's limitations. And Blackwell is quick to add that, at least for a brief period of time, social work was the only profession in which Blacks achieved parity; i.e., their numbers for enrollment in schools of social work exceeded that of the general population. He (Ibid: 275) adds:

> *"At no time in this century has the census-counted black population of the United States reached 12 per cent of the total U.S. population. Throughout the 1970s, the reported black population ranged from 11.1 percent to about 11.6 percent. Using our definition of total access or enrollment parity, black students in first year social work classes not only reached parity but exceeded it in all but the three final years of the decade."*

This led many Blacks to conclude that their decision to select social work as a career option was the best available choice during a period of limited access to other higher education opportunities.

The Black Social Work Alternative

Those involved in the BSWM were seeking an alternative, an organization that they could call their own. It was the merging of interests of social activists throughout the country that resulted in the creation of NABSW. Within a two-year period, NABSW developed a Statement of Purpose, a philosophical base, a Code of Ethics, and a Constitution and By-laws. Its initial Statement of Purpose declared that:

> "The National Association of Black Social Workers, Inc. is a Black organization on the national level with local chapters that provides a structure and forum through which Black Social Workers, workers in related fields of service, and consumers can exchange ideas, offer services, and develop programs in the interest of the Black community.

> It is a non-profit organization, consisting of dedicated Black professionals, community workers, and consumers who, without pay, freely make their skills available to groups, individuals and agencies for the alleviation of the numerous problems confronting the Black community" (NABSW, 1972:1).

The statement further emphasizes the organization's role in the Black community, highlighting the goal of Black liberation as its primary focus:

> "While the social work profession supposedly deals with the common human needs of all individuals regardless of race or ethnic origin, we have found that there are needs peculiar to Black folk that have not been dealt with by the classic social work institutions and agencies. We plan to fill this gap by effectively dealing with those problems deserving high priority in the colonized oppressed

> *Black Community. This, from organizational posture, then means engaging the Black Community in meaningful action toward self determination based on Black Liberation principles as well as deep organizational and personal commitment to collectivity and humanism"* (NABSW, 1972:1).

It is important to note that Black social workers were declaring their "oneness" with all members of the Black community. In so doing, they wanted to emphasize their central focus on racial identity as the "glue" that tied the professional to the community in the struggle for equality. Black social workers, particularly those with college and graduate degrees, were fully cognizant of the emerging class divide in the Black community. They wanted to carefully articulate an openness and acceptance, as equals, of all those involved in the struggle.

The Code of Ethics (Table 1), which drew on the work of Chicago's Black Catalysts, reminded Black social workers of their primary commitment. While NASW focused its attention on the well-being of its members, NABSW shifted its focus to the well-being of the community. The NASW (1977) Code of Ethics required an oath to standards which guided professional behavior with colleagues, employing agencies, other professions and the community. NABSW's Code of Ethics required its members to always function as racially conscious social workers, maintaining their focus on the well-being of the Black community. At a time when the Black community constantly engaged in debate about whether one was a professional who happened to be Black or a Black who happened to be a professional, NABSW put "race first" in front of all considerations. But not all Black social workers would agree.

To Be or Not to Be

From the very beginning tensions arose about the direction of the BSWM and the organization. Two points of contention were evident: integration versus nationalism, and professionalism versus social activism. Conflict around these issues began to divide those who were committed to change but differed philosophically and ideologically as to how change could best occur within social work, and how beneficial that change would be to the Black community and the Black social work professional.

Integration called for the building of an organization and a movement that united all racial and ethnic groups to fight for a common cause; nationalism required

49

Table I
National Association of Black Social Workers Code of Ethics

In America today, no Black person, except the selfish or irrational, can claim neutrality in the quest for Black liberation nor fail to consider the implications of the events taking place in our society. Given the necessity for committing ourselves to the struggle for freedom, we as Black Americans practicing in the field of social welfare, set forth this statement of ideals and guiding principles.

If a sense of community awareness is a precondition to humanitarian acts, then we as Black social workers must use our knowledge of the Black community, our commitments to its determination, and our helping skills for the benefit of Black people as we marshal our expertise to improve the quality of life of Black people. Our activities will be guided by our Black consciousness, our determination to protect the security of the Black community, and to serve as advocates to relieve suffering of Black people by any means necessary.

Therefore, as Black social workers we commit ourselves, collectively, to the interests of our Black brethren and as individuals subscribe to the following statements:
- I regard as my primary obligation the welfare of the Black individual, Black family, and Black community and will engage in action for improving social conditions.
- I give precedence to this mission over my personal interest.
- I adopt the concept of a Black extended family and embrace all Black people as my brothers and sisters, making no distinction between their destiny and my own.
- I hold myself responsible for the quality and extent of service I perform and the quality and extent of service performed by the agency or organization in which I am employed, as it relates to the Black community.
- I accept the responsibility to protect the Black community against unethical and hypocritical practice by any individual or organizations engaged in social welfare activities.
- I stand ready to supplement my paid or professional advocacy with voluntary service in the Black public interest.
- I will consciously use my skills, and my whole being as an instrument for social change, with particular attention directed to the establishment of Black social institutions.

that Blacks unite as a people, clearly defining their own agenda prior to including others in their struggle for freedom and participation. Professionalism suggested that only those with specialized education and training should be included in a Black Social Work Movement and organization; social activism advocated for the inclusion of all concerned Black individuals, from every segment of the society, who were willing to engage in battle with the white-dominated power structure. There were difficult choices to be made.

The activities that culminated in the founding of the NABSW brought together a diverse group of individuals from different regions of the country. All social, political and ideological views were represented. The founding members of the organization were, for the most part, professional social workers with master's level degrees. These individuals were educational achievers and valued their professional accomplishments and careers. Some had been actively involved in the civil rights struggle, which was, overall, an integrationist movement, and believed in the promises of racial unity. Calls by the more militant and nationalist members of the organization to separate themselves completely from professional social work organizations proved difficult for many. Jay Chunn (2009), who emerged as the organization's second national president in 1974, recalls:

> *"I was raised as an integrationist. My mother was a practical nurse; my father had a high school diploma. I was told all of those things that Black children were told who wanted to succeed. You had to be smarter and you had to work harder than the white kids. I was an organizer and leader in NASW before I came to NABSW. I served as president of the NASW Cleveland chapter. I was also a member of CSWE and maintained my membership in these organizations throughout my presidency of NABSW."*

And Chunn was not alone. In addition to their participation in the annual NCSW conferences, many Black social workers were also members of NASW and a few were members of CSWE. Moreover, in the very early stages of the development of NABSW, there remained considerable concern about the relationship the new organization would have with NCSW. For example, during the first conference that was held in Philadelphia in 1969, prior to the election of the first national president, Howard Prunty was elected as chair of the National Steering Committee. Prunty sent a letter to the executive committee of NCSW on May 26, 1969, demanding increases in Black participation at all levels of the organization (Jaggers, 2003:50-51). He also demanded that NCSW "compel" CSWE to increase Black participation at the faculty, staff and student levels in schools of social work. Subsequent discussions within the organization continued to focus on the role of NABSW to NCSW, CSWE and NASW. Many Black social work professionals, as well as those devoted to a belief in the power of integration, were reluctant to sever or cause damage to the relationships that they had with these organizations. Moreover, those with professional education and training were equally vocal about determining which qualifications would be needed for membership in NABSW, and social integrationists and social activists were lodged in both camps. Many of the nonprofessional social activists helped to energize the community, organized and supported marches and rallies and provided vocal testimony against oppressive forms of social injustice. But were these folks to be considered professional social workers? Was the acquisition of essential knowledge, purportedly obtainable only within institutions of higher education, necessary for Black social work practice? And were there certain skills and methods of intervention that could only be obtained through professional training? As the organization moved forward to clarify these issues and concerns, it would strengthen their membership among some populations, but loosen their hold on others.

Moving Forward: The Development of an Organizational Structure

The success of any social movement can be measured by its ability to formally organize the collective into action and provide mechanisms to engage participants in on-going dialogue about the movement's activities (Goldberg, 1991). As the formal base of the BSWM, NABSW needed to find ways to fulfill these basic objectives. It devised an administrative structure and elected national officers and representatives to its National Steering Committee, the policy-making body of the organization. The National Steering Committee would be composed of two representatives from each local affiliate. A four-member officer corps— president, vice-president, secretary, treasurer—would be elected by steering committee delegates. In 1974, two additional seats for member-at-large were added. The organization would later create the position of the executive director. Standing committees and special task forces would address ongoing social and professional issues, including developing and researching new theoretical models and approaches to social work practice that would address and support the Black community's quest for a more liberating society. This effort would prove far more challenging than the early organizers anticipated. However, more than 40 years after its founding, the organizational structure remains relatively unchanged.

Disseminating the Word

African and African American culture is noted for the richness and diversity of its oral traditions (Levin, 1977; Asante, 1988). On countless occasions, "word of mouth" has proven to be an effective mechanism in helping to spread the word, informing community members of political developments, social events, rumors and innuendos. However, during the very early stages of development, organizational leaders decided not to rely solely on word of mouth to disseminate information about the thrust of the movement. Various mechanisms to record the movement's activities developed.

The *Black Caucus Journal*, first published in 1968 by the New York Association of Black Social Workers, became the official journal of NABSW. Described as "an intricate, inseparable part of the Association," the *Black Caucus Journal*:

> "...aims to provide a creative literary, journalistic outlet for its members and others involved with the black community on issues significant to the fields of social work and social services. The Journal was created as an organ for positive change and enlightenment for professionals and laymen interested in social welfare" (Black Caucus, 1969:1).

Acknowledging its uniqueness and nontraditional intentions, the editorial statement proclaimed:

> "We neither want nor solicit conformity on any material presented...We encourage and hope to stimulate controversy. We intend the Journal to be provocative, giving some evidence of considered thought, and a position on things seen by the contributors as important to the black community. Black Caucus does not aim to 'please' or placate, but it certainly will educate!" (Black Caucus, 1969:1)

The *Black Caucus Journal* was published biannually and distributed to members throughout the country. Initially, conference proceedings were published annually (until 1982) and periodically a newspaper was sent to members. In addition, local chapters developed newsletters and other written materials to help disseminate the word, and the local media was utilized to publicize the activities for the movement. The establishment of publication outlets was invaluable to the organization and its members. According to Johnson (1988:14):

> "NABSW offered to African American social workers something which had not been readily available to them in the past, an opportunity to publish their work. Moreover, there was no need to apologize for the focus of the work upon Blacks, this was expected. Nor, was it necessary to do comparative studies of Blacks and Whites. The publication opportunities within NABSW pushed white dominated social work publications to be more responsible to publish African American authors. In addition, more Blacks were appointed to editorial Boards, and were asked to serve as reviewers."

Social Outreach and Social Advocacy

During the formative years, the association developed a reputation as a militant, action-oriented Black organization. The organization's militant stance was reflective of the times and nurtured by the social climate. With sincere articulation, the organization championed the cause of poor Black people who were victimized by societal and institutional racism. NABSW led boycotts and protest marches and developed position statements on issues of concern to the Black community.

For example, members of the New York City chapter organized the United Federation of Black Community Organizations, whose sole purpose was "to unite all black organizations around common issues irrespective of individual ideologies" (ABSW, 1969:9). The New York City chapter also organized the first Afro-American Day Parade in Harlem in 1969, which attracted more than 300,000 people who "paid tribute to their African Heritage and marched with pride and dignity" (ABSW, 1969:10). In New Jersey, Black social workers, having determined the inherent cultural biases in many forms of standardized testing, challenged state testing requirements for child welfare workers in the Division of Youth and Family Services. In addition, through their participation in the National Leadership Roundtable, they helped organize the largest gathering of Black professional leaders and lay persons into a single nonpolitical social action entity—The New Jersey Black Issues Convention.

Racism in social welfare agencies was a frequent target of attack. Traditional social welfare agencies were charged with insensitivity and inadequacy. They were admonished for their failure to effectively service the needs of the Black community. For example, the organization's adamant opposition to transracial adoption, the most widely known and misunderstood of its official position statements, created a storm of controversy, as they demanded that Black children be placed in Black homes. NABSW also demanded that the child welfare system end its systematic discrimination against Black families who were willing to adopt Black children, but often were denied the opportunity to do so by local child welfare agencies (NABSW, 1978).

Conclusion

The foundation had been laid, the Movement launched, and the hard work had begun. NABSW aggressively moved forward to fulfill its mission of organizing the Black social work community as its primary objective. However, the organization's secondary agenda was an attack on societal racism while simultaneously working to strengthen the social fiber of the Black community. Its leaders and members were fully cognizant of the interrelatedness of America's social, economic and political systems and how they impacted the delivery of social welfare services. Moreover, there was a growing awareness of the deleterious effects of these interlocking systems on the Black community. The nation's major social indicators—employment, income, education, housing, wealth, health—revealed that the quality of life for Black Americans was significantly below that of their white counterparts. In the years to come, Black social workers would launch a multitude of community-based initiatives to address these social issues and would fight incessantly to eliminate these social inequities. Thus, the organization viewed itself as one that stood as a vanguard in the protection of the Black individual, the Black family and the Black community. Its agenda was broad in scope. It attempted to tackle not only a myriad of problems endemic to America's social welfare system but a host of complex, interdependent and multifaceted social ills that disproportionately affected the Black community. Now that the organizational body had firmly established its roots, the next big challenge was a question of leadership.

References:

Ambrosino, Rosalie, Joseph Heffernan, Guy Shuttlesworth and Robert Ambrosino (2007). *Social Work and Social Welfare: An Introduction*, Florence, KY: Brooks Cole Press.

Asante, Molefi Kete (2003). *Erasing Racism: The Survival of the American Nation*, New York: Prometheus Books.

_____ (1988). *Afrocentricity*, Trenton, NJ: Africa World Press.

Association of Black Social Workers (1969). *Black Caucus Journal,* New York, ABSW.

Blackwell, James E. (1981). Mainstreaming Outsiders: *The Production of Black Professionals*, Bayside, New York: General Hall, Inc.

Better, Shirley (2007). *Institutional Racism: A Primer on Theory and Strategies for Social Change*, 2nd ed., New York: Rowman and Littlefield Publishers, Inc.

_____(2009). *Personal Interview*, April.

Chandler, Elizabeth Margaret and Marcia J. Heringa Mason (2004). *Remember the Distance That Divides Us: The Family Letters of Philadelphia Quaker Abolitionist and Michigan Pioneer 1830-1842*, East Lansing: Michigan State University Press.

Chestang, Leon (1972). "Character Development in a Hostile Environment," Chicago: Occasional Papers.

Chunn, Jay (2009). Personal Interview, April.

Cohen, Adam and Elizabeth Taylor (2001). *American Pharaoh: Mayor Richard J. Daley: His Battle for Chicago and the Nation*, New York: Little, Brown Publishing.

Cross, William E. Jr. (1971). "The Negro to Black Conversion Experience," *Black World,* July, pp. 13-27.

DuBois, W.E.B. (1968). *Black Reconstruction*, New Haven: Meridian Books.

Franklin, John Hope and Alfred Moss, Jr. (2000). *From Slavery to Freedom*, New York: Alfred A. Knopf.

Goldberg, Robert A. (1991). *Grassroots Resistance: Social Movements in Twentieth Century America*, Belmont, CA: Wadsworth Publishing Company.

Jaggers, Garland (2003). *That Rare Moment in History: A Documented History of the Formation of the National Association of Black Social Workers*, Detroit: Self-Published.

Johnson, Audreye (1988). *The National Association of Black Social Workers, Inc: A History for the Future*, New York: NABSW.

Joseph, Peniel E. (2006). *Black Power Movement: Rethinking the Civil Rights – Black Power Era*, New York: Routledge.

Karenga, Maulana. (2002). *An Introduction to Black Studies*, Los Angeles: University of Sankore Press.

Kirk, John A. (2007). *Beyond Little Rock: The Origins and Legacies of the Central High Crisis*, University of Arkansas Press.

Kirst-Ashman, Karen K. (2009). *Introduction to Social Work & Social Welfare: Critical Thinking Perspectives*, Florence, KY: Brooks Cole.

Larsen, Nella (2000). *Passing*, New York: Random House.

Levine, Lawrence (1977). *Black Culture and Black Consciousness*, Oxford: Oxford University Press.

Miley, K. K., M. O'Melia and B. L. Dubois, (2009). *Generalist Social Work Practice: An Empowering Approach*, 6th ed., Boston: Allyn and Bacon.

National Association of Black Social Workers (1972). *Conference Proceedings, Statement of Purpose*, New York: NABSW.

_____(1978). *Position Paper: Child Welfare and Adoption*, New York: NABSW.

National Association of Social Workers (1977). *Encyclopedia of Social Work*, 17th ed., Washington, DC: NASW Press.

_____(2008). *Encyclopedia of Social Work*, 20th ed., Washington, DC: NASW Press.

National Conference of Black Social Workers (1969). *The Black Family*, Philadelphia, PA.

New York Times, (1967). "Negro Social Workers Organize to Combat Subtle Bias in Their Field," September 5.

_____(1874). "State Board of Charities," nytimes.com/archives.

Reid-Bookhart (1984). "Toward the Third Decade: The National Association of Black Social Workers," (Unpublished Report), New York: NABSW.

Rogers, Daniel and Harry Kitano (1970). *American Racism: Exploration of the Nature of Prejudice*, New York: Prentice-Hall.

Royko, Mike (1988). *Boss: Richard J. Daley of Chicago*, New York: Penguin Books.

Sanders, Charles (1970). "Growth of the Association of Black Social Workers," *Social Casework*, May, pp. 270 – 279.

Sitkoff, Harvard and John Hope Franklin (2008). T*he Struggle for Black Equality*, New York: Hill and Wang.

Slaughter, Thomas P. (2008). *The Beautiful Soul of John Woolman, Apostle of Abolition*, New York: Hill and Wang.

Stewart, Jeffrey C. (1998). *1001 Things Everyone Should Know About African American History*, New York: Doubleday.

Zastrow, Charles (2009). *Introduction to Social Work and Social Welfare: Empowering People*, 10th ed., Florence, KY: Cengage Learning.

Websites

www.cswe.org

www.lib.umich.edu

www.nasw.org

4

A QUESTION OF LEADERSHIP: WHO LEADS IN THE BLACK COMMUNITY?

Perhaps there is no other question more vexing than who should lead in the Black community. Historically, issues surrounding African American leadership have been among the most hotly contested and contentious battles in Black America (Cruse, 1967; White, 1985; Reid-Merritt, 1996; Marable, 1998). Should our leaders be among the most trained and educated, or emerge from the downtrodden, disenfranchised and impoverished masses? Should they be wise, experienced, sage elders, or those who possess the vitality, idealism and fearlessness of youth? Should we choose the giants among the intellectuals or the most charismatic orators? And should they be male or female? These issues, which plagued the Black community in each of the last three centuries, proved to be equally perplexing to those actively involved in organizing the BSWM.

Emerging Black Leadership

During the period of enslavement, there was limited opportunity for Black leadership. Those identified as national leaders or spokespersons were, for the most part, advocates for abolition and resided almost exclusively in the northern states. However, historical evidence of Black Americans' desire to organize in their best interest and provide leadership to the community is well documented. For example, in the 1700s, Prince Hall, Benjamin Banneker, Absalom Jones and Richard Allen emerged as leaders in the Abolition Movement and helped to create the Free African Society (Franklin and Moss, 2000). Allen was also the leader of the Black independent church movement. In the 1800s, activist Sojourner Truth (Isabella Baumfree) was a leading abolitionist and women's rights advocate. Harriett Tubman, a civil rights activist, championed the Underground Railroad, and orator and abolitionist Frederick Douglass traveled the country and the world to speak about Black freedoms. Publisher and abolitionist David Walker admonished the nation about the evils of slavery, and physician, writer and abolitionist Martin R. Delany rallied against efforts to relocate Black Americans to "colonized" settlements in Africa (Ibid).

With the passage of the 13th Amendment, the need for and influence of abolitionists waned. New forms of leadership were needed to help shape and mold the character of the Black community as free men and free women. Believing that most Blacks lacked the capability or resources to assume leadership roles, many northern white liberals and philanthropists lent their support to Black causes, most notably in the establishment of educational and charitable institutions. In fact, many of the nation's historically Black colleges and universities (HBCUs) were founded during this period.

In *Introduction to Black Studies*, Karenga (2002) argues that the failure of Reconstruction, coupled with increased discrimination, segregation and the rise of white terrorist mob violence against African American citizens, resulted in the need for new Black leadership. He identifies three major leaders, as well as three different ideological and strategic approaches: Booker T. Washington chose accommodation; W.E.B. DuBois preferred integration with confrontation; and Marcus Garvey favored Black Nationalism.

Washington was, by most measures, the nation's preferred choice as Negro leader in America during the latter part of the 19th century and early 20th century (White, 1985). Among the first to emerge following Reconstruction, Washington was an ex-slave born in 1856. He was well noted for his contributions to the development of Tuskegee Institute, his leadership of the National Negro Business League and his famous "Atlanta Compromise" speech, which advocated vocational training and skill development as the route the Black community should take in its efforts to uplift the race (Washington, 1968). Concerned about America's refusal to accept African Americans as equal citizens and well aware of the possibility of hostile, violent reactions to Black progress, Washington focused his efforts on helping Blacks to develop usable domestic and trade skills to become economically self-sufficient.

Washington was a highly regarded Black educator. He was an accomplished author, orator, administrator and fundraiser. He was among the first of the race to be invited to the White House (through the front door), received philanthropic support for his educational initiatives and was the recipient of honorary degrees from Dartmouth College and Harvard University (Norrell, 2009; Smock, 2009). However, he was also the target of ridicule and scorn from his northern detractors for his particular methods of social engineering for the transformation of the race, encouraging Blacks to "cast your buckets down where you are" and work in subordinate roles to prove their worth to the white community.

William Edward Burghardt (W.E.B.) DuBois was born on February 23, 1868, in Great Barrington, Massachusetts. DuBois has been described as Washington's foremost critic (Karenga, 2002). A lifelong freedom fighter, DuBois played a pivotal role in the establishment of both the Niagara Movement and the NAACP. Prior to launching the Niagara Movement in 1908, DuBois put forth his famous "Talented Tenth" philosophy as a solution to the leadership crisis in Black America. DuBois envisioned the Talented Tenth as a group of men and women "actively dedicated to black liberation and democratic social transformation" (Rabaka, 2005:443). This group of freedom fighters would "constantly seek self-knowledge, self-realization, and self-control, and possess a serious and sincere spirit of service and sacrifice" (Ibid: 244). DuBois, often accused by his critics as being elitist because of his belief in the leadership abilities of the educated class, experienced many ideological shifts throughout his lifetime. He was, at times, an integrationist, economic segregationist, communist and Pan-Africanist. He was a writer, poet, historian, sociologist and preeminent 20th century intellectual.

DuBois' proclamation for the need of a Talented Tenth led to a further strain in his relationship with Washington. DuBois' and Washington's divergent approaches to educating the masses were the center of the clash between two of America's first Black intellectual leaders. According to Rabaka (2005:444):

> *"Where Washington was firmly for industrial education and trade training, DuBois declared that college education and culture training was a prerequisite for black leadership and black liberation. DuBois did not deny that industrial education was extremely important to black life. He, however, believed that blacks needed broadly cultured men and women in leadership positions to guard against the manipulations and machinations of the white ruling race and class and the hundreds of half-trained black demagogues and opportunists."*

Washington sparred with DuBois about how best to achieve freedom and equality for the Black community until the time of his death in 1917. His death, however, did not elevate DuBois to the most visible and acceptable leader in Black America. Rather, DuBois found himself engaged in an ongoing battle of words and wit with Marcus Garvey.

Marcus Garvey was born in 1887 in Jamaica. His emergence as an international leader in the Black liberation struggle was an unlikely outcome for a printer's apprentice and unsuccessful union organizer (Martin, 1976). An anti-integrationist who admired and publicly supported the work of Washington, Garvey was deeply committed to the concept of racial pride and the uplift of all African people. Garvey's re-introduction of Black Nationalism intensified the struggle for prominence of a leadership role in Black America. Garvey, sometimes described as "the greatest mass leader of African people," (Asante and Abarry, 1996:286) had built his Universal Negro Improvement Association (UNIA) into a major force of contention. In his 1919 address at the First International Congress in New York, he proclaimed:

> *"The Universal Negro Improvement Association for five years has been proclaiming to the world the readiness of the Negro to carve out a pathway for himself in the course of life. Men of other races and nations have become alarmed at this attitude of the Negro in his desire to do things for himself and by himself. This alarm has become*

so universal that organizations have been brought into being here, there and everywhere for the purpose of deterring and obstructing this forward move of our race. Propaganda has been waged here, there and everywhere for the purpose of misinterpreting the intention of this organization; some have said that this organization seeks to create discord and discontent among the races; some say we are organized for the purpose of hating other people. Every sensible, sane and honest-minded person knows that the Universal Negro Improvement Association has no such intention. We are organized for the absolute purpose of bettering our condition, industrially, commercially, socially, religiously and politically. We are organized not to hate other men, but to lift ourselves, and to demand respect of all humanity. We have a program that we believe to be righteous; we believe it to be just, and we have made up our minds to lay down ourselves on the altar of sacrifice for the realization of this great hope of ours, based upon the foundation of righteousness. We declare to the world that Africa must be free, that the entire Negro race must be emancipated from industrial bondage, peonage and serfdom; we make no compromise, we make no apology in this our declaration. We do not desire to create offense on the part of other races, but we are determined that we shall be heard, that we shall be given the rights to which we are entitled" (Ibid: 405).

Marcus Garvey's philosophy on racial pride incorporated his beliefs in racial purity, and he, at times, expressed some disdain for the mixed race, mulatto leaders (which included both Washington and DuBois) who had risen to prominence in the Black community and the African world. At the height of his popularity in the early 1920s, Garvey could claim a following of more than a million in 700 chapters throughout the United States and the African world (Martin, 1976). It was his conviction in 1925 of mail fraud that, eventually, led to his decrease in popularity and the decline of the UNIA.

These men were outstanding leaders. However, Washington, DuBois and Garvey did not remain free from criticism from inside and outside of the Black community. As recognized national leaders, they were vulnerable to constant attacks. Washington was criticized by northern Black leaders for his acquiescence to the southern white power structure, DuBois by the very Black intelligentsia he helped to create through the NAACP, and Garvey by leading Black integrationists who feared his mass appeal to urban Blacks with his unobtainable dream to return back to Africa (White, 1985; Marable, 1998, 1999). What these three men were able to provide were templates for admirable Black leadership roles—*for Black males*! Leadership roles for African American women remained undefined, and at times were considered undesirable.

Black Female Leadership

African American women also faced contentious battles around leadership roles. Noted for their hard work in organizing the struggle and providing the "backbone" that was needed for the race and the nation to survive, African American women have rarely received full credit for their leadership initiatives or success in helping to push forward the struggle for freedom and equality. Truth—who famously raised the question "Ain't I a Woman?"—and Tubman, leading conductor of the Underground Railroad, remain the favorite Black female icons in the struggle for freedom during the period of enslavement. Less is known about Black female leaders like Anna Murray Douglass, Mary Ann Shad Cary, Sarah Parker Remond, Frances Harper, Sarah Mapps Douglass, Eliza Dixon Day and Sarah Forten (Yee, 1992). They were militant, activist abolitionists who also contributed to the struggle for freedom.

At the dawn of the 20th century, Black women continued the battle for civil rights and at the same time organized their own movement (Giddings, 1988). Ida B. Wells-Barnett, Mary Church Terrell, Josephine St. Ruffin and Mary McLeod Bethune were among those who struggled to lead as they faced opposition from males and females, Blacks and whites. They advocated the belief that all of Black America would advance forward by focusing on the need of women and children. Women needed to be educated. They needed to be prepared for productive work and leadership. Not all agreed. For example, Wells-Barnett succeeded in challenging segregated streetcar restrictions in Memphis, Tennessee, led a national anti-lynching campaign and played a formative role in helping to establish the Black Women's Movement. However, as one of only two African American women to sign the call for the founding of the NAACP, she was denied the opportunity to accept a leadership role as secretary in the newly formed organization due to her radical, aggressive and unladylike leadership style (Franklin, 1995; Giddings, 2008).

Bethune was born on July 10, 1875, in Maserville, South Carolina, to former slaves. In addition to her leadership in the Black Women's Club Movement, she was the founder of Bethune-Cookman College. In 1935 she brought together 28 different organizations and formed the National Council of Negro Women (NCNW). NCNW assumed an influential role in getting the country to respond to the needs of Black women. As Blacks began to make advances in the Franklin Delano Roosevelt Adminstration, Bethune emerged as the only female leader, and perhaps the strongest, in Roosevelt's informal Black Cabinet (Sterling, 1988). However, Bethune was always asked to apply her leadership skills to women's issues. She was not a spokesperson for the race.

Sarah Breedlove was a successful business woman, philantropist and civil rights activist. She was the first self-made American woman millionaire. She understood the inherent disrespect that American culture held for Black women and especially Black female leaders. She changed her first name from Sarah to Madame to ensure that she would be treated with dignity and respect in her professional dealings. Thereafter she was known as Madame C. J. Walker (Bundles, 2001).

Nannie Helen Burroughs understood the value of women's work. She was the founder of the National Training School for Women and Girls in Washington, D.C. In 1900 she challenged the National Baptist Convention to create more signifcant roles for women in the church. Much like the dominant white religious organizations, the church successfully institutionalized passive, subservient roles for women. Burroughs' challenge resulted in the formation of the Woman's Convention Auxiliary to the National Baptist Convention, creating one of the largest Black women's organizations in the nation. With all the great successes of Black women in utlizing their leadership skills to help remove the social obstacles that limited Black progress, there still remained an invisible code of conduct that was not be be violated: Don't overshadow the roles of men (Johnson, 2000).

Civil Rights Leadership

The competition for leadership roles marked every stage and aspect of the modern-day Civil Rights and Black Power movements, as well as the battles surrounding which philosophies, ideologies and strategies were best suited to achieve the goals of full citizen participation and equality. Cruse (1967:564) argues that:

"American Negro history is basically a history of conflict between integrationist and nationalist forces in politics, economics, and culture, no matter what leaders are involved and what slogans are used."

Even if Cruse's contentions are true, integrationists also competed with other integrationists. Moreover, nationalists competed with other nationalists, and both integrationists and nationalists competed with each other. The central question still remained: Who should lead in Black America?

Bayard Rustin was a seasoned civil rights leader with a unique set of characteristics: He was a Quaker, pacifist, conscientious objector, nonviolent integration activist, organizer, administrator and gay male. He desired a more prominent role in the movement, but feared his sexual preference would take front and center, overshadowing all of his other leadership abilities (Rustin, Carbado and Weise, 2003; D'Emilio, 2004).

A. Phillip Randolph was once called "the most dangerous man in America." The founder of the Brotherhood of Sleeping Car Porters and the chief organizer behind the historic 1963 March on Washington, Randolph was a freedom fighter who invested most of his energies in the Labor Movement. As a socialist, he believed that jobs and economic security were the basis to achieving equality in American society. As an integrationist, he fought for equal representation and participation of those he believed to be the underdogs, including Blacks, Hispanics, Native Americans and poor white Americans. He opposed Black Nationalism and Garvey's back to Africa sentiments. Respected by presidents, union organizers and civil rights and community leaders, he found his role as preeminent Black leader eclipsed in his prime by a young, extremely articulate orator and preacher from the South named Martin Luther King, Jr. (Anderson, 1973; Pfeffer, 1990).

As the Civil Rights Movement began to unfold, it was Dr. King who emerged as the dominant figure on the national scene. Dr. King was an unlikely choice, having been pushed to take the lead in the growing civil disobedience protests that were occurring in the South. In addition to his intellect, charisma and courage to take a stand, Dr. King benefited from his position as a Baptist minister, the occupation of choice for many Black leaders during the civil rights era. Black men of the cloth enjoyed freedoms often denied to their brethren. Religious leaders and institutions were often described as the only sector in the community that was controlled by Blacks. In his brief lifetime, Dr. King worked assiduously at keeping the issues of jobs, freedom, voting privileges and other basic human and civil rights at the forefront of the Civil Rights Movement. He was viewed as a skillful orator, nonviolent strategist and charismatic leader by some; a dangerous, uppity Negro agitator by others. The FBI, under J. Edgar Hoover, felt Dr. King was dangerous enough to maintain ongoing surveillance of all of his activity (Garrow, 1983). But why select Dr. King for such a coveted leadership position? Was he the right man, at the right time, for the job? What about the other gifted leaders of the era, including Randolph, Representative Adam Clayton Powell, DuBois, Andrew Young and others who had years of experience in the freedom struggle? Or were we following a pattern established in the early days in the emergence of Black leadership, only allowing one Black leader to be the designated spokesperson for the entire race at any given time (referred to in the Black community as the HNIC—Head Negro in Charge—syndrome). As the movement progressed from passive, nonviolent confrontation to the more militant, self-defining and self-dignity stance of the Black Power Movement, Dr. King's leadership became much more palatable to the American establishment. Much to the chagrin of the nation, leaders like Malcolm X, Huey P. Newton, Bobby Seale and Maulana Karenga were unwilling to wait passively to obtain their constitutionally guaranteed rights. They would no longer accept second-class citizenship. For many, the integrationist movement had proven to be ineffective. As noted by Franklin and Moss (2000:518), "the feeling, bolstered by bitter experience, that justice and equality were not to be extended to blacks under any circumstances" gave birth to the Black Power Movement. Their calls were for freedom…now! Their commitments were to Black Power, Black Pride, Self-Determination and Black Cultural Nationalism. As they struggled to make their voices heard in white America, they would face internal leadership battles within their own newly developed organizations as well (Deale, 1970; Jones, 1998; Karenga, 2002).

Black women have written volumes about leadership opportunities, or the denial thereof, in both the Civil Rights and Black Power movements (Brown, 1993; LeBlanc-Earnest, 1998; Matthews, 1998; Cleaver and Katsiaficas, 2001; Collier-Thomas and V. P. Franklin, 2001; Forbes, 2007; Spencer, 2008). Rosa Parks may have been noted as the mother of the Civil Rights Movement, but following her protest in Montgomery, her leadership role was more ceremonial than real. Ella Baker, Fannie Lou Hamer and Victoria Gray made tremendous contributions as organizers and leaders of the civil rights struggle in the southern Black belt, yet their efforts were overshadowed by the contributions made by their male counterparts—most Americans, Black or white, cannot recall their roles in history. The Reverend Willie Barrow worked with Dr. King and Jesse Jackson on a number of civil rights initiatives. As she shared her story in *Sister Power* (Reid-Merritt, 1996), she recalled that she was often denied opportunities, pushed aside because of her diminutive stature and because she was a woman. A rarer exception may have been the role that Dorothy Height played in the Civil Rights Movement when she changed the role of the "big five" into the "big six."

Height was born on March 24, 1912, in Richmond, Virginia. Following her graduation from New York University, she began her career as a caseworker for the New York City Department of Welfare. Her career as a civil rights activist began when she joined the NCNW in 1937. Height would eventually serve the organization for more than 70 years, nearly 50 in the role as president and chairman (NCNW, 2009). A protegee of Bethune, she is credited with inspiring women in the South to fight for their rights and to get involved with the voting rights movement (Reid-Merritt, 1996). In 1957, Height became president of NCNW. The council was a major supporter of the 1963 March on Washington. When *Time* magazine (1963) proclaimed the "big five" leaders of the Civil Rights Movement to be Roy Wilkins of the NAACP, James Forman of CORE, Dr. King of SCLC, Whitney Young of NUL and James Farmer of SNCC, Height took exception. She insisted upon taking her place, as the representative of NCNW and all Black women, front and center along with the other male leaders (Height, 2005).

Women in the Black Power struggle were more vocal about the denial of leadership roles in the Movement. In "Engendering the Black Freedom Struggle: Revolutionary Black Womanhood and the Black Panther Party in the Bay Area California," Spencer (2008:90) notes:

> *"The notion of black male emasculation at the hands of superpowerful black women clearly shaped the context for the emergence of Black Power. As a result, the Black Power movement has been inextricably linked to 'the belief in black male dominance' and the restoration of a manhood that was 'separate from (and even antagonistic) to Black womanhood' in the scholarly literature and in the popular imagination."*

Elaine Brown, who was among the first of the Black Panther women to publicly denounce the blatantly sexualized posture of the party, was far more critical in her assessment. Brown was born in 1943 and raised in the heart of

North Philadelphia's ghetto community. In 1968 she joined the Black Panther Party, where she willingly sold newspapers, cleaned guns, sang songs, edited the newspapers and performed other tasks deemed essential to the success of the Movement. Brown ascended to a position of leadership in the party at precisely the same time a leadership vacuum existed due to the number of male leaders no longer available to assume leadership responsibilities due to their imprisonment. According to Brown (1993: 357):

> *"A woman in the Black Power movement was considered, at best, irrelevant. A woman asserting herself was a pariah. If a black woman assumed a role of leadership, she was said to be eroding black manhood, to be hindering the progress of the black race. She was an enemy of the black people...and acting in alliance with counter-revolutionary, man-hating lesbian, feminist white bitches."*

She quit the party in 1977, when she could no longer tolerate the sexism and patriarchy that dominated the organization. However, Spencer (2008) cautions that this blanket indictment belies other realities regarding leadership roles for women in the Black Panther Party. She (Ibid: 99) asserts:

> *"The Panthers created images that valorized the armed, revolutionary black woman at a time when the dominant sociological and public policy arguments said that strong black women were detrimental to the family and therefore the community, and both liberal integrationist and conservative nationalist rhetoric promoted patriarchy. In stark contrast to the image of women spontaneously and individually engaging in self-defense, which emerged from the civil rights movement, the Panthers posited black women as proactive and organized – acting alongside men as defenders of the black community."*

The intensity of the battles may vary from careful conversation to openly hostile public debates. However, the literature provides abundant evidence that issues of sexism, chauvinism and patriarchy were major, and oftentimes unresolved, challenges all movement activity.

Black Social Work Leadership

During a period in which many Black professionals distanced themselves from mainstream organizations, and many others had to choose between social integration or Black Nationalism as their guiding principle, one of the nation's prominent civil rights leaders emerged as the president of the National Association of Social Workers (NASW). The choice of Whitney Young suggested progress to some but more acquiescence to others.

Young was, symbolically, a "typical" offspring of a middle-class Black family or "what a sociologist might describe as the educated elite of a subordinate color caste" (Fredrickson, 1995:268). Born on July 31, 1921, in Lincoln Ridge, Kentucky, his parents had secured respectable employment as an educator and postmaster. Young attended Kentucky State University, a historically Black university, where he earned a bachelor's of science degree. He later earned his MSW from the University of Minnesota in 1947.

As a newly minted social worker, Young began his professional career with the Urban League in St. Paul, Minnesota, where he was also able to assume his first leadership role. In 1950, he became president of the Urban League of Omaha, Nebraska. He would later assume the position of director of NUL. However, in the interim, Young was appointed dean of the Atlanta School of Social Work. As dean, "Young supported alumni in their boycott of the Georgia Conference of Social Welfare. The organization had a poor record of placing African Americans in good jobs" (NASW, 1971). One must assume that Young was fully cognizant of the problems of race and racism in social work. Young left the deanship to accept the position of director NUL. Under his leadership, the organization experienced unprecedented growth, expanding from 38 to 1,600 employees in four short years, some of which could be attributed to the availability of federal funding from Johnson's War on Poverty program (nul.org/history). However, he maintained his involvement with professional social work organizations.

Young assumed the presidency of NASW at precisely the same moment NABSW was founded. He served from 1969 to 1971. According to NASW archives, Young "spent his tenure as President of NASW ensuring that the profession kept pace with the troubling social and human challenges it was facing" (NASW, 1971:1). In addition, he called upon social workers to address social welfare through poverty reduction, race reconciliation and putting an end to the Vietnam War. It was a daunting task, one he attempted to accomplish when increasing numbers of Black social workers were questioning the viability of getting the professional association to set an agenda that aggressively addressed the needs of America's inner city and rural Black communities. The ultimate measure of Young's ability to work within NASW and be responsive to the call and demands of Black social workers in the Movement remains unknown. Young's tenure as a civil rights and social work leader was cut short, unfortunately, by his untimely death due to drowning in 1971 at the age of 50.

NABSW Leadership Mantra

Understanding the role of leadership, especially in regards to the presidency of NABSW, might best be described as the competition between males and the women that supported them. Patriarchy, sexism and chauvinism were key areas of concern, for some, in the Civil Rights and Black Power struggles in the wider community. These issues were present within the BSWM as well, although the expressions of such were covert, and rarely, if ever, elevated to a level of open discourse among organization members. These topics were considered taboo, prohibited by their perceived detrimental impact on the essential components of nation building. Males were the chosen, preferred leaders, and the desire to place males in dominant leadership roles within the organization would persist for decades to come.

The first two years of organizing on the national level were both exciting and tumultuous. As local leadership continued to gather to formalize the association into a national body, there were many questions about leadership. Who was best suited to head up the organization? There were a number of viable choices: T. George Silcott in New York, Garland Jaggers in Detroit, Audreye Johnson in Chicago and Nawab Shah II in Los Angeles. Additionally, there were a number of individuals who helped to organize the walkout in San Francisco—Shirley Better, Joan Coleman, Howard Prunty, Douglass Glasglow and William K. Wolfe—and continued to support the building of a national organization. And there were other recent newcomers—Howard Brabson, Jay Chunn, LaVerne McCummings and Audrey Russell—who had taken a keen interest in the organization. These were the credentialed professional men and women with diverse visions as to how the organization could grow, contributing not just to the social work profession but to the larger movement that had swept through the country as well. And giving birth to any new entity invariably results in differences of opinions and more than a few conflicts.

71

Jaggers (2003:55) was one of the founding members of NABSW. He served as its first national convener. However, within the first two years he noted that "those who initiated this group in Washington in 1968 are drifting away or being pushed aside." Why? There were a variety of reasons given for leadership conflicts over the future direction of the organization. For certain, there were philosophical differences around the mission, purpose and goals of the new association. There were ideological differences, too. What was the meaning of professionalism for Black folks? Who should be included or excluded? Brabson (2009), who would assume leadership as the organization's third president in 1978, recalls the focus of the conflict in the early years:

"We had to decide what kind of organization we were going to be. Some viewed us as another civil rights organization. Others wanted it to be more professional, catering to the desires of those who had achieved graduate level education. There were conflicts between the East Coast and the West Coast, conflicts that almost divided the organization at the very beginning. Some people wanted a chief executive officer, others wanted a president. However, what it really came down to was how to include and be fair to all those people who had worked in poverty programs, providing direct help in the neighborhoods. Should they be called social workers? These local-level workers were, for the most part, non MSWs. The original leaders were MSWs. That's when we decided that all Black folk working on behalf of the community would be welcomed. A lot of professional, graduate level social workers left the organization, but continued to use us when it was convenient for career advancement."

The first national election that was held at the second annual conference in Washington, D.C., in 1970 resolved some of the dilemmas faced by the organization but created new ones for those who had nurtured its development. The struggle for leadership proved to be a competition among men. Competing for the coveted position of first national president were Chunn from Ohio, Shah II from California, McCummings from Philadelphia and newcomer Cenie J. Williams from New York. Following rounds of voting and several contentious verbal exchanges, a winner finally was able to declare victory. And much to the surprise of all those who had struggled to reach this point, the newly elected president was Williams.

He would be joined by "Nawab Shah II of Carson, California, as Vice President; Chester Wright of Oakland, California, as Treasurer; and James Madry of Detroit, Michigan, as Acting Secretary" (Jaggers, 2003). If questions were raised about gender diversity, they were not viewed as an organizational priority. It was time for Black men to take their rightful place as leaders of the Movement. As one former official stated, "The sisters were behind the brothers 100 percent. Thank God for the sisters!" Leora Neal (2009), a child welfare and adoption activist for more than 40 years, was a graduate student at the Columbia University School of Social Work when Williams and Abe Snyder recruited her and others into the Movement. For Neal, being a part of the Black social work organization was important because "it was the only professional social work organization that was primarily concerned about issues affecting the Black community." She recalls the very conscious choice some Black women made about leadership of the organization:

> *"When NABSW began, it was the women who decided that they would not seek to run for the office of president because we wanted Black men to be in the lead, as they were often not allowed to be leaders in the general society."*

This sentiment persisted. Black males were elected into the office of the president every other year in each election over the 16-year biannual voting cycle. It would be 32 years before a Black woman, Judith Jackson from Detroit, would have the opportunity to do the same.

Cenie "Jomo" Williams

More than 40 years following the historic first election, those who were involved in the process continued to describe it as the "ultimate political coup." For example, many of those who were interviewed about the early organizing experience offered, with a great amount of emotional emphasis, the following assessments:

> *"It was like the New York Mafia had arrived and taken over the organization."*

73

"I don't believe that anyone ever thought that Cenie Williams would leave the room as president. We didn't even know who he was!"

"New York City arrived at the conference with five busloads of people. They all claimed to be members and wanted to vote. We had not worked out all the details about one vote per chapter. Cenie's people were vocal, and somewhat fearless. They were not about to be denied."

"Cenie came in and stole the election. He knew he stole it. We all expected that Jay Chunn would be voted in as the first president. It just didn't happen that way."

"Cenie had no intention of going to Washington for the purpose of running for office or taking over the organization. Cenie was a community organizer. He had the ability to bring people along with him. We didn't decide to make a run for it until after we arrived at the conference. We were challenged on the rules, but we fought back. Yes, we were from New York and we had much more experience with the strategic aspects of the political process than those who were in the running for office."

Williams was born on June 12, 1938, in Conway, South Carolina. He attended South Carolina State College, graduating with a Bachelor of Arts degree. He began his career as a caseworker in the New York City Department of Welfare. It was during this period that he became acutely aware of the needs of the city's welfare workers as well as the clientele they served. A member of CHARMA, Williams had honed his skills in political confrontation and community organizing. After several years, he decided to pursue a career in social work "with the concept of providing services to mankind for uplifting and building the Black community" (NABSW, 1983). Williams entered New York University and received his Master of Social Work degree in 1968. He was not a part of the NCSW walkout that triggered the national movement. In 1969, he was elected president of the New York City Chapter of the Association of Black Social Workers, a leadership position that he unexpectedly wrested from Silcott. Gil Raiford (2009), Williams' colleague at the New York City Department of Welfare, recalls the circumstances that thrust Williams into leadership. In 1966, Raiford was serving in a supervisory role when he and 24 other employees in the welfare department were given the opportunity to attend graduate school to pursue their master's degrees. According to Raiford:

> "The year that we started school, the department provided full scholarships for 25 African American welfare employees. Additionally, they paid our full salary for the two years. About a dozen of us matriculated at NYU. I think that it might have had something to do with the fact that Commissioner Dumpson was in leadership at that time. It was in 1967 and we were just beginning the second semester of our MSW program at NYU when Cenie approached me to say that he was very dissatisfied with the conservative direction that ABSW was going, and that it was possible for us to take over the organization and redirect it. At the time, I did not take him seriously. After all, although we were adults, we were still students, and to make this seem more impossible, one of the primary leaders of ABSW at that time was our CO [Community Organizing] professor, George Silcott. But Cenie was a superior organizer. Anyway, we went to the meetings with a solid plan to take over the organization. To my everlasting amazement, it worked. I kept thinking: 'now what?'"

Under Williams' leadership, the association, only in its third year of existence, reportedly "increased membership by 90 percent in one year" (ABSW, 1983). He is credited with building the New York City chapter into the largest in the world.

Williams was employed as the director of special projects for the New York Urban League when he assumed the position as the first national president of NABSW. His emergence to the top was unexpected. Yet he became the embodiment of a Black leader who was dedicated to the cause of freedom, liberation and equality. It was a role he embraced with unbridled enthusiasm, 24/7. It was Williams who set the direction and agenda for the national organization. Under his leadership, NABSW would emerge as a militant Black group grounded in nationalist beliefs. It was open to membership to all Black people willing to embrace the organization's philosophy and work toward the full empowerment of the community. The decision to emphasize practice over theory and research further divided the organization, with many members and potential members asserting that NABSW could not meet the needs of the "true" social work professional, i.e., those with MSW degrees. Throughout the early years there were heated debates about the viability of joint membership in NABSW and NASW. Some often described the organizations as being "diametrically opposed" and felt it was necessary for Black social workers to make a choice. However, many MSW-level social workers decided to maintain their membership in both. The discourse over dual membership persisted throughout the years and intensified when NASW began its push for state licensing, a move that NABSW viewed as a blatant, elitist attempt to rein in the radical members of the profession and control all aspects of social work practice.

However, NABSW continued to experience unprecedented growth. Aided by the successful linkage of Black social workers and human service professionals throughout the country, the development and implementation of an organizational structure and the social climate, which sustained the calls to Black Consciousness, the BSWM continued to grow in popularity. What's critically important to note is that Black social workers did not limit their activities to the formal organization, but engaged in many forms of social activism.

Based on written and verbal accounts, the pinnacle of NABSW's existence was during its first five to seven years when Williams served as president. Indeed, the period may aptly be described as the organization's and the Movement's heyday. At one point (1975–76), NABSW could boast of a national membership that created more than 180 chapters. Although exact membership figures are unknown, exaggerated claims that more than 50,000 individuals were affiliated during the first decade of the organization's existence were frequently made (Reid-Bookhart, 1984).

A succession of strong, vocal leaders on the local and national levels— including Prunty, Silcott, Johnson, Preston Wilcott, Chunn, McCummings, Jaggers and Russell—accounted for much of the organization's initial success. But none were like Williams. Viewed from the outside, one may have easily concluded that the organization stood solid as a rock. NABSW had succeeded in spearheading a national Black Social Work Movement and continued to serve as the organization's focal point for Black social work activity.

Williams, whose southern dialect and limited oratorical skills masked his brilliance as a thoughtful leader and community organizer, managed to build the organization while continuing to support social activism in the larger community. He constantly encouraged Black social workers throughout the country to plan, join, lead, agitate and fully participate in protest activity on the local level. Williams understood the potential impact of the BSWM beyond the formal organization. In his 1972 address to thousands of conference delegates in Nashville, Williams shared his views on the role of Black social workers in the struggle for freedom:

"My fellow colleagues, the question before us this weekend is not whether or not you are going to make a contribution to the liberation of 30,000,000 blacks, but whether or not you are willing to sacrifice or endure some pain so that others will be relieved of their pains, which means making a total commitment to the Black Cause. In order for us to follow the route of 'self-help,' progress and nation building, there must be self-sacrifice. We must not ask ourselves about selfish goals, but be concerned about how our brothers and sisters in the community will benefit. I don't know what the future holds, but I do believe that we are willing to accept this challenge.

...with the various issues confronting us today, we must ask ourselves – Are we truly ready to sacrifice – to struggle? We must also keep in mind that today's struggle is greater than yesterday's because we are struggling not only against national forces, but also international. But because our cause is a just cause – And

Like Toussaint L'Ouverture, we must have courage and strength,
Like Nat Turner, we must have determination,
Like Malcolm X, we must have wisdom,
Like Marcus Garvey, we must have pride,
Like Martin Luther King, we must believe that justice will conquer injustice, that good will conquer evil, that right will conquer wrong, and that the forces of oppression and racism will come tumbling down, and never rise again.

77

And Black Social Workers will stand in the middle of the crossroad joining hands with our black brothers and sisters throughout the world, regardless of their philosophies, regardless of their ideologies, regardless of their religion – saying to the world that we are now united into one. And that our proud black spirit seeks justice and decency everywhere – that it seeks a newer world and a better tomorrow" (NABSW, 1972:9-10).

For Williams, there was no other cause more righteous than the call for Black social workers to assume a leadership role in the struggle for freedom, liberation and the preservation of the Black family. It was their moment to rise to the occasion and do the right thing. His passion for the Movement, his belief in self-determination, his fight to end racism and his commitment to social justice contributed to the expansion of the membership base of NABSW, as well as catapulting the organization to national prominence. Headquartered in New York City, under Williams' leadership the organization sharpened its militant stance, developed policy statements and initiatives and forged relationships with other Black organizations. Williams was, in the words of Marcus Garvey, a "race man." However, his love for the race did not make him "anti-white." Raiford (2009) emphasized:

Although Cenie was extremely pro-Black, he was never anti-white. This became clear to me one day when I was riding with him through Harlem. A white man had stopped at a traffic light and a Black teenager reached into the car and grabbed the man's wallet and ran down an alley. Seeing this, Cenie stopped his car in the middle of the street and dashed into the alley behind the boy—and caught him. He took the wallet, gave the boy a good shaking and let him go. Then he returned it to the white man's car and handed him the wallet, demanding that he look through it to see if anything was missing. Still shaking, the man said everything was there and, not knowing what else to do, held out some bills for Cenie. Cenie just gave him a very disdaining look and said: "Get the hell out of here."

Williams gained the admiration of thousands of Black social work professionals, paraprofessionals, politicians and community activists. But he was not without his detractors. Throughout his administration, Williams faced criticism about his leadership style. East Coast/West Coast rivalries deepened with the election of Williams, and the decision to locate the national office in New York, home to the largest (and most powerful) chapter in the organization, was viewed as a salting of the wounds. Moreover, Williams continued to serve as local chapter president; his wearing "two hats" caused confusion for some and resentment for others. However, when Williams' term ended, newly elected president Chunn, along with the delegates of the National Steering Committee, moved quickly to appoint Williams as the executive director. In his new role, undoubtedly created just for him, Williams continued his work as spokesman for the organization. When the organization launched its opposition to transracial adoption, it was Williams whose face and comments were synonymous with the fight to keep Black children in the Black community. He was ridiculed by scholars, practitioners, journalists and professionals who opposed NABSW and Williams' harsh comments about racism in America.

In addition to his administrative duties as executive director, he worked to mobilize other Black social workers around the nation by helping them to establish new chapters. Within one decade the number of affiliated chapters had expanded from eight to 188. Williams continued in his role as executive director under the administration of Brabson, who assumed the third presidency from 1978 to 1982. Even with his tremendous success as an organizer, Williams also faced criticism about his administrative abilities. And on at least one occasion, Williams' inability to articulate the policy and position statements of the organization led one leading Chicago Black newspaper, *The Defender*, to label the organization as "Confused Social Workers" (Armstrong, 1982). The final blow occurred on April 7, 1982, at a news conference for the opening of the 14th annual conference of NABSW in Chicago. Reporter Charles B. Armstrong described both Williams and President Brabson as "confused" and "ignorant," with the language facility of "a second grade dropout" (Ibid: 4/10/82).

It was an embarrassing moment for Williams, President Brabson and NABSW. Faced with mounting dissatisfaction with his performance, the National Steering Committee voted to terminate his services at the quarterly meeting held at the conclusion of the conference. The significance of this action cannot be understated.

The decision to terminate the service of the organization's first president and executive director was a difficult barrier for many members to overcome. The allegiance and intensity of commitment that many organizational members felt for Williams produced a sharp emotional divide within the organization. Some members refused to support the organization without him. Furthermore, the financial restraints and limitations facing NABSW resulted in the decision not to hire a new executive director or national administrator to assume the roles and responsibilities formerly carried out by Williams. This would prove deleterious to the organization. Finally, the most devastating blow was Williams' tragic and unexpected death less than a year following his departure from the national body. Williams' tenaciousness in the fight for Black freedom often resulted in a neglect of his own personal health needs. And on March 1, 1983, Williams died at Harlem Hospital. The cause was, at that time, an unknown disease called sarcoidosis. He was only 44 years old.

Conclusion

Black social workers resolved their leadership questions with the selection of strong male representatives that reflected traditional choices for the Black community. Williams epitomized a new form of passionate, militant leadership that helped catapult NABSW to national prominence. His death sealed his reputation as a freedom fighter and warrior who gave his life for the cause of Black liberation. In death he was transformed from the organization's last perception of him as a bumbling, ineffective administrator into the first martyr of the BSWM. New presidential leadership would emerge, including: William T. Merritt, Morris Jeff, Gerald Smith, Leonard Dunston, Rudy C. Smith, Jackson and Gloria Batiste-Roberts. However, all of the leaders to follow would be measured against Williams' greatness.

References:

Anderson, Jervis B. (1973). A. *Phillip Randolph: A Biographical Portrait*, New York: Harcourt Brace Jovanovich.

Armstrong, Charles B. (1982). "Confused Social Workers," *The Defender*, April 7.

Asante, Molefi and Abu S. Abarry (1996). *African Intellectual History: A Book of Sources*, Philadelphia: Temple University Press.

Association of Black Social Workers, New York City (1983). *News*, New York: New York.

Brabson, Howard (2009). Personal Interview, April.

Brown, Elaine (1993). *A Taste of Power: A Black Woman's Story*, New York: Pantheon Books.

Bundles, A'lelia (2001). *On Her Own Ground: The Life and Times of Madame C. J. Walker*, New York: Scribner.

Cleaver, Kathleen and George Katsiaficas (eds.) (2001). *Liberation, Imagination and the Black Panther Party: A New Look at the Panthers and their Legacy*, New York: Routledge Books.

Collier-Thomas, Bettye and V. P. Franklin (eds.) (2001). *Sisters in the Struggle: African American Women in the Civil Rights-Black Power Movements*, New York: New York University Press.

Columbia Encyclopedia (2007). 6th ed., "Booker Taliaferro Washington," New York: Columbia University Press.

Cruse, Harold (1967). *The Crisis of the Negro Intellectual*, New York: Quill.

D'Emilio, John (2004). *Lost Prophet: The Life and Times of Bayard Rustin*, Chicago: University of Chicago Press.

Forbes, Flores Alexander (2007). *Will You Die With Me? My Life and the Black Panthers*, New York: Simon & Schuster.

Franklin, John Hope and Alfred Moss, Jr. (2000). *From Slavery to Freedom*, New York: Alfred A. Knopf.

Franklin, Vincent P. (1995). *Living Our Stories, Telling Our Truths: Autobiography and the Making of African American Intellectual Tradition*, Oxford: Oxford University Press.

Fredrickson, George M. (1995). *Black Liberation: A Comparative History of Black Ideologies in the United States and South Africa*, Oxford: Oxford University Press.

Garrow, David J. (1983). *The FBI and Martin Luther King, Jr. From Solo to Memphis*, New York: W.W. Norton and Company.

81

Giddings, Paula (2008). *Ida: A Sword Among Lions: Ida B. Wells and the Campaign Against Lynching*, New York: Harper Collins.

Height, Dorothy (2005). *Open Wide the Freedom Gates: A Memoir*, Cambridge: Perseus Books.

Jaggers, Garland (2003). *That Rare Moment in History: A Documented History of the Formation of the National Association of Black Social Workers*, Detroit: Self-Published.

Johnson, Karen (2000). *Uplifting the Women and the Race: The Lives, Educational Philosophies and Social Activism of Anna Julia Cooper and Nannie Helen Burroughs*, New York: Garland Publishing.

Jones, Charles (ed.) (1998). *The Black Panther Party Reconsidered*, Baltimore: Black Classic Press.

Karenga, Maulana. (2002). *An Introduction to Black Studies*, Los Angeles: University of Sankore Press.

LeBlanc-Ernest, Angela D. (1998). " 'The Most Qualified Person to Handle the Job': Black Panther Party Women, 1966-1982," *The Black Panther Party Reconsidered*, Charles E. Jones, ed., Baltimore: Black Classic Press.

Marable, Manning (1998), *Black Leadership*, New York: Columbia Press.

_____ (1999). *Black Leadership*: Four Great American Leaders, New York: Penguin Books.

Martin, Tony (1976) *Race First*, Westport: Greenwood Press.

Matthews, Tracye (1998). " No One Ever Asks What a Man's Role in the Revolution Is: Gender and the Politics of the Black Panther Party, 1966-1971," *The Black Panther Party Reconsidered*, Charles E. Jones, ed., Baltimore: Black Classic Press.

National Association of Black Social Workers (1972). *Diversity: Cohesion or Chaos – Mobilization for Survival*, New York: NABSW.

_____, *Newsletter*, Vol.1, No. 4, March.

National Association of Social Workers (1971). *NASW News*, Washington, D.C.: NASW.

National Council of Negro Women (2009). "Celebrating Dorothy Height," Program Brochure, Washington, D.C.

Neal, Leora (2009). Personal Interview, April.

Norrell, Robert J. (2009). *Up from History: The Life of Booker T. Washington*, Cambridge: Belknap Press/Harvard University Press.

Pfeffer, Paula F. (1990). *A. Philip Randolph, Pioneer of the Civil Rights Movement*, Baton Rouge: Louisiana State University Press.

Rabaka, Reiland (2005). "Talented Tenth," *Encyclopedia of Black Studies*, Molefi Asante and Ama Mazama, (eds.), Thousand Oaks, CA: Sage Publications, pp. 443 – 445.

Raiford, Gil (2009). Personal Interview, April.

Reid-Bookhart (1984). "Toward the Third Decade: The National Association of Black Social Workers," (Unpublished Report), New York: NABSW.

Reid-Merritt, Patricia (1996). *Sister Power: How Phenomenal Black Women Are Rising to the Top*, New York: John Wiley and Sons.

Rustin, Bayard, Devon W. Carbado and Donald Weise (2003). *Time on Two Crosses: The Collected Writings of Bayard Rustin*, Berkeley, CA: Cleis Press.

Seale, Bobby (1970). *Seize the Time*, New York: Random House.

Smock, Raymond (2009). *Booker T. Washington: Black Leadership in the Age of Jim Crow.* Chicago: Ivan R. Dee Press.

Spencer, Robyn Ceanne (2008). "Engendering the Black Freedom Struggle: Revolutionary Black Womanhood and the Black Panther Party in the Bay Area, California," *Journal of Women's History*, Vol. 20, No. 1, 90 – 113.

Sterling, Dorothy (1988). *Black Foremothers: Three Lives*, New York: The Feminist Press at the City University of New York.

Washington, Booker T. (1968). *Up From Slavery*, New York: Magnum Books.

White, John (1985). *Black Leadership in America: 189- 1968*, New York: Logman Group Limited.

Yee, Shirley (1992). *Black Women Abolitionists: A Study in Activism*, 1828-1860, Knoxville, University of Knoxville Press.

Website:

www.nul.org

5

PRESIDENTIAL LEADERSHIP, DEVELOPMENT AND SOCIAL RESPONSIBILITY

One of the most coveted roles within the BSWM was to assume the position as president of NABSW. There was an undeniable popularity that accompanied the Movement's emergence as a culturally conscious, radically infused professional organization among many Black social workers. For the most part, professionally trained Black social workers were denied key leadership roles within mainstream social work organizations. NABSW offered both leadership training and leadership opportunities for those wishing to serve. However, the organization's form of participatory democracy—only allowing steering committee representatives to cast votes in national elections—resulted in a handful of individuals empowered to make key decisions about leadership choices and the future direction of the organization. Once elected, the president assumed the role of commander and chief and was held responsible for the continued growth of the organization.

Cenie J. Williams left an indelible print on the organization, and many aspiring leaders who followed hoped to rise to his level of prominence. A review of NABSW's presidential leadership provides a brief glimpse into the many issues that challenged the Movement and the organization from its early beginnings into the 21st century.

Chunn Administration (1974–78)

Jay C. Chunn, having lost the first presidential election, was in line to succeed Cenie J. Williams as the organization's second president. Howard Brabson of Michigan would serve in his first term as vice-president. Chunn was an experienced social work administrator, organizer and newly appointed dean of Howard University's Graduate School of Social Work. He was committed to keeping the Movement and organization moving forward. He understood the major obstacles that impeded the growth and development of NABSW, including sharp political and ideological differences among organizational members. Chunn served as president of NABSW during a period of high interest and demand for newly minted Black social work professionals. The success of the Civil Rights and Black Power movements—coupled with the War on Poverty, community action, Model Cities programs and the general expansion of the industrial complex needs of urban America (Harrington, 1962; U.S. Department of Labor, 1965-75; Clark and Hopkins, 1970; Harrison, 1972; Murray, 1984) —resulted in the creation of job opportunities for those in the social service arena. The small group of progressive, socially conscious Black social workers who had organized in 1968 now included thousands of paying members. Interest in the association remained high, but many challenges existed. Chunn was deeply aware of the organization's potential strengths and existing obstacles. He established three major priorities: (1) development and implementation of annual conferences; (2) development of organizational infrastructure; and (3) expansion of the membership base with the addition of new chapters.

During the Chunn administration, successful conferences were held in Detroit, Baltimore, New Orleans and San Francisco, helping to buttress the organization's claim as a legitimate national body. Thousands of Black social workers converged on the various cities to participate in the professional gatherings. The staging and production of a national conference was a new experience for Black social workers and the organization's fragile infrastructure was severely tested and strained. Chunn relied on Williams, the newly appointed executive director, to further develop and help maintain a national office.

Black social workers continued to organize themselves into local chapters and sought affiliation with NABSW. Multiple chapters, including those organized on college campuses, existed in Arkansas, California, Florida, Georgia, Illinois, Indiana, Louisiana, Maryland, Michigan, New Jersey, New York, North Carolina, Ohio, Pennsylvania, Texas, Tennessee and Virginia. There was a constant flow of energy and information exchange throughout the country, with significant connections to chapters established in the international communities of Nassau, Bahamas; London; Johannesburg; Montreal; and Nova Scotia.

For many Black social workers, the motivation to engage in Movement activity was social, personal, professional, political and/or some combination of all of the above. There was a confluence of conflicting issues and agendas. On the national level, political and ideological differences continued to unfold within the organization and threatened the growth of the Movement. Chunn (2009) recalled his main concerns and greatest accomplishments as he turned the leadership over to Brabson, the organization's third president, who had beat back a challenge from Lorna Hill of California. Hill was the organization's vice-president in Chunn's second term and the first woman to run for the presidency:

> *"I was worried about a split in the organization. Throughout my administration, we had some difficulty holding the East Coast and the West Coast together. As my presidency ended, I no longer felt that the organization was unstable. Howard Brabson, who had served a term as my vice-president, was able to benefit from the cohesiveness that resulted from years of effort by me and Cenie, who organized the East Coast as I organized the West. There were about 65 chapters when I entered office and about 120 when I left."*

As Chunn concluded his presidency, the organization fulfilled one of the major goals of the Movement: successfully solidifying its membership base.

Brabson Administration (1978–1982)

As Brabson began his term as president, with Audreye Johnson as vice-president, NABSW had firmly established itself in the professional social work community as evinced by its presence in major cities, social welfare policy discussions and schools of social work (NABSW, 1976–84). Brabson was a seasoned federal employee working as the local program director of Chicago's Walker, Madame C. J. when he first became involved with the BSWM. An active participant from the very early stages, he was careful not to assume a public leadership role while fulfilling his responsibilities as a federal employee. When Brabson joined the faculty at the University of Michigan in 1969, his position afforded him the academic freedom needed to work on professional and community issues relevant to the needs of the Black community. Even prior to his election, Brabson visited social agencies, community programs and schools of social work throughout the nation, where he focused on the need to develop and support an independent Black social work organization.

The Brabson administration would maintain the policies and programs established by the previous administrations of Williams and Chunn. The continued growth of the association through the expansion of its membership base was of paramount concern. However, while modest levels of interest continued to be evident, the decline in social activism that followed the end of the Black Freedom Movement era (Franklin and Moss, 2000; Karenga, 2002) had a significant impact on the organization's ability to generate high enthusiasm among Black human service professionals. Brabson continued the conference tradition, but was faced with increasing external challenges from those who began to question the legitimacy, if not legality, of the organization and its gatherings. The organization's reputation for building a "Black only" membership was fairly well known to social service agencies and questioned by many administrators and supervisory personnel, who often determined which conferences would be supported with the agency's professional development funds. Members began to report that their agencies refused to support their attendance at educational programming sponsored by Black social workers, primarily due to the fact that whites were not permitted to attend. And the organization's militant stance around social issues impacting the Black community did not endear it to traditional social work professionals or local authorities. Julius Hayes (2009), a MSW trained worker recalls:

"There was a time when just the mention of Black social workers meant that your agency dare not support your request for conference travel. Our image and presence was larger than our actual strength. Somewhere along the line, all that changed. Supervisors felt that they could deny you without any severe consequences."

Moreover, Reaganomics, the economic recession of the early 1980s and the subsequent downturn in the economy left many social agencies strapped for funds to support employee professional development (Sethi, 1982).

NABSW had developed into an organization that was firmly committed to a philosophy of self-help and self-determination. And President Brabson agreed to continue this approach, always encouraging individuals to renew their commitment to the struggle for Black freedoms. However, the organization's steadfast commitment to Black independence came at a cost. Concerned about the role of government funding in controlling the direction and activities of civil rights and social activist organizations, NABSW, on the national level, refused all forms of outside funding and was totally self-sufficient, relying on membership fees and the income earned from the annual conferences. In order to survive, the organization needed to extract from the Movement more individuals who were committed to a new approach to Black social work and were willing to fund the sponsored activities of NABSW with their own personal resources. Many proved willing to make the necessary sacrifice. This actualization of self-determination principles strengthened the organization's resolve to protest against social injustice in any form deemed appropriate and effective.

While the annual national and international gatherings remained a top priority for the organization, other important issues emerged. During the four years of the Brabson administration, there appeared to be a tremendous surge in the growth of the organization— there was a 33 percent growth in the number of affiliated chapters. As Brabson prepared to leave office, developing a financial and administrative structure that could support a national body with close to 200 chapters was a growing concern. According to Brabson (2009):

"At the time of my administration, it was clear to me that the organization had grown up. We had national and international impact. We met with congressional representatives and expressed our concern about social welfare issues here at home and in Africa.

And we were able to draw attention to the needs of people in Africa because of our international conferences. NABSW continued to grow. There were more than 188 chapters at the end of my term. A lot of that organizing was the result of Cenie, who was the executive director at the time and who was basically running the organization. We had more chapters, but our membership was down. People all over the country listed themselves as members but refused to pay. And we had money problems. Members wanted more accountability. We had to stop thinking so much about social action and ask ourselves if we could administer a national organization with a national office and staff. I had grave concerns as I turned the leadership over to Bill Merritt."

The Second and Third Decades

Much had changed since the BSWM was launched in the late 1960s. During the 1970s, which marked the organization's first full decade, the nation experienced a decline in social activism and an end to the modern-day freedom movement (Karenga, 2002; Franklin and Moss, 2004). In the 1980s, the mood of the nation vacillated from pessimism to optimism, depending largely on which party occupied the nation's highest office. On one hand, we were confronted with the oppressive socio-political polices of Reaganomics (1981–89) and Gulf War politics of George Bush, Sr. (1989–1993); on the other, a vision of possibilities regarding change. While the calls for Black Power had subsided, a record number of Blacks had been empowered by their election, as Democrats, to political office, including Philadelphia Mayor Wilson Goode in 1984, Chicago Mayor Harold Washington in 1983, New York City Mayor David Dinkins in 1989 and Virginia Governor Douglas Wilder in 1989. And Jesse Jackson mounted a respectable campaign for the U.S. presidency in 1984 and 1988. Moreover, there was a significant increase in the number of Blacks elected and appointed to political office on the local, state and federal levels (Joint Center for Political and Economic Studies, 1978, 1981, 1985, 1993).

By the early 1990s, many were eager to refocus the civil rights struggle on concerns about domestic issues, including jobs, housing and health care. When the Democrats and President William Jefferson Clinton (1993–2001) wrested the White House from Republican control, Blacks felt that they had a friend at the highest level of government. This coincided with other important developments in the Black community, including the historic Million Man and Million Woman marches, the Los Angeles Rebellion—which placed Rodney King at the center of the civil rights controversy—and the famous Thomas-Hill confrontation, which demonstrated to America that Ivy-league-educated Blacks existed on both sides of the political spectrum (Karenga, 2002). Maintaining public interest in the BSWM would prove to be a daunting task. College-educated Black professionals were no longer limited to a few select career choices like education, nursing and social work. And even those with social work training were attracted to other special interest groups, such as Blacks in Government, Blacks in Criminal Justice, and 100 Black Men and Women. Those who felt that the Black social work organization and conferences were important gatherings for socially conscious professional activists now had other equally viable options. Moreover, the need for Blacks to support traditional Black organizations appeared to be on the wane. National organizations began to articulate their concerns about dwindling enrollments, specifically as it related to a younger generation embracing the activism of the old (Johnson and Stanford, 2002; Dickerson, 2007). These issues and social concerns would have a significant impact on the BSWM.

Merritt Administration (1982–1986)

In the early 1980s, William T. Merritt unexpectedly became the fourth president of NABSW when he defeated Audreye Johnson, one of the organization's founding members. Paul Hubbard of Detroit would serve as Merritt's vice-president. Johnson's defeat renewed interest in the questions about female leadership: Was it possible that gender played a role in leadership selection? In addition to Johnson's role as a founder, she also served as a steering committee member, conference vice-chair, recording secretary and vice-president. Leadership opportunities had been plentiful for Johnson and other women in the organization, but the position of president was still out of reach. And most members denied that sexism or chauvinism was an issue. As indicated by one member, "There were more women in the membership than men. If the organization could or would not elect a woman, it was because the women would not allow it to happen, not the men." Sexism may or may not have been a pertinent issue; however, the Merritt administration would face a new set of more serious challenges that eventually would lead to a steady contraction of members and local affiliates.

91

As previously indicated in Chapter Four, the Merritt administration coincided with the dismissal of Cenie J. Williams, the organization's first executive director and president. This action produced far-reaching consequences for the organization and created a new, unintended role for the organization's president—executive administrator. It was a heavy burden to bear. In addition, the Merritt administration would mark the beginning of presidential leadership steeped in social service administration and supervisory experience, skills that were highly valued during a period of dwindling financial support. There appeared to be diminishing leadership roles for social work scholars and educators who had assumed more prominent roles in the organization during earlier stages of development.

Merritt, a 42-year-old Plainfield, New Jersey, native, received his MSW from Rutgers University in 1967. He was employed as executive director of Girls Center of Essex County, a residential treatment center for girls, and was serving as a city councilman in Plainfield when elected to office. He was no stranger to power and politics. Merritt had been actively involved in the organization for ten years, serving two terms as member-at-large and as conference chairman. In New Jersey, Merritt was the face of Black social work. Serving six years as state president, he had successfully organized local chapters in various counties in the state. Moreover, he had led a successful protest against the state's division of child welfare services, targeting unfair and biased employee practices that were injurious to Black employees.

Merritt assumed the presidency without administrative support. As executive director during both the Chunn and Brabson administrations, Williams was able to fulfill the goals and objectives of the organization by devoting his full energies to the promotion of NABSW and the expansion of BSWM activities. At the time of his departure, NABSW could legitimately claim affiliate representation in 35 states, with additional chapters in the international community. Unfortunately, financial constraints and other limitations resulted in the decision not to hire a new executive director or national administrator to assume the roles and responsibilities formerly carried out by Williams. Subsequently, the national office experienced a prolonged period of understaffing.

Administrative decision making and program implementation tasks were dependent upon voluntary efforts assigned primarily to the organization's executive committee. This resulted in the overtaxing of the organization's executive officers, particularly the new president, who attempted to assume a dual role as executive director/CEO and president. It also marked the point when the maintenance and preservation of the organization was prioritized over all other activity. In essence, NABSW, and its local affiliates, had replaced the BSWM as the most critically important work for many Black social work activists.

The organization's major communication mechanisms were also affected by its financial exigency. Publication of the *Conference Proceedings* was suspended in 1983. The *Black Caucus Journal,* which was published biannually, was now published annually and at times less frequently. Fortunately, the organization's policy statements were published in *Position Papers* in 1983 and again in 1985, and *Preserving Black Families: Research and Action Beyond the Rhetoric* was published in 1986. The latter publication was of particular importance. Not only did it clarify and expand upon NABSW's commitment to quality service for Black children in the child welfare system seeking foster care and/or adoption, the document cast the issue of transracial adoption in clearer perspective. And while the organization was unable to assume a high level of visibility in terms of national leadership in the Black community, there remained an unrelenting concern over NABSW's position on transracial adoption. The push to "eliminate barriers" by encouraging more white families to adopt Black children was now a congressional policy issue. On June 25, 1985, Merritt was called for congressional hearings held by the Committee on Labor and Human Resources: Barriers to Adoption, chaired by Utah Republican Senator Orrin Hatch, and asked to provide testimony in defense of the organization's opposition to transracial placements. (A fuller discussion of NABSW's child welfare platform and transracial adoption can be found in Chapter Eight.)

For a brief period, an interim executive position was created in 1985 to provide administrative and research support to the national office. A social work faculty member on sabbatical leave (this author) was utilized to conduct a major review of the organization's national policy initiatives and assess affiliate activity. Among other findings, it was noted that the effectiveness of the national communication network was diminishing and that local leadership evinced marked unfamiliarity with the organization's policy and position statements. Both circumstances posed serious threats to the continued viability of the organization. However, it was also noted that local leaders were enthusiastically committed to NABSW and expressed pride in local activity and accomplishments (Reid-Bookhart, 1985).

The interim executive's final report, "Toward the Third Decade: Local Implementation of the NABSW Thrust," included recommendations to: develop a formalized mechanism to receive feedback on successful local projects and programs for duplication around the country; operationalize a regional network to increase effectiveness of intra-organizational communication; create organizational structures to promote information exchange between committee chairs; institutionalize a mechanism to orient, develop and educate new leadership; reissue the organization's Position Papers and provide a forum for discussion of content; formalize ties with other national Black organizations via written statements of agreement and articulation; appoint a historian; and promote efforts to secure an interim executive on an annual basis to continue research and development activities (Ibid). Unfortunately, few of the recommendations were implemented.

Limited financial resources would also impact decision making around the annual conferences. The ongoing success of the national conferences remained a critical component in the organization's activities and was clearly linked to the economic survival of the organization. Moreover, it was the primary mechanism used to connect Black social workers from all over the nation with the message of the Movement, which continued to promote social action, social advocacy and social justice for members of the Black community. It was during the Merritt administration that the organization's leaders took note of the link between America's popular cities and national conference attendance. As funds for Black social workers continued to dry up, many conference participants chose to use their personal resources and also used the annual events as quasi-vacations. It was important to select major cities with easy travel access and those rich in culture, heritage and entertainment to help guarantee that the conferences would generate crowds large enough to net a profit for the organization. As a result, a decision was made to strip the local affiliates of their responsibility to organize, implement and manage the national conferences. To ensure quality, consistency and fiscal accountability, the annual conferences were nationalized. While providing more stability to the national body, this move contributed to a power shift from the local affiliates to the national office.

The organization was undergoing a major transition. Chapter and individual memberships declined but rebounded in 1985 and 1986. And, interestingly enough, while NABSW fought incessantly for increased participation of Blacks in schools of social work, the increased number of Blacks who obtained graduate degrees did not expand the organization's membership base. As indicated in Table II, Black enrollments in schools of social work (MSW programs) increased significantly from 1969 until 1973, only to follow a continuous decline from 1974 to 1987, with 1988 to1990 showing the beginnings of a reversal in this trend. Yet, from 1970 to1980 alone, approximately 11,000 new Black MSWs joined the professional ranks, with an additional 7,000 to 8,000 being added from 1981 to1990. Ironically, as the number of Black social work professionals increased, membership in the organization decreased.

It is important to note that Black social workers reported their involvement in other professional associations. Black membership in NASW and CSWE increased, with Black social workers establishing a separate Black Caucus within CSWE to address their unique needs. The expansion of membership cannot be reported for NABSW. From 1980 to 1990, there were fewer than 4,000 members and 100 local chapters affiliated with the organization in any given year. It seems apparent that in the decade following America's social upheaval, calls to Black consciousness and social activism among Black social work professionals produced diminishing returns. However, the data also suggests that a strong correlation exists between the organization's heyday and the peak period of Black student enrollment in graduate schools of social work. During the early 1970s, when the organizing of Black social workers reached fever pitch, Black student participation at the graduate level was also at an all time high. One might conclude that a symbiotic relationship existed between these two developments. The reciprocal effects added strength and vitality to the Movement.

Finally, following a series of cost-cutting measures, prudent budgeting and many successful fundraising efforts, NABSW regained financial solvency in 1985. Again, NABSW was primed to direct more of its focus on professional development, relevant social issues and the revitalization of the Black Social Work Movement as Merritt turned the reins of leadership over to the fifth president, Morris X. F. Jeff of New Orleans.

TABLE II

BLACK STUDENT ENROLLMENT
GRADUATE SCHOOLS OF SOCIAL WORK
1969–90

| YEAR | TOTAL | FULL-TIME MSW STUDENTS | | | | POST/DOCTORAL | |
| | | 1ST YR. | | 2ND YR. | | | |
		#	%	#	%	#	%
1969	1531	888	14.2	607	10.7	36	8.9
1970	1901	975	14.5	872	14.3	54	11.7
1971	2146	1067	14.9	1049	15.3	30	13.3
1972	2439	1226	15.8	1126	15.4	87	15.4
1973	2516	1185	14.4	1227	15.6	104	16.8
1974	2230	1004	12.7	1093	12.6	133	17.4
1975	2109	933	11.9	1093	12.4	123	17.3
1976	1969	836	10.5	1013	11.3	120	15.6
1977	1927	864	10.2	947	10.5	116	13.4
1978	1901	844	10.3	930	9.8	127	15.5
1979	1846	799	9.9	928	9.9	119	12.5
1980	1778	737	9.8	934	9.8	107	13.0
1981	1475	679	9.0	796	8.8	120	13.8

| YEAR | TOTAL | FULL-TIME MSW STUDENTS | | POST/DOCTORAL | |
		#	%	#	%
1982	1565	1435	9.5	130	14.1
1983	1349	1247	8.8	102	11.9
1984	-	1225	8.7	104	13.0
1985	1209	1129	8.1	80	11.4
1986	1104	1014	7.3	90	15.0
1987	1269	1165	7.9	104	14.7
1988	1519	1399	8.7	120	14.1
1989	1538	1423	9.0	115	13.4
1990	1760	1624	9.3	136	16.2

Source: Statistics on Social Work Education in the United States, 1969-90. Council on Social Work Education. Washington, D.C.

Jeff Administration (1986–1990)

New Orleans native Jeff proved to be one of the more charismatic leaders of NABSW. Born in 1938, Jeff was, perhaps, destined to continue in the footsteps of his father, Morris F.X. Jeff, Sr., a lifetime advocate of civil rights and social justice for Black children and the community. Jeff received a bachelor's degree from Xavier University, a master's degree in social work from Atlanta University (later to be renamed Clark Atlanta University) and a DSW from Tulane University. Active on the local level, he had served as chapter president prior to assuming the position as national president. He was a lifelong learner and focused much of his studies on African and African American history and culture. Robbie Little of West Palm Beach, Florida, would serve as his vice-president.

Unlike previous presidents, Jeff was an administrator of a public welfare agency, where support for vital human services is mandated by public policy. Jeff had limited experience with the Herculean task of fundraising for a nonprofit organization or managing a large all-volunteer organization where passion and dedication combined with idiosyncratic eccentric behaviors to produce were the norm. This proved detrimental to his administration.

The Jeff administration undertook another major review in the fall of 1986, launching "a planning process to help develop, implement, and evaluate the organization's future directions" (NABSW, 1986:1). Following a survey of the organization's local leadership conducted by Detroit member Geneva Williams, five major priority areas were targeted: social issues and programs; membership; finance and administration; planning; and communication. (It is interesting to note that professional role development, professional issues or the development of social work practice methodologies were not listed as priority areas.) While the organization was unable to fully embrace and implement the five policy recommendations, the National Steering Committee did vote to relocate the national office from New York City to the campus of Clark Atlanta University, a historically Black college. In addition, and equally important, a new executive director, E. Hill Deloney, was hired in 1986. These two actions required substantial ongoing financial support and the development of an organizational infrastructure that could support a freestanding independent Black organization.

A strong proponent of preserving the African American family, Jeff never hesitated to speak out in support of unifying Black families and communities. Jeff, like the presidents before him, became the public face of Black opposition

97

to transracial adoption. This issue remained a hotly debated topic nearly 15 years after NABSW issued its position statement opposing transracial placements (see Chapter Eight, Table IV). Jeff made numerous appearances on national media shows, including the *Today* show, *Nightline*, *Night Watch* and the *Oprah Winfrey Show*, defending the position of the organization. Unfortunately, the new notoriety, much like the old, was steeped in negativism and projected the organization as one that was blinded by a singular issue. NABSW's purpose and accomplishments, and the extent to which it articulated the concerns of thousands of Black human service workers, remained ambiguous and obscure.

Jeff, who was committed to the public affirmation of one's African identity through social rituals, is credited with moving the organization toward a stronger connection to its African heritage and an African philosophical worldview. His creation and development of the Harambee Ceremony provided conferees with the opportunity to celebrate and reaffirm their African identity and dedication to an African-based value system.

The Harambee celebration was first held at the 16th annual conference in April 1984 during the Merritt administration as a tribute and memorial for Williams. It was an elaborate ceremonial event that included a leadership processional, libations and call to the ancestors, spoken word, call and response, and African drumming and dancing. Jeff requested that all conferees attend the program in traditional African clothing. While some of the leaders and conferees were reluctant to embrace the concept, the Harambee Ceremony eventually grew to be among the most popular conference events. In this politically and professionally safe environment, full expressions of the African heritage became more visible. Throughout the four-day gathering, many conferees shed their western clothing for traditional African attire. However, other participants questioned the increasing overt emphasis on African culture and heritage. As stated by one regular conference attendee: "I came here because I wanted to be Black. I don't know about all of this African stuff."

Even after his departure from the office of president, Jeff continued to take an active role in moving the organization closer to embracing an African identity. On March 1998, he was enstooled as an African chief—Sankofaheme Barima Odi Akosah—in Kibi, Ghana. Jeff, who had unofficially assumed the title as African cultural ambassador, continued to fulfill the role as chief guru until his untimely death in June 2003.

Smith Administration (1990–1994)

In many ways, the presidency of Gerald K. Smith symbolized the philosophy and values of the larger Movement and the organization. Smith, not a social worker by education, joined the organization as a social advocate. Born July 19, 1942, in Cincinnati, Smith received his Bachelor of Science in history and government from Ohio University. He held a master's degree in education from Xavier University. Once he relocated to Detroit, he continued to pursue his education: He received a Master of Arts degree in sociology and urban affairs from the University of Detroit, Mercy and eventually obtained a doctorate in education in administration and supervision from Wayne State University. As a member of the Detroit chapter, Smith's success in the field of social services was well noted. Smith was employed as a corporate manager for Proctor and Gamble when he resigned to take a position with Family and Neighborhood Services of Western Wayne County. His concern for youth and families led him to accept a position as executive director of a settlement house. He would later join the W.K. Kellogg Foundation, where he focused on the needs of inner-city urban youth. Smith would leave Kellogg to become the founder and chief executive officer of Youthville, Detroit. Smith was a community activist who organized and joined several initiatives that focused on Black youth, families and community. Eventually he emerged as a recognized leader on both the local and national levels.

As Smith entered office with Barbara Baldwin of Houston as his vice-president, he was fully aware of the new challenges that he faced. The organization was teetering on a slippery slope, facing the possibility of bankruptcy. The organization's move to the campus of Clark Atlanta University was a short-lived experiment that failed to serve the best interest of the national body. In addition, the organization found that it could not financially support a full-time national administrator. While NABSW had built a solid reputation as a leader in the field of Black family services and Black child advocacy, their ability to maintain an independent freestanding national office remained a challenge. The National Steering Committee voted to relocate the office to Detroit, providing easy access for the new president as well as an opportunity to utilize the support and resources of the local chapter, which had grown to be one of the largest in the organization. Smith, a skilled administrator and successful fundraiser, would focus his attention on the need to implement new administrative procedures and strengthening the policy positions of the organization. Additionally, he sought to devise new ways of delivering the core message of the Movement to the people.

Not withstanding the financial crisis that faced the organization, there was never any doubt that conference organizing and planning would move forward. For more than a few social workers, the ability to connect with other like-minded Black professionals on an annual basis was a necessary "fix" needed to survive predominantly white, bureaucratic social service organizations. However, Smith was searching for newer innovations that would help strengthen the base of the organization.

Under the Smith administration, an important mechanism designed to help the membership keep abreast of critical social issues was the National Public Policy Institute (NPPI). The NPPI was launched in October 1990. The institute, chaired by G. Rosaline Preudhomme and Katey Assem, both of New York, targeted everything from family preservation to traumatic social conditions and sought to empower the organization to create "a bold, purposeful and powerful agenda" (NASBW, 1994). In the more than 30 years since its founding, the organization continued to "cast the net widely," always focusing, with limited success, on a plethora of social ills that impacted Black America. It was, as suggested by Sanders (1970), one of the ongoing dilemmas faced by NABSW: attempting to address too many of the major social problems in the Black community.

Deviating from past practices, a policy institute was held at every quarterly Steering Committee Meeting and at the annual conference. Institute leaders included Jualeyne Dodson, John Bess, Bette Pierce-Denise, Aminifu Harvey, Marina Barnette, Tawana Ford Sabbath, Thaddeus P. Mathis, S.B. Chapman, Geoffrey Canada, Yolanda Burwell, Sylvia Parker, Paul Snead, Barbara Conover, Megan McLauglin, Barbara Sabol, Eddie Ellis, Waayl Shahie, Iris Carlton-Laney, Anjanette Wells, Jodi Brockington, Peter Brown, Toni Oliver, Leora Neal and Zena Oglesby. These individuals were representative of different regions in the country and shared their expertise on the need to develop critical policy statements on social issues facing the Black community. Unfortunately, the measurable impact of these initiatives was often limited by the broad range of issues that were part of the organization's action agenda. However, the local leadership remained informed about critical social issues impacting Black America.

Smith's wise use of local leadership, coupled with his extraordinary administrative skills and experiences, helped the organization regain its financial footing. He was creative in his approach to fundraising, including borrowing money from the membership with the promise that they would be paid back in full. Smith achieved that goal and more. Smith established new managerial and operational procedures that would become a permanent part of the organization. As he prepared to leave office, it was noted that chapter and individual memberships remained relatively unchanged. Capturing the next generation of Black social workers was a major concern, one that Smith would share with the incoming administration. Smith continued to contribute his support and expertise to the organization until his passing in August 2008.

Dunston Administration (1994–1998)

Leonard G. Dunston, a North Carolina native, would make his mark in social work and human services as a resident of New York. Dunston graduated from Livingstone College in Salisbury, North Carolina, with a Bachelor of Arts in sociology and secondary education. Following a two-year stint in the U.S. Army, Dunston began his career as a street gang worker in New York City. He later received a MSW degree in social work administration from Hunter College School of Social Work. Dunston would eventually work his way up to the position of commissioner of the New York State Division for Youth (currently known as the Office of Children and Family Services), a position he held when elected to the presidency of NABSW. Marva Anderson of Los Angeles. would serve as his vice-president.

Dunston joined the BSWM in the late 1960s, having been influenced by the organizing and leadership abilities of Williams in New York City. He served as steering committee representative for the Westchester chapter and national member-at-large. He was unopposed in his bid to be the organization's seventh president.

The concepts surrounding Afrocentricity had entered the lexicon of Black social workers. The new theory of social work practice was one that was African-centered, based on knowledge, values, skills and a philosophy generated by the advances in Black intellectual thought in the fields of the humanities, social and behavioral sciences and the professions. Wedding African-centered knowledge to contemporary social work practice was the new goal. During the earliest days of the Movement, the desire to develop a new foundation for practice within the Black community was a driving force behind the creation of the organization. What was now needed was a mechanism by which this new knowledge could be transferred to Black social work professionals. The Dunston administration launched the National Academy for African-Centered Social Work in 1996 to serve that purpose.

The academy was the creation of Patricia Reid-Merritt, professor of social work and Africana Studies at the Richard Stockton College in New Jersey, and Thaddeus P. Mathis, professor of social work administration at Temple University in Philadelphia. Mathis was the founder and director of the Institute for Africana Social Work at Temple in 1993; Reid-Merritt, on sabbatical leave, served as the associate director. Reid-Merritt and Mathis had been engaged in a number of projects that examined the link between Africana studies and social work. In numerous workshops and presentations, they often bemoaned the lack of advancements in social work that specifically addressed the needs of the Black social work practitioner. They were not alone in their concerns. According to Dunston (2009):

> *"I remember being introduced to the whole concept of African-centered social work in a workshop given by Pat Reid-Merritt and Thad Mathis. They talked about replacing Eurocentric knowledge and beliefs with an African-centered foundation. I was intrigued by that.*

> *When I became president, I wanted my administration to reflect our African culture and heritage, and thought about ways in which I could incorporate African customs and practices into the organization. I also challenged Pat and Thad to come up with something that could translate their small workshops into something more beneficial to the larger organization and membership. They created the Academy for African-Centered Social Work."*

Reid-Merritt and Mathis developed a curriculum of study for Afrocentric social work practice (see Chapter Nine). The first graduating class in April 1997 included 55 social work professionals—all with masters and some with doctorate degrees—from throughout the country.

Dunston expanded the Afrocentric thrust of the organization, introducing a spiritual awakenings/call to the ancestors at the opening of all steering committee meetings and national conference sessions. The majority of these openings were performed by academy graduates who were in the best position to articulate the connections between African-centered thought and African-centered social work practice. The added emphasis on embracing African culture was a welcome addition by many, but caused concerns for others. As one conference participant indicated: "For me, it was never about being African. All I wanted to be was Black."

The Dunston administration, with strong support from the Office of Student Affairs and national representative Tricia Bent-Goodley, also placed greater emphasis on increasing youth participation in the organization. Dunston renewed interest in developing student chapters and organized youth forums, which were held in each host city. Pre-conference summits and community activity days were also held as a method to forge stronger connections between Black social workers and the local community. These summits focused specifically on identifying some of the most adverse conditions that impacted Black communities. The *Black Caucus* was published on a semiannual basis, and increased attention was given to intra-organization communication. According to Dunston, his administration was buoyed, somewhat, by an increased level of social awareness generated by such events as the Million Man March, the Million Woman March and the popularization of rap music that spoke to awakening the social consciousness of the emerging generation (Karenga, 2002). He (2009) states:

> "I was aware of everything that was going on around me at the time. I was able to participate in the planning of the Million Man March. As president of NABSW, I had a platform to talk about our major issues. We were focusing on the need to locate more Black homes for Black children. After my initial pleas during the march, we received more than 3,000 phone calls from people all over the country expressing their interest in the NABSW adoption and child welfare programs. Our local programs in Atlanta, Detroit, New York and Los Angeles benefitted tremendously from this effort."

Dunston is also credited with renewing formal ties to other national Black organizations, seeking to develop collaborative efforts that would best serve the interest of the respective organizations, as well as the needs of the Black community.

The Fourth Decade—21st Century America

As America entered the 21st century, there appeared to be endless possibilities. African Americans had made significant advances in many areas, including social work. In fact, the role of Blacks in the field of social work was no longer in question. While Blackwell (1981) spoke to the decline in parity in Black participation in graduate school enrollments that occurred in the mid-1980s, African Americans had achieved leadership milestones in every professional arena. African Americans were repeatedly elected to leadership roles in all of the professional social work organizations, including the Council on Social Work Education, the NASW and the Association of Baccalaureate Program Directors. They were deans of schools of social work, and many had been appointed as human service commissioners at the state level. And in 2008, America would elect its first African American president, spawning talks about a "postracial era."

However, the problems of inequality and inequities in the distribution of social resources and the quality of Black life were still of major concern. Black social workers continued to feel the need to fight for increased social opportunities and social justice for all. Many viewed the continued survival of NABSW as vitally important.

Smith Administration (1998–2002)

Rudy C. Smith became NABSW's eighth president as another woman (this author) sought election to the organization's highest office. Reid-Merritt (who was also now married to the organization's fourth president) argued that the organization could not continue its practice of male-only presidents. The body, predominantly female, was in dire need of some consciousness-raising to highlight the role that gender played in leadership selection. Reid-Merritt was a strong advocate of Black female leadership and was noted for her groundbreaking work on Black women and power (1996). The election was held in April 1998 at the annual conference. Smith was the overwhelming choice.

Smith was born in Harlem in 1943. He attended the City College of New York, graduating in 1964 with a B.A. degree in sociology. He attended the University of California, Berkeley, where he received his MSW degree in 1966. Smith was licensed as a clinical social worker in California in

104

1969. He was first introduced to the BSWM while living and working in the San Francisco Bay area, where one of the early local chapters had been established.

During his military career, Smith served in the U.S. Air Force as a psychiatric social worker and director of Military Community Mental Health Services at Sheppard Air Force Base. Smith continued his work in direct services and developed a stellar career as a clinical social worker, supervisor and director. He had recently retired from full-time practice in order to devote his energies to the office of the president. Judith Jackson of Detroit would serve as his vice-president.

Smith inherited a high-spirited organization, but one that was somewhat divided by lingering questions of gender and leadership in the organization. However, coupled with the remarkable progress that Blacks had made in the field of social work since the beginning of the Movement, the continued success of the organization was not in jeopardy. The responsibility to keep the organization moving forward now rested with Smith and the new administration. It would prove to be an overwhelming task. According to Smith (2009):

> "I was ready to assume the role of president and [was] proud to have been elected to continue the presidential tradition of excellence. However, I felt challenged by the disjointed, unprofessional aspects of the national office, the unyielding organizational structure, and the ability to mesh together a cast of characters, all of whom had a deep passion for the Movement and the organization. It was a tremendous responsibility."

Altering the basic format of the national or international conferences was not an option for Smith or any other president. These gatherings served as a mechanism to maintain the communication network among Black social workers and remained a core aspect of the organization's purpose and identity. What Smith did inherit was a shift in conference planning that moved the national gatherings from major cities to "second-tier" cities that would presumably be more attractive to potential conferees due to lower travel and hotel costs. During Smith's second term of office, conference attendance dropped by more than 25 percent. While

105

it is difficult to isolate a single cause, the selection of smaller second-tier cities may have been a contributing factor. Additionally, questions were raised about the possibility of declining interest in Black social work as an independent platform for social activism in the 21st century.

Stabilization, not growth, became Smith's priority. He focused his attention on the move of the national office from Detroit to Washington, D.C., the nation's capital. Given the long history of NABSW, Smith felt that the organization needed to center itself in the midst of policy makers. He achieved that goal when the organization moved into temporary quarters in Washington, D.C., in 2002. The steering committee supported Smith's request to hire a national consultant, Sandra Mitchell, who would oversee operations in the national office. Smith also moved the organization toward the greater use of technology, developing and maintaining a national website and communicating to members electronically.

Smith was aware of the changing social milieu. The social movement was dormant, protest activities produced diminishing returns, and being Black and proud was no longer in vogue. There may have been a decreased emphasis by some on the needs of the Black community, but social advocacy was still needed. With a dwindling number of paid chapters, it was more important than ever that Black social workers target their limited resources on those areas that would yield the greatest impact. Smith wanted to continue the organization's focus on preserving Black families and creating quality service programs for their care. Developing new initiatives and programming around kinship care was one of his carefully chosen social action agenda items.

Jackson Administration (2002–2006)

In 2002, Judith D. Jackson became the first female president of NABSW. It was 32 years after the first male had been elected to office. She was unopposed in her quest to be president, and everyone agreed that it was time. Jackson had numerous leadership experiences before she assumed the presidency. She had served as president of the Detroit chapter, National Steering Committee representative, national conference co-chair, national treasurer and national vice-president. She may very well have been the most "seasoned" of all NABSW presidents. This first-time achievement was celebrated by the members of the organization and viewed as a major milestone by many. As Cheryl Dozier, newly elected vice-president from the University of Georgia, proclaimed, "The women are now in charge!" Jackson was fully cognizant of the significance of her role and knowledgeable about the organization's history around gender issues. She was careful not to engage "in any activity that appeared too feminine" in fear that it might split the organization. She was also appreciative of the tremendous support she received from the past presidents. For Jackson, it would be business as usual as she attempted to stay the course, making certain that NABSW did not falter in its responsibility to maintain national and international forums for Black social work activists to share their issues and concerns. She would, however, devise creative management and leadership strategies to help strengthen the organization.

Jackson was born and raised in Marion, Indiana. She received her bachelor's degree in sociology from the University of Indiana. Jackson received her MSW in administration and planning from the George Warren Brown School of Social Work at Washington University in St. Louis. She had just completed her graduate training when she was first exposed to NABSW. Jackson recalls looking for work when she attended the fifth annual conference in New York City and immediately saw the connection between social work and the real world. After a brief experience in clinical social work, Jackson relocated to Detroit and began her career in policy and management. She had been mentored in various capacities, and for many years, by Gerald Smith, NABSW's sixth president. Jackson was the executive vice-president of Youthville USA, a comprehensive youth service organization where Smith was serving as president, when she assumed the position of president.

Jackson was aware of the shifting patterns of support via conference attendance and membership affiliation. She recalls that there were many discussions about the ongoing relevance of the organization. According to Jackson (2009):

> "During my years as president, I remember struggling with the membership issues. I wanted to focus more attention on bringing in new, younger members. They didn't always come with the depth of understanding about the history and purpose of NABSW. Many of them wanted to revisit the issue about why whites were not permitted to be members or attend the membership meeting and conferences. Within the organization, we have a very captive old guard who weren't as receptive to the younger members and were even less tolerant when it came to discussing the reasons for our existence."

107

Discourse about the relevance of Black organizations was certainly not limited to NABSW. Many groups who had emerged in the 1960s were questioning their future survival. While some were experiencing declining membership (e.g., NAACP, CORE, National Conference of Black Lawyers) others were no longer in existence (e.g., SNCC, Congress of Black Churches). For NABSW, reaching out to social work professionals in the African diaspora remained an essential part of the organization's objectives.

Much like Rudy C. Smith, Jackson was aware of the unyielding nature of the organization's steering committee structure. There were as many committees, subcommittees and special task forces to equal the number of national representatives. Jackson suggested streamlining the steering committee functions by creating four focus groups, including: (1) family preservation; (2) health and wellness; (3) youth development; and (4) civil liberties. While child welfare issues would remain an organizational priority, NABSW needed to reconsider its social action agenda.

As with other presidents, there was no escaping the issues surrounding transracial adoption. The success of numerous congressional acts forced the organization to modify its strategies, working to put into place new guidelines governing the placement of Black children in homes outside of the community. However, it is important to note that the organization remained morally and philosophically committed to the belief that the needs of Black children were best served when they were placed with Black families.

Jackson was able to advance policy discussions and positions beyond the realm of child welfare. Of particular importance was the ongoing discussion around the issues of domestic violence in the Black community. Black-on-Black assault—social, physical, sexual and emotional—was a difficult topic to engage. Under the guided leadership of Tricia Bent-Goodley, the organization was able to make significant headway around educating local leadership about the necessary steps that needed to be taken to forcefully address the issue in the Black community. This is perhaps one area in which female leadership made a difference.

Jackson continued the push to elevate the visibility of NABSW and its national policy positions by securing their presence in the nation's capital. Under the Jackson administration, and for the very first time, the organization purchased property, establishing a permanent home for its national headquarters in Washington, D.C., in 2004.

Roberts Administration (2006–2010)

In 2006, Dr. Gloria Batiste-Roberts from Houston followed Judith Jackson as the second female president of NABSW. She ran unopposed and was joined by the newly elected Vice-President Cheikh Ahmadou Banba Mbacké from Detroit.

Roberts was born in New Orleans and reared in New Roads, Louisiana. She graduated from Texas Southern University in 1972 before moving on to Howard University, where she received an MSW in 1973. Returning to Houston, she became involved with the BSWM in 1974 during the early days of chapter organizing. She served in numerous leadership roles, including president, vice-president and steering committee representative. On the national level, she also served two terms as member-at-large before assuming the role as president. Following years of service in the field of public health, Batiste-Roberts received her Dr.P.H. in 2000 from the University of Texas School of Public Health.

Batiste-Roberts was serving as president of the Houston chapter when Hurricane Katrina hit New Orleans. Thousands were evacuated to other cities, including Houston, which received significantly larger numbers of residents seeking shelter (Cha-Jua, 2005; Allen, 2007). The ability of the Houston chapter to establish and implement a model of intervention for emergency services was extraordinary. According to former president Jackson (2009):

> *"Most people are unaware of the impact that the Houston chapter had on emergency service intervention in Houston and around the country. As president of NABSW, I was contacted by federal officials who were uncertain how to respond to these new communities in need. Many of those who were suddenly displaced were members of the African American community. The federal officials were struggling with ways in which they would begin to integrate them into the community. It was the Houston model that was lifted up to be shared with all those seeking effective solutions to the problems that followed the Katrina disaster. It was one of the most successful initiatives ever developed by an NABSW chapter."*

Batiste-Roberts' 30-year history with the organization convinced her of her ability to set NABSW on a new course. She was cognizant of the steady decline in membership but confident that a new, energetic administration would help to revitalize the membership base and attract new, younger members to the organization. Batiste-Roberts was familiar with the local chapter projects that were under way in cities across the nation. The activities were diverse and included: youth educational and scholarship programs; voter registration and education; HIV/AIDS educational and service programs; fundraising to support their own initiatives; and networking with other organizations dedicated to uplifting the Black community. And there were specialized, successful efforts under way in cities where the local NABSW chapter presence had existed for decades. For example, there were child welfare and black family adoption agencies in New York City, Los Angeles, Detroit, Charlotte, Harrisburg, Pennsylvania, Pittsburg, St. Paul, Richmond, Silver Springs, Maryland, Jackson and Atlanta. Intergenerational and rites of passage programs existed in Westchester, New York, and Philadelphia. Social advocacy and health care programs were established in Lansing, Michigan, and Cleveland. Teen pregnancy, prevention and parenting programs were created in Mobile, Alabama, Washington, D.C., and Atlanta. In Minneapolis, the local chapter established a community-based anti-violence program. In Indianapolis, counseling services were established for survivors of violent death. Batiste-Roberts was ready for the challenge of the presidency, but nothing quite prepared her for the controversy surrounding the organization's planned 40th anniversary conference in Los Angeles in 2008.

The national and international gathering of Black social workers was the glue that held NABSW together. As mentioned previously, once the conferences were nationalized under the Merritt administration, each subsequent administration inherited a conference theme, location and keynote speakers that had been planned years in advance. Such was the case with Batiste-Roberts. The 39th annual conference in Detroit, with its theme "Building on Our Strengths: Infusing New Leadership," suggested that new leadership challenges were forthcoming. And from the moment she assumed office, Batiste-Roberts struggled with making executive leadership decisions that would be in the best interest of the organization.

During the previous administration, a contract had been negotiated with a local independent hotel in Los Angeles as the conference host site. Unfortunately, in the year prior to the event, the organization was notified of pending strike activities, which pitted the independent hotel owner against organized labor. The issues were complex. The powerful, national union insisted that the workers

110

wanted to unionize. However, the workers showed a marked lack of enthusiasm for the initiative. Moreover, the elderly Asian hotel owner was more representative of an independent minority group member struggling against organized labor and corporate conglomerates. Furthermore, the organization faced the dilemma of fulfilling their commitment to the hotel via signed contractual agreement. Reneging on the agreement could have resulted in the loss of revenue, the inability to follow through with the national conference, perhaps even deliver a financial death blow to the organization.

After heated debate, visits to the hotel site and national and local investigations, the National Steering Committee voted to move forward and honor the signed agreement. The decision resulted in many longtime organizational and union members refusing to attend the conference and left lingering feelings of emotional turmoil in the organization. While the conference was a programming success, the loss of revenue, coupled with ongoing concerns about a declining membership base, were felt immediately. Yet the organization remained high-spirited, searching for new ways to add strength and vitality to the movement. And Batiste-Roberts began to concentrate her efforts on other important issues.

The Communication Information Network (CIN) was a major initiative undertaken by the Batiste-Roberts administration to improve the flow of information among local chapters and organizational members. Chapters were encouraged to share news about successful local programming worthy of duplication in other areas of the country. The utilization of information technology assisted in the rapid transfer of information. And e-blasts offered the capability of informing thousands of members of critical issues on a daily basis. Batiste-Roberts also renewed interest in producing scholarly work, focusing on the need to provide historical documentation of the BSWM and the emergence of NABSW.

The political enthusiasm surrounding the candidacy of Barack Obama renewed the organization's active leadership role in voter education and registration. According to Batiste-Roberts, NABSW local chapters assisted in the registration of more than 50,000 new registered voters. And the election of the nation's first African American president was viewed as a major milestone in achieving social equality for members of the Black community.

Finally, Batiste-Roberts achieved another important "first" for the organization. In 2008, NABSW entered into a partnership agreement with NASW to support and promote the passing of the Social Work Reinvestment Act (H.R.

5447), legislation designed to aid in the development of social work education and services while recognizing two African American pioneers in the field of social and civil rights activism: Whitney Young and Dorothy Height. Would this action serve as an example of contemporary social work leadership and organizational practices in the "postracial" era?

Conclusion

The presidency of NABSW offered many individuals the opportunity to develop and exercise their leadership skills. The responsibility of national leadership was, undoubtedly, a novel experience for all of the organization's leaders. Each administration was challenged to discover innovative ways to preserve the spirit and intent of the Movement and the organization. And they succeeded. NABSW has experienced struggle and strife. Yet because the organization and its members are still standing, ready to engage in the next battle for equality and social justice for the African American community, they have emerged triumphant.

References:

Allen, Troy (2007). *"Katrina: Race, Class and Poverty: Reflection and Analysis,"* *Journal of Black Studies*, (March), 37, 466 – 468.

Batiste-Roberts, Gloria (2009). Personal Interview, April.

Blackwell, James E. (1981). *Mainstreaming Outsiders: The Production of Black Professionals*, Bayside, New York: General Hall, Inc.

Brabson, Howard (2009). Personal Interview, April.

Chu-Jua, Sundiata (2006). "Hurricane Katrina," Guest ed., *Black Scholar*, Vol. 36, no. 4.

Chunn, Jay (2009). Personal Interview, April.

Clark, Kenneth and Jeannette Hopkins (1970). *A Relevant War Against Poverty: A Study of Community Action Programs and Observable Social Change*, New York: Harper Press.

Council on Social Work Education (1969-90). *Statistics on Social Work Education in the United States*. Washington, D.C.: CSWE.

Dickerson, Deborah (2007). "The NAACP's Sad Decline," June 19, Salon.com.

Dunston, Leonard (2009). Personal Interview, April.

Franklin, John Hope and Alfred Moss, Jr. (2000). *From Slavery to Freedom*, New York: Alfred A. Knopf.

Harrington, Michael (1963). *The Other America*, New York: Macmillian Company.

Harrison, Bennett (1972). *Education, Training and the Urban Ghetto*, Baltimore: John Hopkins Press.

Hayes, Julius (2009). Personal Interview, April.

Karenga, Maulana. (2002). *An Introduction to Black Studies*, Los Angeles: University of Sankore Press.

_____ (1967). *The Quotable Karenga*, Inglewood, CA: Kawaida Publications.

Jackson, Judith (2009). Personal Interview, April.

Johnson, Ollie and Karin L. Stanford (eds.) (2002). *Black Political Organizations in the Post—Civil Rights Era,* New Brunswick: Rutgers University Press.

Joint Center for Political and Economic Studies (1978, 1981, 1985, 1993). "Black Political Participation," jointcenter.org.

Merritt, William T. (2009). Personal Interview, April.

Mitchell, Sandra (2009). Personal Interview, April.

Murray, Charles. (1984). *Losing Ground: American Social Policy, 1950—1980*, New York: Basic Books.

National Association of Black Social Workers (1970-82). Annual Conference Proceedings, New York: NABSW.

_____(1969-2009) *Annual Conference Brochures*. New York: NABSW.

_____ (1986). *Plan for the Future*, New York: NABSW.

_____(1994). *National Public Policy Institute*, New York: NABSW.

Reid-Bookhart (1984). "Toward the Third Decade: The National Association of Black Social Workers," (Unpublished Report), New York: NABSW.

Rodney, Walter (1974). *How Europe Underdeveloped Africa*, Washington, D.C.: Howard University Press.

Sanders, Charles (1970). "Growth of the Association of Black Social Workers," *Social Casework*," May, pp. 270 – 279.

Sethi, Parkash (1982). The American Federation of State, County and Municipal Employees (AFSCME) AFL-CIO Advocacy Campaign Against Reaganomics (Center for Research in Business and Social Policy), Special Report.

Smith, Rudy C. (2009). Personal Interview, April.

U.S. Department of Labor (1965-75). *Manpower Reports of the President (Annual)*, Washington, D.C.: U. S. Government Printing Office.

PART II

INNOVATIVE FRAMEWORKS FOR SOCIAL WORK PRACTICE

6

THEORY MEETS PRACTICE: KAWAIDA, AFROCENTRICITY AND BLACK INTELLECTUAL THOUGHT

The BSWM successfully achieved many of its initial goals and objectives with the organizing of Black social welfare advocates and the establishment of a formal organization to maintain focus on the Movement's activities. As indicated previously in Chapter One, by the late 1960s, Black social workers and other groups of Black professionals began to question the relevance of their knowledge and skills as it related to the advancement of Black freedom. Many sought clarification on the roles they would play in the Civil Rights and Black Power movements.

As social rebellion and turmoil continued to unfold in the Black community, there were many questions being raised by and about Black social work professionals. For example, as social workers, had they been exposed to information about the history, heritage and culture of African people? If not, what attributed to their lack of knowledge? Did the process of becoming an educated professional strip away one's cultural identity? Were Black social workers being trained as liberators or oppressors? Moreover, there were broader questions that plagued the entire Movement. For example, what provided the basis for Black intellectual thought? Which scholars and intellectuals were worthy of further study? And how did one begin the process of transforming the mind, making certain that erroneous views and perspectives on the Black community and Black culture were replaced with accurate, culturally reinforcing knowledge?

The cultural and intellectual renaissance of the 1960s had far-reaching effects on the Black community. The emergence of new literature in history, psychology, sociology, political science and biography was of particular significance to Black social workers. Culturally conscious Black social workers were eager to apply relevant, newly acquired knowledge to practice as they began to search for an intellectual foundation that would support a more liberating form of social work practice.

Educating the Black Mind

Scholars and intellectuals in the Black community have a long and rich history surrounding their quest for knowledge about the cultural heritage of African people (Woodson, 1969; Meier and Rudwick, 1986; Asante and Abarry, 1996; Dagbovie, 2004). African American historians were among the first to question the accuracy of historical facts and the absence of historical recordings that detailed the experience of Africans in the world and the contributions they made to human development. While 20th century America witnessed an explosion of interest in African American history, there were several noted pre-20th century historians as well, including George Washington Williams, Robert Benjamin Lewis, John Wesley Cromwell, James W.C. Pennington, William Wells Brown, William Still and Benjamin Brawley (Logan and Winston, 1982; Cromwell, 2007). These men and women were engaged in historical research during a period of heightened racist attacks on the Black community. Yet they persevered, setting an example for future generations to follow.

In 1915, Carter G. Woodson, considered the father of Black history, and Jesse E. Moorland founded the Association for the Study of African American Life and History (ASALH). One of the many contributions that ASALH made to the advancement and dissemination of knowledge about Black life was the creation of the *Journal of Negro History* in 1916, which was renamed the *Journal of African American History* in 2002. The journal provided an outlet for those interested in Black history to publish their research and commentaries on Black history, life and culture. In addition, it offered alternative views and perspectives on Western and American history. The first few years included works by leading writers and intellectuals of the time, including Monroe N. Work (1916), Henry E. Baker (1917), Alice Dunbar-Nelson (1917), Delilah L. Beasley (1918) and Charles H. Wesley (1919) (Gutenberg.org).

Carter G. Woodson's (1969) publication of *The Mis-education of the Negro* in 1933 also marked a pivotal point in African American intellectual history. Woodson was among the first to call attention to the ways in which the educational system, through ignorance, benign neglect and misinformation, built its teachings on inaccurate and incomplete historical facts, and in the process corrupted the minds of African American youth and the entire community. Woodson's groundbreaking work was followed by critical analysis of the European version of American and Western history by such noted historians as J. A. Rogers (1947), Benjamin Quarles (1961) and John Henrik Clarke (1992). Moreover, in the decades to come, African American historians would continue to provide groundbreaking insights into African and American history throughout the Civil Rights and Black Power eras as they focused their attention on investigating contributions by Black men and women who had not been included in traditional texts (Drake and Clayton, 1962; Adams, 1969; Franklin, 1974; Van Sertima, 1976).

African American scholars and researchers in the social and behavioral sciences also questioned the body of literature on which they built their careers. The field of sociology provides just one example of Black scholars' initiatives to bring a new voice and new vision to intellectual inquiry and scholarly discourse.

W.E.B. DuBois, who was also a noted historian, was the first African American to receive a Ph.D. in sociology from Harvard University in 1895. He immediately began to focus his attention on understanding the social organization and social development of the Black community. DuBois' classic field study, *The Philadelphia Negro*, laid the foundation for sociological research in urban communities. Following the completion of his work in Philadelphia, he moved to Georgia, where he was hired by Atlanta University.

Furthermore, as James Stewart (2004:251ff) has maintained, his vision of the development of the Black college project provides an important insight in the intellectual and practical struggles for Black liberation. Especially relevant to the transformation of ideas and practices in social work were W.E.B. DuBois': 1) advice to end the "rift between theory and practice"; 2) recognition of "the complementarity of methodologies"; (3) "recognition of the limitations of traditional science alone as a vehicle of liberation"; 4) stress on "the critical role of research in his overall program of social uplift"; and 5) concept of intellectuals and "leaders as servants of the people." These essential concepts found their way into the general Black Liberation Movement discourse in various forms and from various quarters, and helped lay a foundation for the transformation of how Black social workers saw and approached their work.

Sociologist E. Franklin Frazier gained fame in the late 1930s with his publication of *The Negro Family in the United States* (1939). Frazier, whose background training in social work undoubtedly influenced his decision to focus on the Black family, argued that the historical burden of slavery and the discrimination and segregation that followed left the Black family at a socially disadvantageous position in American society. Frazier's writings, along with his public verbal attacks on the old vanguard of civil rights leadership in the 1930s, resulted in his being viewed as a radical voice in the fight for social justice. However, Frazier's assessment of Black family life has also been viewed by some scholars as inadvertently contributing to the establishment of a pathological view of Black family functionality. According to Maulana Karenga (2002:318):

"The pioneering African American sociologist, E. Franklin Frazier (1939), unintentionally, may have helped to lay the basis for the pathology school in his research on the Black family. He believed that enslavement, urbanization and racism prevented perpetuation of the African family relations and forms and imposed severe strains on the Black family's ability to function effectively. Thus, it developed negative situational adaptations to handle this legacy of oppression and exploitation. From this, he noted, came the matriarchal character of the Black family with its strong women and ineffective and marginal men; its unstable marriages; the prevailing norm of casual sex, and the loss of folk culture cohesiveness in the urbanization process. However, it is important to note here, as indicated above, that Frazier attributed these problems to social causes and to social policies not to an inherent deficiency of Black people and the community."

Frazier created more controversy with the 1957 publication of the *Black Bourgeoisie*. In this widely read text he accuses the middle-class Black community of creating a culture based on the imitation of European society. He denounced those who would not look to their own ancestral homeland, Africa, to select the very best aspects of their own heritage to preserve for future generations. However, Frazier did prove to be a man before his time. He promoted an Afrocentric philosophy even before the concept was introduced and developed by Asante (1980). In 1962, the year of his death, he wrote "The Failure of the Negro Intellectual" in which he admonished the Black intellectual community for not seizing control of their own destiny. The publication of his article in Joyce Ladner's *Death of White Sociology* (1971) renewed interest in Frazier's work. In it he (1971:66) argues:

"I want to emphasize this by pointing out that if the Negro is ever assimilated into American society his heritage should become a part of American heritage, and it should be recognized as the contribution of the Negro, as one recognizes the contributions of the English, Irish, Germans and other people.

But this can be achieved only if the Negro intellectual and artist frees himself from his desire to conform and only if he overcomes his inferiority complex.

It may turn out that in the distant future Negroes will disappear physically from American society. If this is our fate, let us disappear with dignity and let us leave a worthwhile memorial—in science, in art, in literature, in sculpture, in music—of our having been there."

As the Civil Rights and Black Power movements unfolded, Black sociologists offered new analyses on social organization, community and Black family life (Billingsley, 1968; Staples, 1976; McAdoo, 1981; Sudarkasa; 1981). They, too, wanted to make a significant contribution to contemporary Black intellectual thought. Prior to and during the civil rights era, sociology had provided a proliferation of literature explaining the condition of the "Negro," much of it incorrect. The early works of white sociologists produced an abundance of views on the culturally deprived, socially maladjusted, pathological behaviors of the Black community (Moynihan, 1965; Coleman, 1966; Lewis, 1966). Theories on family function, male/female relationships, community organization and culture were, for the most part, negatively viewed and were grounded in biased research perspectives that viewed the Black community as pathological. Even writings by white, liberal social scientists who presumably had no racist intent were limited by the racially biased literature that served as their foundation (Liebow, 1967; Ryan, 1972). Black sociologists attempted to produce new works that offered insights into the Black socialization experience (Billingsley, 1968; Hill, 1972; Ladner, 1973). Much of this work took a reactive approach, providing a defense of the Black community and Black family functioning in a racist and socially oppressive society.

The mid-1960s also marked the beginning of a proliferation of literature that questioned not only the validity of the concepts and theories that portended to explain the Black condition, but also the roles and contributions of the Black intellectual community who were positioned as the new vanguard in Black intellectual thought. In 1967, Harold Cruse, a brilliant intellectual who never obtained a college degree but assumed the position as professor of African American studies, published *The Crisis of the Negro Intellectual*. In this work, Cruse argues, rather vehemently, that Black intellectuals had the responsibility to assume a lead role in the fight for radical social change. Often described as a social critic, Cruse's work arrived at a critical time in Movement history. A young, newly empowered generation was questioning America's collective intellectual wisdom, and Cruse provided enough fodder to engage scholars, intellectuals, professionals and social advocates about the future direction of the Movement. Cruse's perspective appealed to those who wanted to utilize their intellectual prowess to make a contribution to the fight for Black equality, liberation and freedom.

However, for many social activists, Franz Fanon (1967) was the ultimate revolutionary thinker and intellectual. Fanon was born in 1925 in Martinique. His socialization in a French-colonized Caribbean island provided unique insights into the struggles of those victimized by racism in the places that they called home. Fanon was a medical doctor and a trained psychiatrist who began to focus his attention on the relationship between race, culture, political subjugation and psychopathology. Fanon's *The Wretched of the Earth* (1968) provided a searing analysis of class struggle and strife between the perpetrators of social oppression, the white colonizers and the victims, most often identified as the indigenous populous masses struggling to be free. He argued that "freedom must be taken, never given" and warned of the violence that would accompany the people's fight for justice.

Fanon's writings and call for the liberation struggle influenced the Black Power Movement in a profound and sweeping way. The major organizations and leaders of the period, students and community activists of varied ideological tendencies all quoted Fanon and cited his *Wretched of the Earth* as required reading. Among Fanon's concepts that most appealed to the Black Power Movement are: the indispensability of struggle; the central role of culture in struggle; the unavoidable and key task of the people in the liberation struggle; and the essentiality of the mass education and involvement of the masses.

Fanon (1968:210) argues that the question of culture rises especially in the context of the role of colonialism and oppression in distorting and destroying the culture of the ruled. He says:

> *"Colonialism is not satisfied merely with holding a people in its grip and emptying the native's brain of all form and content. By a kind of perverted logic, it turns to the past of the oppressed people and distorts, disfigures and destroys it."*

This creates what Fanon calls "cultural estrangement," or cultural alienation, and demands a corrective found in struggle on both the subjective and objective level.

Fanon (1968:233), again linking culture and struggle, contends that "to fight for national culture means in the first place to fight for the liberation of the nation. ..." In this national struggle for cultural and political liberation, Fanon views the education of the masses as indispensable. He (Ibid: 197) states further that ". . . in the end everything depends on the education of the masses, on raising the level of thought." This means "opening their minds, awakening them and allowing the birth of their intelligence. ..." And it means teaching them "that everything depends on them; that if we stagnate, it is their responsibility, and that if we go forward it is due to them too. ..."

Woodson, DuBois, Frazier, Cruse, Fanon and others provided a socio-historical foundation for those seeking alternative views and insights on African and African American experiences. The Movement era opened up the intellectual floodgates. Emerging young scholars and intellectuals exhibited an insatiable quest for new knowledge that could be utilized in providing a solid foundation for analyzing and understanding social oppression and social functioning in the Black community. This knowledge was fundamental in the fight for freedom, equality, liberation and Black empowerment.

Social Work Knowledge Base

As a practice discipline, social work has long been dependent on research provided by other disciplines, especially in the social and behavioral sciences, for the foundation needed to understand the human condition. Required courses in sociology and psychology were needed to understand how humans functioned as individuals and in groups, while political science and economics were required to understand how humans functioned in their socially constructed environments. Research in psychology and sociology has been especially crucial to social work education. During the early stages of development, social work, lacking a research base of its own, borrowed heavily from these two related disciplines. In sociology, students were exposed to theories by Karl Marx to facilitate an understanding of class conflict, David Émile Durkheim to comprehend social isolation and anomie, and Max Weber on social stratification (Appelrouth and Edles, 2006; Edles and Appelrouth, 2009). Theories in psychology were used to analyze individual behavior. Sigmund Freud, Otto Rank, Erik Erikson, Alfred Adler, Abraham Maslow and Carl Jung were leading European psychology disciples who had a profound impact on the profession (Gay, 1990; Beckett, 2002; Cameron, 2002). However, as the various movements began to reach the academy and Black participation reached a critical mass, Black students and faculty began to question the legitimacy of research findings based on studies that did not include Blacks or those that were based on negative views of the people and the culture. A frequently asked question in the classroom and in scholarly discourse was: How inclusive were the populations used to draw conclusions about the social functioning of the entire human race?

In the 1960s, the academy was the new battleground for both social and intellectual activism. It was time to target "brain central," i.e., America's institutions of higher learning, responsible for producing pseudo-scientific theories of human and social development that guided and shaped the nation's social policies. And schools of social work would fall prey to a heavy dose of social and academic scrutiny. However, it is important to note that all of the professions and academic disciplines had a history of racial exclusion. There are no exceptions (Blackwell, 1981). It was during the Civil Rights and Black Power movements—coupled with the expanding needs of the industrial economy—that African Americans seized upon the opportunity to force their way into the Ivy Towers, disciplines and professions that had limited their opportunities in the past. Black students and scholars wanted their views heard. The humanities, social and behavioral sciences, as well as many of the professions, witnessed an explosion of Blacks who wanted to participate in the scholarly pursuit of knowledge and the application of intellectual wisdom. And the success of the BSWM depended heavily on the ability of Black intellectuals and scholars to produce substantive literature that could serve as the foundation for Black social work practice.

Desperately seeking alternative information and literature, which would provide insights into the Black experience and hopefully cast a positive light on African Americans, Black social workers began to gravitate toward any and all literature that countered standard Eurocentric theories in the social and behavioral sciences. In the process, they explored the various schools of Black psychology for alternative perspectives. As Jones (1991:xii) states, Karenga has "identified three schools of Black psychology—the traditional school, the reformist school and the radical school"—which "provide a useful framework" for understanding these writings and their use by Black social workers (Karenga, 2002:505-533). For example, early writings by Kenneth Clark (1965),William Grier and Price Cobb (1968) and Alvin Poussaint (1972) were must reads for aspiring Black social workers. These writings, described by Karenga (2002) as being part of the traditional school of Black psychology, attempted to explain the Black condition based on theoretical models provided by traditional psychological theories used to explain the human condition. These approaches to Black psychology were also adopted by schools of social work as they began to struggle to alter their curricula to include content on African Americans. Lacking any other resources, these traditional approaches were accepted as truths and embraced by those wanting to equip themselves with specific knowledge about members of the Black community. As indicated previously, Black psychologists began to express dissatisfaction with traditional psychology in the late 1960s. Just as civil rights activists, scholars, intellectuals and other professionals involved in the Civil Rights and Black Power movements, psychologists, too, struggled to find their voice.

Recognizing the inadequacy of their traditional training and equipped with ineffective theories about behavior and mental health functioning in the Black community, Black psychologists began to question insights gained from the sacred canon of psychological literature. They, too, were confronted with the same issues as Black social workers: fight for modifications to current acceptable theories of behavior by including a Black perspective, or develop new theories in psychology that were grounded in the Black experience. By the early 1970s, Black psychologists began to produce literature that attacked traditional theories of learning, which invariably concluded that Blacks were somehow genetically inferior to whites. In the area of clinical practice, Black psychologists questioned the use of racist theories to treat mental illnesses and emotional disorders in the Black community. However, as younger, more militant voices emerged in the field of psychology, they began to question the wisdom of the elders, both Black and white.

William Cross' 1971 publication of "The Negro to Black Conversion Experience" provided the kind of innovative theory in Black psychology and mental health that many members of the Black social work community were seeking. According to Cross, historical conditions, combined with continued social oppression in America, had created a community of Negroes unfamiliar and most unwilling to embrace their own culture. Cross argued that Negroes could be transformed into African Americans by passing through a series of stages— Nigrescence—which ultimately led to a racially conscious, self-accepting, proud Black individual. His theory of Nigrescence validated many African Americans' true life experiences with racial identity formation. Other, more radical psychologists soon followed. Bobby Wright's *The Psychopathic Racial Personality* (1975), Amos Wilson's *The Developmental Psychology of the Black Child* (1978), Na'im Akbar's "Awareness: The Key to Black Mental Health" (1974) and Kobi Kambon's "Black Psychology and Black Personality" (1976) were viewed as groundbreaking publications. And scholars like Wright, Wilson, Kambon and Akbar interacted frequently with those involved in the BSWM and were regular presenters at NABSW gatherings. Wade Nobles (1980), Linda James Myers (1988) and others offered theoretical approaches that were grounded in the Black experience, or what later would be identified as African-centered approaches. These contemporary theorists offered a new psychological framework that Black social workers could use as a foundation for understanding learning and behavior in the Black community.

Combined with the availability of new literature on all aspects of the Black experience, Black social workers would discover new ways to integrate and utilize these theories and approaches into social work practice. For example, Leon Chestang's "Character Development in a Hostile Environment" (1972) offered a powerful analysis of the impact of the Black experience on personality development. Citing the works of Clark (1965), Cleaver (1968), Frazier (1968), Ellison (1953), and Grier and Cobb (1968), Chestang deviated from traditional European socio-psychological analyses, which were required reading in schools of social work. According to Chestang (1972:1):

> "...social work practice in its efforts to effect changes in individuals or in social systems has been confounded by charges of 'irrelevance' and 'insensitivity.' These charges, made largely by black people in high and low places, stem from the persistent awareness of the failure of traditional concepts about black people to provide a basis for confronting their personal and social problems effectively. Laden with notions that assign to the victims responsibility for their condition, traditional concepts tend to skirt the peculiar nature of the black experience and its impact on character development and transracial interaction."

He states further:

> "...social work must devise and be guided by concepts that comprehend the nature, structure, and dynamics of the black experience as a social syndrome that develops out of the values, norms, and beliefs projected and acted upon by the larger society and dealt with and integrated by members of the black community."

In the near future, Black social workers would become fully engaged in the process of transforming traditional social work knowledge into new paradigms reflective of contemporary Black intellectual thought.

Kawaida

One of the most significant developments in 20th century Black intellectual thought was Karenga's introduction of Kawaida philosophy as a guide to social change (Karenga, 1978, 1980, 1997, 2008; Asante, 2009). Karenga (2002) played

127

a leading role in the Civil Rights, Black student, Black studies, Black Arts and Black Power movements. During the height of Movement activity, he emerged as an important activist-scholar committed to working toward social change in the Black community (Karenga, 1978, 2008; Asante, 2002:190-193; 2009:16-18). Moreover, Karenga, as Marable (2000:15) states, has been "central to the development of the discipline of Africana Studies." He has written the most widely used introductory text in the discipline (Karenga, 2002) and played a major role in the development of the discipline's professional organizations, the National Council for Black Studies NCBS and AHSA. Marable goes on to say that "unquestionably two intellectuals have been most pivotal as interpreters and political forces in the development of Black Studies—Maulana Karenga and Molefi Asante." As argued below, this represents an intellectual exchange, continuity and common ground that were of major importance to the Movement, the discipline and NABSW. Finally, for a brief period Karenga was employed as a social worker during the 1960s at the Los Angeles County Bureau of Public Assistance and worked with the National Welfare Rights Organization during the presidencies of Johnny Tillmon-Blackstone and Catherine Jermany.

At the peak of the social activism that gripped the Southern California area and the entire nation in the mid-1960s, he founded the organization Us, a cultural nationalist and social change organization, and created Kawaida theory as a philosophical framework to guide the organization's development and its work and struggle in the community and larger society. Karenga (1997:12) states that "Kawaida philosophy evolved in the 1960s, forged in the crucible of the struggle for freedom. It, of necessity, bears the tone and texture of an organization (Us) and a Movement engaged in intense ideological and practical struggle to change society and the way we think about it." He lists as some of the critical issues engaged and struggled around in the United States: "discourse about the good and just society; the role of culture; the meaning of Black; the relevance of Africa; and the road to revolution or radical and progressive societal change." He (1997:15) concludes that "Kawaida then evolves in the *crucible of practical and ideological struggles of the 1960s*, struggles not only directed toward the established order, but [also] internal struggles to establish ideals and achievable goals, define the most appropriate 'road to revolution' and to build the local and national African American community in the process."

Kawaida, which in Swahili means "tradition," was expanded by Karenga to mean a synthesis of both tradition and reason, and is defined as "an ongoing synthesis of the best of African thought and practice in constant exchange with the world" (Karenga, 2008:3). Key to understanding Kawaida is Karenga's stress on culture and cultural revolution. When he first introduced it in the mid-1960s, Karenga (1993:173) described Kawaida as a philosophical position that:

> "...centered around the contention that the key crisis in Black life is the cultural crisis, i.e., a crisis in views and especially, values. The need, thus, is for a cultural revolution which would break the monopoly the oppressor has on Black minds and begin to rescue and reconstruct Black history and humanity in their own image and interests."

It was and remains one of his most fundamental contentions that "the struggle for liberation is first and foremost at its foundation a struggle to free ourselves culturally in the fullest sense" (Karenga, 2008:4-5). He defines culture as "the totality of thought and practice by which a people creates itself, celebrates, sustains and develops itself and introduces itself to history and humanity" (Ibid:5). In his conception of culture, he lists as vital seven basic areas: "spirituality and ethics (religion); history; social organization; economic organization; political organization; creative production (art, music, literature, dance); and ethos—the collective psychology shaped by activities in the other six areas" (Karenga, 1967:14).

Perhaps Karenga is best known for his creation of the African American and pan-African holiday of Kwanzaa and the Nguzo Saba, or the Seven Principles (Karenga, 1993). He (1993:173) stated that:

> "It is Kawaida out of which this author developed Kwanzaa and the Nguzo Saba. The Nguzo Saba (Seven Principles) were advocated as a communitarian African value system necessary to build community and serve as social glue and moral orientation for cultural practice."

Karenga (Ibid: 174) goes on to argue that the Nguzo Saba, or principles of Kawaida and Kwanzaa, "has become the basis for the philosophical orientation of many independent schools, rites of passage, community and professional organization's programs." When one examines the activities of Black social workers, especially within NABSW and the many community-based programs

129

sponsored by the local chapters, this statement is essentially correct. The Nguzo Saba, with its seven basic concepts of unity, self-determination, collective work and responsibility, cooperative economics, purpose, creativity and faith, appealed to those who were seeking an alternative view and value system for the Black community. Aided by the introduction of Kwanzaa celebrations to millions of African Americans, Karenga's views on cultural nationalism and cultural affirmation spread rapidly across the nation.

Many Black social workers embraced the Nguzo Saba as a practical guide to organize programs and projects in the local community. Efforts were made to unify the Black community by breaking down perceptual barriers between professionals and community members. Black social workers emerged as visible advocates in the local community. Cultural projects, including Kwanzaa, rites of passage, parades and other culturally based celebratory programs, sprang forth throughout the nation. For example, The Philadelphia Alliance of Black Social Workers purchased a house in the midst of North Philadelphia's ghetto community where Black social workers developed projects to engage local residents and to help strengthen the neighborhood. In New Orleans, the local chapter developed a partnership with the local schools and established youth programs in the community. New York City partnered with other Black cultural organizations to launch the African Heritage Parade. Greater Los Angeles established an adoption agency to connect Black families with children in need. Black social workers organized community-based Kwanzaa celebrations in hundreds of cities throughout the nation, including Philadelphia, New Orleans, Lansing, Michigan, New York, West Chester, Newark, San Francisco, Chicago, Durham, North Carolina, Miami, Baltimore and Boston. Kawaida was also used as a foundation to develop culturally specific models of Black social work practice.

Thaddeus P. Mathis (1972:2), responding to the charge of the first national gathering of Black social workers to develop a theory of practice "based on liberation rather than adjustment," offered the nation-building approach. He (Ibid) attempted to "suggest a beginning framework for reconceptualizing the nature of social work practice within the Black community." The ultimate goal of nation building, as described by Mathis, was the liberation of the Black masses from "the shackles of physical, emotional, economic, and political dependency." Nation building required that Black social workers: root themselves in an understanding of the extended family in the African American community; commit themselves to the development of independent Black institutions; free themselves from white social work values and concepts; and operate from a value system based on African communalism. This new form of practice would be based on the Nguzo Saba principles as developed by Karenga.

Also utilizing the Nguzo Saba principles as the basic value system, Gwendolyn Gilbert (1974) offered the "Survival-Liberation Model for Social Work in the Black Community." In this practice approach, she called for "a fundamental change in the primary goal of the profession" to make it more liberating than oppressive. She argued further that the neo-colonial conditions that existed in the Black community required new knowledge, concepts and theories to understand the social and economic victimization of the community, and to explain how the Black community survived. The social worker needed to identify ways in which the community could be brought to a greater sense of self-realization, self-fulfillment, self-actualization and liberation. According to Gilbert (1974:47):

"The model is conceived out of a value stance which explicates black aspirations, undergirded by a social theory of humanism that rejects all human oppression. Consistently then, the goal of social work in the black community is re-defined as non-oppressive social functioning. Neo-colonialism defines the oppressive reality that abuses and obstructs the complete human development of black individuals, families and communities."

Kawaida concepts were firmly planted among many of those who were active members, workshop presenters and conference participants with NABSW, as well as those who sought greater involvement with the BSWM. From the beginning of its introduction to the present, many Black social workers used Kawaida theory to guide, justify and expand their professional interactions with members of the Black community (NABSW, 1970 -1985; Harvey, 1997; Monges, 1997; Graham, 2003; Bent-Goodley, 2003).

Karenga's Kawaida philosophy also served as a foundation and inspiration for the next major African American theory to inform Black social work and intellectual discourse in the community and the academy, i.e., Molefi Asante's Afrocentricity. Asante (1988:21) noted in his seminal text on the subject that "Kawaida, the philosophy expounded by Maulana (Karenga) is—the most extensive development of a cultural ideology to grow out of the 1960s," and he states that his Afrocentric project "builds upon that foundation in its social and cultural work." He (2007:7) reaffirms this position in his most recent book on Afrocentricity, stating that "Karenga's political essays and philosophical works, particularly around the importance of culture in the liberation of the mind, became useful guides in the evolution of my own theory of Afrocentricity."

Afrocentricity

Molefi Asante's 1980 publication *Afrocentricity: The Theory of Social Change* shook the foundation of intellectual thought in the Black community. Asante's theory entered scholarly discourse at a time when many scholars struggled to reformulate and reconceptualize their basic orientation to the study of African people. Asante synthesized the very best of Black Nationalism, Black humanitarian philosophy and self-loving Black intellectual thought to create a new conceptual framework and language to guide scholarly examination of the Black experience. A prolific scholar, he is considered by his peers to be one of the most distinguished contemporary African scholars and influential African American leaders of our era (Mazama, 2008).

Asante's approach to understanding the African world provided a much needed framework for radical Black social workers. In brief, Asante's theory of Afrocentricity posits that African descendant people's experience of "disorientation" and "dislocation" in the contemporary world results from a process of "decentering" emanating from European domination and colonization of Africa and the holocaust of enslavement that followed in the Americas. In an effort to gain a positive social and cultural identity, individuals seek to reclaim their African identities by centering themselves in their own values, history and culture, and embracing what is a reflection of their true heritage, or more specifically, locating themselves in an "Afrocentric reality" (Asante, 1980, 1990; Reid-Merritt, 2008).

Asante's work had a tremendous impact on contemporary Black intellectual thought. His conceptualization of the African worldview helped to shape the discipline of Africana studies. In addition, Asante's impact on the academy, the development of Afrocentric scholarship, education and Blacks in the helping professions is undeniable. Educators, social workers, psychologists, historians, writers and other professionals have created new scholarship and ways of interpreting their professional worlds using constructs from Afrocentricity as the basis of their analysis (Schiele, 1997; Richardson, 2000; Mazama, 2002).

In the first decade of the BSWM, the descriptive adjective "Black" was inserted in every aspect of discussion that attempted to bring a new perspective reflective of the African American experience. The desire was to move toward an understanding of traditional approaches of learning by including the word "Black." Thus, much of the discourse focused on the importance of transforming traditional disciplines and professions with the infusion of a Black perspective. Including the word "Black" signaled a change in focus, perspective, or use of informational materials. However, a fundamental change in how these disciplines viewed the Black world was not always the case. Black was a state of being; it did not, in and of itself, provide a systematic or methodological approach to the study of Black people.

By the late 1980s, Black social work activists began to alter the language, substituting the word "Afrocentric" for Black. The words "Afrocentric," "Africentric," "Afrocentricity" or "African-centered" (these words were used interchangeably) frequently appeared in papers and discussions on new approaches to social work practice and the liberation of Black people (NABSW, 1988–2008; King, 1994; Swigonski, 1996; Schiele, 1996, 1997; Harvey, 1997; Graham, 1999). The desire for African cultural connections, self-determination and, in the language of Afrocentricity, the right to obtain "agency" of one's being, altered the direction of NABSW and those who wanted to be involved in the BSWM. For the next two decades, Black social workers began to focus their discourse around the need for "Afrocentric knowledge," "Afrocentric philosophy," "Afrocentric approaches," "Afrocentric values," "Afrocentric family services" and "Afrocentric social work practice" (NABSW, 1988–2008). A new generation of social workers sought racially and culturally specific knowledge to support their work in the Black community. The theory of Afrocentricity helped to fill that void.

Faculty members at schools of social work may have been aware of the explosion of new literature that offered challenging theories and new perspectives on Black America. But just as Lawrence (1969) predicted at the very beginning stages of the BSWM, the pace of change at many schools of social work would be slow. The much needed transformation of school curriculums continued to lag for years to come. Social workers throughout the nation continued to be drawn to the BSWM due to their feelings of professional inadequacy as they attempted to begin their careers in social work. Jerry Brooks (2009), who received an MSW degree in 1985, shared this poignant insight:

"I worked hard throughout my two years at Temple. I read all of the materials. I wanted to be a great professional. I had my degree, but something was missing. I didn't feel like I was prepared to work with my own people. And I was concerned about doing them harm. That's what led me to seek out the Black social workers and become more involved with their form of social work practice."

Conclusion

Contemporary Black intellectual thought had a profound impact on the BSWM. Black social workers, seeking alternative approaches to understanding the Black community, utilized emerging theorizes and philosophies in Black psychology, Black sociology and other social science disciplines to modify the social work knowledge base. The introduction of Karenga's Nguzo Saba and Kawaida philosophy offered a value base that emanated from an African worldview. Asante's theory of Afrocentricity provided the language and cultural grounding needed to guide Black social workers toward the development of nontraditional alternative approaches to understanding the Black community from an African-centered perspective. These intellectual contributions aided Black social workers in their search for the development of more liberating theories and approaches to social work practice.

References:

Adams, Russell L. (1969). *Great Negroes Past and Present*, Chicago: Afro-Am Publishing Company.

Akbar, Na'im (Luther X. Weems) (1974). "Awareness: The Key to Black Mental Health," *Journal of Black Psychology*, Vol.1, 1 (August), pp. 30 – 37.

_____(1981). "Mental Disorders Among African Americans," Black Books Bulletin, 5, 2, pp.18 – 25.

Appelrouth, Scott and Laura Desfor Edles, (2006). *Sociological Theory in the Contemporary Era: Text and Readings*, Thousand Oaks, CA: Pine Forge Press

Asante, Molefi Kete (1980). *Afrocentricity: A Theory of Social Change*, Trenton, NJ: Africa World Press.

_____ (1990). *Kemet, Afrocentricity and Knowledge*, Trenton, NJ: Africa World Press.

_____ (2002). *100 Greatest African Americans: A Biographical Encyclopedia*, Amherst, New York: Prometheus Books.

Asante, Molefi Kete and Abu S. Abarry (1996). *African Intellectual Heritage: A Book of Sources*, Philadelphia: Temple University Press.

Beckett, Chris (2002). *Human Growth and Development*, Thousand Oaks, CA: Sage Publishing Co.

Bent-Goodley, Tricia (ed.) (2003). *African American Social Workers and Social Policy*, New York: The Haworth Press.

Better, Shirley (1972). *"The Role of the Black Social Worker,"* *Black World*, November

Billingsley, Andrew (1968). *Black Families in White America*, Englewood Cliffs, NJ: Prentice-Hall, Inc.

Blackwell, James E. (1981). *Mainstreaming Outsiders: The Production of Black Professionals*, Bayside, New York: General Hall, Inc.

Brooks, Jerry (2009). Personal Interview, April.

Brown, Scot (2003). *Fighting for US. Maulana Karenga, the US Organization, and Black Cultural Nationalism*, New York: NYU Press.

Cameron, Noel (2002). *Human Growth and Development* (17th ed.), San Diego: Academic Press.

Clarke, John Henrik (1992). *Christopher Columbus and the African Holocaust: Slavery and the Rise of European Capitalism*, New York: A and B Book Distributors, Inc.

Clark, Kenneth (1965). *Dark Ghetto*, New York: Harper and Row.

Cleaver, Eldridge (1968). *Soul on Ice*, New York: Rampart Books.

Coleman, James S. (1966), *Equality of Educational Opportunity*, Washington, D.C.: U.S. Office   of Education.

Cress, Welsing Francis (1970). *The Cress Theory of Color Confrontation and Racism (White Supremacy)*, Washington, D.C.: C-R Publishers.

Cromwell, Adelaide M. (2007). *Unveiled Voices, Unvarnished Memories: The Cromwell Family in Slavery and Segregation*, 1692-1972, Columbia, MO: University of Missouri Press.

Cross, William E. Jr. (1971). "The Negro to Black Conversion Experience," *Black World,* July, pp. 13 – 27.

Cruse, Harold (1967). *The Crisis of the Negro Intellectual*, New York: William Morrow.

Dagbovie, Pero Gaglo (2004). "Black Women Historians from the Late 19th Century to the Dawning of the Civil Rights Movement," *The Journal of African American History*, Vol. 89.

Drake, St. Claire and Horace Clayton (1962). *Black Metropolis*, New York: Harper and Row.

Edles, Laura Desfor and Scott Appelrouth (2009). *Sociological Theory in the Classical Era: Text and Readings*, Thousand Oaks, CA: Pine Forge Press.

Ellison, Ralph (1953). *The Invisible Man*, New York: Signet Books.

Fanon, Frantz (1967). *Black Skin, White Masks*, New York: Grove Press.

_____(1968). *The Wretched of the Earth*, New York: Grove Press.

Franklin, John Hope and Alfred Moss, Jr. (2000). *From Slavery to Freedom*, New York: Alfred A. Knopf.

Frazier, E. Franklin (1973). The Failure of the Negro Intellectual," *in The Death of White Sociology*, Joyce Ladner (ed.), New York: Vintage Books, pp. 52 – 66.

_____ (1939). *The Negro Family in the United States*, Chicago: University of Chicago Press.

_____(1968). "Negroes in Policy-Making Positions: A Study of Black Powerlessness," Mimeographed, Chicago: Urban League.

Gay, Peter (1990). *The Id and the Ego: The Standard Works of Sigmund Freud*, New York: W.W. Norton and Company.

Gilbert, Gwendolyn C. (1974). "The Role of Social Work in Black Liberation," *The Black Scholar,* (December), Vol. 6.4. pp16 – 23.

Graham, Mekada (1999). "The African Centered Worldview: Developing a Paradigm for Social Work," in *British Journal of Social Work 29*, (2) pp. 252 – 267.

Grier, William H. and Price M. Cobb (1968). *Black Rage*, New York: Harper and Row.

Harvey, Aminifu (1997). "Group Work with African American Youth in the Criminal Justice System: A Culturally Competent Model," in G.L. Greif and P.H. Ephross (eds). *Group Work with Populations at Risk* (pp. 160 – 174), New York: Oxford University Press.

Hill, Robert. (1972) *The Strengths of Black Families*, New York: Emerson Hall.

Jones, Reginald (1980). *Black Psychology*, New York: Harper and Row.

Kambon, Kobi (1976). "Black Psychology and Black Personality: Some Issues for Consideration," *Black Books Bulletin*, Vol. 4, 3:6 – 11.

Karenga, Maulana (1980). *Kawaida Theory: An Introductory Outline*, Inglewood, CA: Kawaida Publications.

_____ (1967). *The Quotable Karenga*, Inglewood, CA: Kawaida Publications.

_____ (2002). *An Introduction to Black Studies*, (3rd ed.), Los Angeles: University of Sankore Press.

_____ (1993). *An Introduction to Black Studies*, (2nd ed.), Los Angeles: University of Sankore Press.

_____ (2008). *Kawaida and Questions of Life and Struggle: African American, Pan-African and Global Issues*, Los Angeles: University of Sankore Press.

King, A. E. (1994). "An Afrocentric Cultural Awareness Program for Incarcerated African-American Males," *Journal of Multicultural Social Work*, Vol. 3 (4), p. 20 – 29.

Ladner, Joyce (1973). *The Death of White Sociology*, New York: Vintage Books, Inc.

Lewis, David Levering (1994). *W. E. B. DuBois: Biography of a Race, 1868-1919*, New York: Owl Books.

Lewis, Oscar (1966). "The Culture of Poverty," *Scientific America*, October 1966.

Liebow, Elliot (1867). Tally's Corner: *A Study of Negro Streetcorner Men*, New York: Little Brown Publishing Company.

Logan, Rayford and Michael R. Winston (eds.) (1982). *Dictionary of American Negro Biography*, New York: W.W. Norton.

Mathis, Thaddeus P. (1972). "Social Work and Nation Building in the Black Community," Proceedings of Fourth Annual Conference, pp. 159 – 177, New York: NABSW.

Mazama, Mambo Ama (2002). "Afrocentricity and African Spirituality," *Journal of Black Studies*, 11, Vol. 33: pp. 218 – 234.

_____ (ed.) (2008) *Essays in Honor of an Intellectual Warrior: Molefi Kete Asante*, Paris, Menaibuc.

Marable, Manning (2000). *Dispatches from the Ebony Tower*, New York: Columbia University Press.

McAdoo, Harriette (1981). *The Black Family*, Beverly Hills, CA: Sage Publications.

Meier, August and Elliott Rudwick (1986). *Black Historians and the Historical Profession 1915-1980*, Urbana: University of Illinois Press.

Monges, Miriam Ma'At-Ka Re (1997). Kush —The Jewel of Nubia: *Reconnecting the Root System of African Civilization*, Trenton: Africa World Press.

Moynihan, Daniel (1965). *The Negro Family,* Washington, D.C.: Office of Planning and Research, U.S. Department of Labor.

Myers, Linda James (1988). *Understanding an Afrocentric World View: Introduction to an Optimal Psychology*, Dubuque, IA: Kendall/Hunt.

National Association of Black Social Workers (1970–1985). *Conference Brochures,* New York: NABSW.

Nobles, Wade W. (1976). "Black People in White Insanity: Issues for Black Community Mental Health," *Journal of Afro-American Issues*, Vol. 4, 1, pp. 21–27.

Poussaint, Alvin F. (1972). *Why Blacks Kill Blacks*, New York: Emerson Hall Publishers.

Quarles, Benjamin (1961). T*he Negro in the American Revolution,* Chapel Hill: University of North Carolina Press.

Reid-Merritt, Patricia (2008). "The Spread of Afrocentricity Among the People," in Mazama, Mambo Ama (ed.) *Essays in Honor of an Intellectual Warrior: Molefi Kete Asante*, Paris: Menaibuc.

Richardson, Elaine (2000). "Critique on the Problematic of Implementing Afrocentricity Into Traditional Curriculum: The Powers That Be," *Journal of Black Studies,* 11, Vol. 31: pp. 196 – 213.

Ryan, William (1972). *Blaming the Victim*, New York: Vintage Books.

Schiele, Jerome (1997). "The Contours and Meaning of Afrocentric Social Work," in *Journal of Black Studies*, Vol. 27 (6) p. 803.

_____(1996). "Afrocentricity: An Emerging Paradigm in Social Work Practice," Social Work, (May), 41 (3) pp. 284-94.

Staples, Robert (1973). "What is Black Sociology," *in The Death of White Sociology*, Joyce Ladner (ed.), New York: Vintage Books.

_____(1976). *Introduction to Black Sociology,* New York: McGraw Hill.

Sterne, Emma Gelders (1971). *His Was The Voice, The Life of W. E. B. DuBois*, New York: Crowell-Collier Press.

Sudarkasa, Niara (1981). "Interpreting the African Heritage in Afro-America Family Organization," in *Black Families*, Harriette P. McAdoo (ed.), Beverly Hills, CA: Sage Publications.

Swigorski, M. (1996). "Challenging Privilege Through Africentric Social Work Practice," *Social Work* Vol. 41 (2): 153 – 161.

Van Sertima, Ivan (1976). *They Came Before Columbus*, New York: Random House.

Williams, Robert (1974). "A History of the Association of Black Psychologists: Early Formation and Development," *Journal of Black Psychology*, Vol. 1, 1 (August), pp. 7 – 24.

Willie, Charles (1970). *The Family Life of Black People,* Columbus, OH: Charles Merrill.

Wilson, Amos (1978). *The Development Psychology of the Black Child,* New York: Africana Research Publications.

Woodson, Carter G. (1969). *The Mis-education of the Negro*, Washington, D.C.: Associated Publishers.

Wright, Bobby E. (1975). *The Psychopathic Racial Personality*, Chicago: Third World Press.

Websites

www.Gutenberg.org

7

NATIONAL NETWORKS/ INTERNATIONAL LINKAGES

One of the most successful outcomes of the BSWM was the establishment of NABSW and the ability of the organization to create and maintain a communication network among thousands of Black social workers, human service professionals and paraprofessionals, community organizers and social activists in the nation and the African diaspora. For more than 40 consecutive years, NABSW conferences linked members with nonmembers, practitioners with educators, intellectuals with social advocates, policy makers with social service administrators, and the Black social worker with the Black community. Like most professional organizations, conferences are used to provide members with the opportunity to connect with colleagues, share information about advances in the field, and plan for future beneficial endeavors. However, with its constant calls for cultural consciousness and racial solidarity, NABSW was able to offer all of the traditional benefits to its members and so much more. In an extended family environment, it offered a safe haven for Black social workers to plan, develop and implement professional programs and community projects consistent with their professional values, beliefs and code of ethics. Moreover, the annual conferences provided consistency, continuity and an operational framework for each new administration. And the organizational and leadership skills of each new president were often measured by the degree of success in maintaining and expanding the organization's major communication mechanisms and other program offerings. A cursory review of four decades of national and international conferencing offers insights into the value of these meaningful experiences.

Responding to the Call

For the Movement's organizers, the first half of the '70s decade was high-spirited. Black human service workers across the nation responded to the call to join a newly established professional Black social work organization. With only ten members needed to constitute a chapter, and with membership criteria that permitted any Black person working in the helping professions or those committed to Black empowerment eligible for membership, local affiliates sprang forth in virtually every region of the nation. These individuals were the backbone of the national conference gatherings. Other nonmembers also found the activities of the organization appealing and participated in the annual conferences that crisscrossed the nation.

The yearly conferences were a mainstay of NABSW. As indicated in Table III, the organization sponsored national conferences across the country that focused on pertinent issues and concerns to members of the Black community. The conferences provided a forum for Black social workers to discuss common problems, issues and the state of the art of social work practice in the Black community. By conscious and deliberate design, the conferences were open only to people of African descent, thereby creating an environment in which participants felt free to discuss sensitive issues of racism and discrimination without inhibition. Coming to grips with one's own sense of "blackness" was viewed as both a personal and professional issue.

Following the success of the first national conference in Philadelphia under the Williams administration (1970–1974), subsequent conferences were held in Washington, D.C., Chicago, Nashville, New York and Los Angeles. The conferences benefited from the heightened sense of awareness that was an integral part of the Black community in the early 1970s. As the movement expanded, the ability to attract new recruits to social and professional activities offered through national conference gatherings remained a main focus of each administration.

142

TABLE III
NABSW NATIONAL CONFERENCES 1969–2010

Year	Theme	Location
1969	The Black Family	Philadelphia., PA
1970	The Black Social Worker as an Agent for Change	Washington, DC
1971	Blueprint for Black Unity	Chicago, IL
1972	Diversity-Cohesion or Chaos: Mobilization for Survival	Nashville, TN
1973	Nation Building	New York, NY
1974	Survival and Beyond	Los Angeles, CA
1975	Promises of Power: Actual or Potential	Detroit, MI
1976	Black America: Reawakening for the Future	Baltimore, MD
1977	Strategies for Liberation	New Orleans, LA
1978	Silhouettes of Past Promises-Definitions of Future Faces	San Fran., CA
1979	Continued Struggle For Liberation	St. Louis, MO
1980	Developing an Action Plan: Social, Political and Economic Direction for the Black Community	Washington, DC
1981	Strength in Unity: Developing the African American Community for the 1980s	Atlanta, GA
1982	Building the African American Community Through the Effective Use of Resources: Our Mission for the '80s	Chicago, IL
1983	Fortifying African American Networks	Miami Beach, FL
1984	Private Troubles, Public Issues: Advocating for Social, Political and Economic Justice	Detroit, MI
1985	The Past We Inherit—The Present We Create: Social Work and Social Action	New Orleans, LA
1986	The Black Community: Unity and Strengths—Conceive—Believe—Achieve	Houston, TX
1987	African-American Family: Our Past, Present and Future	Boston, MA
1988	Entering Our Third Decade: Challenges and Expectations	San Fran., CA
1989	Mobilizing the African-American Community	Richmond, VA
1990	African-American Visions: Past Successes/Future Directions	Los Angeles, CA
1991	Preserving African American Families: Research and Action Beyond Rhetoric	Atlanta, GA
1992	A Holistic Approach to African American Family and Community Preservation	Washington, DC
1993	Erasing the Pain: Combating Violence in the African American Community	New Orleans, LA
1994	African-Centered Social Work: Historical Solutions for Today's Issues	Philadelphia, PA
1995	Intergenerational Approaches to African American Intergenerational Family Preservation	New York, NY
1996	Building on our Heritage: A Source of Power	Houston, TX
1997	Approaching the New Millennium: A Call to Action	Detroit, MI
1998	Harambee: 30 Years of Unity: Pulling Together and Changing Systems	New Orleans, LA
1999	Sharing Our Strengths: Building on our Successes	Atlanta, GA
2000	African-Centered Social Practice & Policies in the New Millennium	Los Angeles, CA
2001	Guided by Our African Legacy: Addressing Strategies for Current Social Work Issues	Charlotte, NC
2002	Embracing Our Ancestral Wisdom: African-Centered Social Work for Community Empowerment	Albuquerque, NM
2003	Making a Difference: Implementing Effective African-Centered Social Work Policies and Practices	Jacksonville, FL
2004	Building African-Centered Partnerships for an Effective Social Work Agenda	Pittsburgh, PA
2005	Fortify the African American Family: Educate, Rejuvenate and Motivate	New Orleans, LA
2006	In the Spirit of Sankofa: Facing the Challenges	Houston, TX
2007	Building on Our Strengths: Infusing New Leadership	Detroit, MI
2008	Ma'at, Sankofa & Harambee: 40 Years Strong	Los Angeles, CA
2009	The Black Family: Combating Challenges and Building on Strengths	Louisville, KY
2010	Keepers of the Village: The Role for Community Organizers	Philadelphia, PA

--Source: NABSW Conference Brochure, 2009

The second annual conference in Washington, D.C., cemented the focus and direction of NABSW by confirming the organization's commitment to remain open and accessible to all Black people dedicated to the common goal of enhanced social functioning, human dignity, freedom and liberation. With both the membership and leadership questions resolved, the organization moved forward, focusing its attention on galvanizing those who had initiated similar types of movement activities throughout the country. In subsequent years, the organization gathered strength as it continued to attract Black social service workers as well as key leaders and intellectuals in the Black community.

Examples of the organization's ability to bring together Black intellectuals, politicians and religious leaders with members of the social service community are plentiful. For instance, at the third annual conference in Chicago, Congressman Ronald V. Dellums provided the keynote address, where he emphasized and celebrated the day-to-day contributions made by Black social workers. Dellums, taking great comfort in knowing that he was speaking to members of his own community, stated:

> *"You have the potential to be the most influential organization of people—bar none—in America, because you understand the plight of Black people in this country. You work with Puerto Rican brothers, Chicano brothers, Asian brothers, Native American brothers, poor whites, lower class-whites, middle- class whites, urban and rural whites. You know everybody's problems. And let me just lay the real heavy point: You are potentially the most powerful leaders in America" (Dellums.1971:4).*

Dellums, recognizing the significant number of women in attendance, also cautioned the conference delegates on remaining mindful of the role that sexism and discrimination played in the Movement and the Black community. He stated further:

> *"We have Black women all around here who are not message carriers: they are not mediocre people; they should not be relegated to remedial tasks. They are competent pros. They went to school to put down the mop, to do something for the movement. So you have to respect their competence and ability. How can we talk about Black*

freedom, when we talk about oppressing our own women? I want you to know that I don't have a woman by the door as tokenism…I have a very competent, very beautiful, very able young woman, twenty-six years old, A.B. degree, M.S.W., graduated from law school at UCLA in June and joined up in June. She came here in March and, dig, the brothers didn't see her as the competent person that I had selected as administrative assistant. They're busy worrying about trying to go to bed with the sister. I don't raise that as a point of embarrassment; I raise that as a point to deal with what is happening with us. I selected her because she was the pro, the best in the country, as I saw it. She had brilliance, dedication, commitment, and integrity. The fact that she is beautiful is just a byproduct" (Ibid:17).

Other keynote presenters included Lerone Bennett, senior editor of *Ebony Magazine,* and Rev. Jesse Jackson, national president of Operation PUSH. In addition, there was a plethora of workshops dealing with every major issue in the Black community and every stage of the life cycle. The conferences also issued resolutions, providing an action agenda for conferees to follow when they returned to their local communities.

The fourth annual conference was equally impressive. Held in Nashville, the conference drew more than 1,000 participants hoping to address issues related to the survival of the Black community. Workshops were held in areas related to: Black community structure; institutional racism; politics; social planning; funding; health; education; employment; mass media; religion; law; corrections; and family and child Welfare. Social work professionals—Douglass Glasglow, Lawrence Gary, Shirley Better, Charles Sanders, James Craigen and Jay Chunn—and others were joined by professionals from various disciplines to discuss the harnessing of energy that the Movement continued to generate. The goal: to continue to motivate participants to work for social change. Of special note was a workshop presented by Rachel Brown, William Perry and Thaddeus P. Mathis, all from Temple University's School of Social Administration, entitled "Social Work and Nation Building in the Black Community." Mathis (1972), who submitted a paper for publication in the *Conference Proceedings,* offered an analysis of the Black social work community's efforts to move toward new social theories and social work practice that would aid in the struggle for Black liberation. As previously indicated, it was here that he introduced Karenga's (2002) Nguzo Saba as the value base of such a new approach. In the following year, the organization would focus the entire conference on the nation-building theme.

As conference attendance continued to increase each year, thousands were attracted to the message of the Movement. Reportedly, the largest conference, with the theme of nation building, was held in New York City in 1973 and attracted 4,000 to 5,000 individuals (Reid-Bookhart, 1984). This, too, was a memorable event. According to one (male) participant:

> *"I remember that conference very well. It seemed like there were thousands of us jammed into the hotel convention center. Louis Farrakhan of the Nation of Islam was giving the keynote address on a Friday night. We were there to talk about nation building and get more information on NABSW. By this time, everyone knew that it was the conference to attend. And the sisters were everywhere. We were all young, enthusiastic and, some of us, still very much into chasing the women. But he concluded by admonishing all of us with "lust in our hearts" to stay away from trouble in the hotel rooms. He hollered, 'I know what's going on up in there!' We left that session with our hands in our pockets and a commitment to focus on the need to rebuild our community and nothing else" (Anonymous, 2009).*

Minister Farrakhan did offer a powerful speech. He focused on the need for members of the Black community to become more independent and less dependent on the white community for securing their freedoms. He discussed the need for Blacks to "free your minds" from years of education that supported the ongoing oppression of Blacks in America. And he talked about the destruction of the Black man and the Black family. It was within this context that Farrakhan (1973) chose to address conferees' responsibilities:

> *"You came here for a social convention, but you know what you have in your mind. You know what's going on in the parties, you know what's going on in the rooms and you know what's going on as soon as I finish. You don't have a serious mind, you have a party mind. You've got a finger-poppin' mind, so how in the world can you build a society for Black people? The Black man has been made a goodtime party*

man, a clown. He wants to be a clown, a lover man. Romance all the women he can get his hands on! How in the world are you going to build a society if you've got a weak-minded man?" (1973:24)

Farrakhan went on to remind the conferees of their promised commitment to rebuild all of Black America, and complete dedication to the cause was the only way to fulfill that goal. Finally, he concluded by stating that until *the learned* and *the educated* use their knowledge to uplift all of our people, "we are not yet properly educated" (Ibid:27).

It is important to note that the national gatherings offered a new, mind-boggling experience for most of the young Black social work professionals. For many, it was a first-time travel experience. They were exposed to luxury hotel rooms, suites and penthouse accommodations. There were numerous receptions with free food, drinks and an endless amount of late-night social interactions, including emotionally charged debates about the controversial issues of the day. The experience was mesmerizing. According to one young participant:

"I remember attending my first conference in New York. To be honest, I had never stayed in a hotel. I had had a motel experience, but this was something totally different. I couldn't believe it when the president invited us up to the penthouse after the evening session. I remember seeing a spiral staircase that led up to a second floor. Sisters seemed to be lined up on every step in the most glamorous outfits. It was like a scene out of a Hollywood movie. 'This is power!' I thought to myself. But really, it was probably how white folks were living all along" (Anonymous).

The fifth annual conference continued to draw leaders in the field and those actively involved in the Black liberation struggle. Andrew Billingsley, Yosef ben-Jochannon, John Henrik Clark, Floyd B. McKissick and others discussed the need to develop an African consciousness and discover ways to connect and strengthen the African diaspora. Major problem areas like housing, health services, education, the family and theory building were ongoing topics of concern. It was within this context that Williams, who was in his second term as the organization's president, felt the need to connect Black social workers with the struggles of those in the African diaspora.

147

International Conferences

Following the success of the national conferences, international conferences were initiated in 1974. The purpose was threefold: (1) to forge linkages with people of African descent in the diaspora; (2) to examine the status of social welfare programs in foreign countries; and (3) to provide an additional fundraising source for the association. Williams, on his first international trip, traveled to South Africa to examine social conditions, specifically the racial oppression endured by Blacks under the system of apartheid. Black Americans felt a special infinity toward those suffering in South Africa. Apartheid, for many, was reminiscent of the system of enslavement in the United States. A still imprisoned Nelson Mandela united those in the African diaspora and those who believed in freedom and justice in a worldwide campaign that sought his release from prison (Mandela, 1994). Williams, who was given the name "Jomo" in a renaming ceremony, organized the first international chapter, the Association of Black Social Workers in South Africa, during his initial visit. The very next year, the organization's local president attended NABSW's conference in Detroit.

In subsequent years, the organization hosted international conferences in the Caribbean, North America, South America and Africa. Hundreds of professionals in a variety of disciplines, as well as nonprofessional and community members, traveled with the organization on the educational tours. The focus of these conferences was not limited to a visit to an exotic and foreign land; rather, the organization sought to explore the unique social conditions and social welfare needs of Blacks in diaspora. This initiative further legitimized NABSW as both a professional and social action organization with a national and international agenda. And strengthening the bridge between African Americans and those in the diaspora emerged as one of NABSW's most dominating organizational themes. The organization would also extend its support to special projects that focused on human service needs. For example, responding to the request for financial aid for the starving people in Africa in 1974, NABSW donated $11,000 to Congressman's Charles Diggs' Hunger Campaign in the Sahel.

Continuing the Tradition

For each presidential administration, the highest priority was given to the continuation and success of the annual national and international conferences. It was not only the glue that held the organization together; each conference was part of a carefully woven fabric that represented the organization's history, strength, vitality and insistence upon keeping the BSWM alive.

During the Chunn administration (1974–1978), conferences were held in Detroit, Baltimore, New Orleans and San Francisco. The conference themes, as always, served as the clarion call and focal point for discussion. Power, liberation and freedom from social oppression were common themes. For example, "Promises of Power: Actual or Potential" was the theme for the seventh annual conference in Detroit, and "Strategies for Liberation" was the theme for the ninth conference in New Orleans. The thrust of the conferences was in concert with leading ideological discussions of the era (Cruse, 1967; Karenga, 1967; DuBois, 1968, 1969; Baraka, 1972; Rodney, 1974). Keynote addresses by some of the most progressive Black thinkers of the time, including Francis C. Welsing, Barbara Solomon, Congressman Parren Mitchell, Congressman Charles Diggs and Na'im Akbar, fueled the imagination with talk and promises of change. Workshop discussions centered on the delivery of social services to members of the Black community; community organization; social, political and economic reform; and the development of new social work practice models that were sensitive to the needs of Black people.

In addition to the national conferences, local, state and regional conferences emerged in areas in which the BSWM had gained momentum. Regular state conferences were held in California, Illinois, Indiana, Maryland, Michigan, New Jersey, New York, North Carolina, Ohio, Pennsylvania and Texas. In the Southwest, Texas, Oklahoma, Arizona and New Mexico held regional conferences to help connect those living and working inside major metropolitan areas with those in suburban and rural areas. And in New England, Connecticut, Rhode Island and Massachusetts joined together to host annual regional conferences, as well as contribute to the development of community outreach projects.

In the first half of the second decade, conferences were held in St. Louis, Washington, D.C., Atlanta and Chicago during the Brabson administration. Speakers such as Benjamin Mays, Andrew Young, Bobby Wright and John Jacobs continued to share their visions about an empowered Black America. Advocacy, social justice and social activism were always part of the Black social work agenda, and conferees often participated in activities that benefited from the large gathering of Black social workers. For example, the social activism of NABSW during the 11th annual Conference in St. Louis remains legendary among conference regulars and many local residents. Following the initiative of the local chapter, the organization mounted an attack on the city hospital, which maintained "the racist practice of separate but equal facilities" (*St. Louis Dispatch*: April 1979). Conferees from around the country linked hands with their brothers and sisters on the local picket line to protest discriminatory practices and demand immediate change. The action, which attracted both local and national media attention, left an indelible print on the minds of many.

NABSW also demonstrated a willingness to engage in protest action with brothers and sisters in the international community. Upon the organization's arrival in Trinidad for the fifth international conference, 1978, conferees were thrust into the midst of a hotel workers' strike, which pitted local indigenous workers against the European-controlled hotel conglomerates. With the support and encouragement of the national leadership, conferees supported the workers' strike by joining their protest actions and refusing to utilize hotel support services (food, entertainment, etc.). Conferees relied on local residents to help secure alternative services.

Under the Merritt administration (1982–1986), conferences were held in Miami Beach, Detroit, New Orleans and Houston. The format and focus remained unchanged. The message was consistent: empowerment, freedom, liberation and cultural preservation. The mounting of the national conferences was a costly endeavor for an organization that was operating with extremely limited resources. However, at times, it appeared that the organization was operating on sheer will. Black scholars, intellectuals, politicians, academics and religious leaders, as well as Black human service workers and other professionals, were welcomed conference participants and continued to support NABSW. Sonia Sanchez, Wade Nobles, Jawanza Kunjufu and Congressman Walter Fauntroy were a few of the noted contributors who provided emotionally charged, inspirational messages specifically targeted to the Black social work professional. In fact, Congressman Fauntroy's appeal to the Black social workers to support the launching of the National Black Family Plan during his keynote luncheon address in 1985 resulted in an impromptu "pass the plate collection" that netted more than $3,000 in contributions.

The ongoing success of the international conferences was also undeniable. During the Merritt administration, NABSW hosted international conferences in Jamaica, Barbados, Grenada, Kenya, Egypt and Brazil, where social workers in the African diaspora connected with the message of the BSWM. The impact was, at times, profound. According to Merritt (2009):

> *"We could see the excitement among the Black social workers when we arrived in the country. So many of them expressed an interest in what we were doing. They endured a number of hardships just to come to the conference. Some walked for miles just to meet us. Most had limited financial resources and could not afford to register, but we allowed all the locals to attend for free. But we even had to extend ourselves and offer to buy food and drinks because the costs of these items at the local hotels were out of reach. The people were very emotional, indicating that they had never had an opportunity to gather and talk about the specific needs of the Black community. They talked about the discrimination and oppression they faced in their own country. And I recall that we were very supportive and encouraging. However, when they asked that we gather with them and talk about ways in which we could support their planned revolutionary activities, I don't think we were quite ready for that."*

The strong, emotional reaction to Black social workers in the international community was not an isolated incident. Sandra Mitchell (2009), who served as the organization's international conference co-chair and as national administrative consultant, summarizes her experiences:

> *"The experiences that we had over the years were overwhelming. There were times when the local Black social workers would begin to cry, uncontrollably, as they attempted to thank us for our presence in their country. They often talked about how they had never received validation as Black social workers and the role that racial identity played in their day-to-day work. I believe, for many, having the opportunity to interact with Black social workers from America was a life-changing experience."*

While each administration was held accountable for the success or failure of the annual conference, the primary responsibility for the planning and implementation of these gatherings was assigned to conference committees and the designated co-chairs. These roles were assumed by many, including Alan Coates, Chunn, James Craigen, Paul L. Hubbard, Barbara Carter, Stella Browne, Merritt, Zelma Smith, Sandra Mitchell, Barbara Baldwin, Margaret Penn and Judith Jackson, all of whom gained valuable leadership experiences and organizational skills in the process.

During the Jeff administration (1986–1990), conferences were held in Boston, San Francisco, Richmond and Los Angeles. There were international gatherings in Venezuela, Aruba, Togo, Benin and Egypt. The conferences continued to invite speakers who were close to the political left, including Lerone Bennett, Tony Brown, Wade Nobles, Patricia Russell-McCloud, Robert Staples and others.

Under President Gerald K. Smith (1990–1994), national conferences were held in Atlanta, Washington, New Orleans and Philadelphia. Rev. Jeremiah Wright, Molefi Asante, Lawrence Gary and Andrew Billingsley delivered powerful keynote addresses, reminding conferees of the critical role they played in the nation as representatives of the Black community. International conferences were held in Ghana, Morocco, Brazil and Senegal as Black social workers continued to focus on the active liberation struggles in the African diaspora. International representatives from the Patrice Lumumba Coalition and the African National Congress also participated in the national conferences. NABSW continued to focus on issues related to family preservation, youth development, social violence, substance abuse, and professional development. Workshops, scholarly papers, presentations and keynote addresses consistently reinforced those themes, and the Harambee Ceremony provided an uplifting, spiritual reconnection to the African heritage.

As the conferences crisscrossed the country from New York to Houston, and Detroit to New Orleans during the Dunston administration (1994–1998), the organization moved closer to fully embracing the concept and the language of Afrocentricity. Asante's (1980, 1990) work was gaining popularity among scholars, intellectuals and the general public (Reid-Merritt, 2007). Increasingly, "Afrocentric" was the word used to describe one's embrace of the African cultural heritage. Within this context, keynote speakers like Rev. Benjamin Chavis, Jr., Min. Robert Muhammad, Linda James Myers, Conrad Worrill, Bishop John Hurst Adams, Iyanla Vanzant, Gil Noble and Adelaide Stanford continued to provide a sharp focus on the specific needs of the Black community, some invoking the Afrocentric paradigm to explain their positions. During this same period, international gatherings were held in South Africa, Zimbabwe, Ghana, and Trinidad and Tobago, further strengthening the connection to those in the African diaspora.

Rudy C. Smith was serving as the organization's president (1998–2002) when the decision was made to move the national conferences from major cities to "second-tier" cities. Atlanta (1999) and Los Angeles (2000) were major host cities that drew large numbers of conferees. However, when the national conference moved to Charlotte (2001) and Albuquerque (2002) there was a noticeable decline in conference attendance. The Jackson administration (2002–2006) would also struggle with the impact of hosting annual conferences in second-tier cities, as gathering in Jacksonville, Florida, (2003) and Pittsburg, (2004) continued the downward trend, before returning to the major host cities of New Orleans (2005) and Houston (2006). Given the strong, rich heritage of utilizing the annual conferences to link and maintain the communication network among Black social workers, the decline in conference attendance generated tremendous concern. NABSW's focus on the Black family, the Black community and African-centered approaches to social intervention had not changed. Unfortunately, it appeared that fewer Black social work professionals were responding to the message.

During the first decade of the 21st century, international conferences were held in Belize, Barbados, Kenya, Tanzania, Panama, Costa Rica, South Africa, Brazil, Gambia and Cuba. By traveling to Cuba, NABSW defied years of presidential administrative policy (Bush, Clinton, Bush, Sr., Reagan, Carter, etc.) to forge a connection with the Black social work community. According to Jackson (2009):

> *"I was especially proud of our taking more than 100 Black social workers to Cuba. We were so well received by the government. They were anxious to talk about race and color issues and wanted our expertise in other areas. We met with Castro's representatives and the president of Parliament as well as mayors of a couple of cities. In my mind, it was quite an historic trip for a number of reasons. Notably, we were probably one of the last groups to tour before Bush shut down all travel."*

As detailed previously in Chapter Five, president Batiste-Roberts (2006–2010) describes her initial experience with conference planning as the organization's leader as "a baptism by fire." There were many goals for the 40th anniversary

153

conference in Los Angeles (2008), the most important of which was celebrating NABSW's longevity and revisiting the purpose and goals set by the Movement's founders. Settling on the conference site proved to be a difficult process. There was ongoing controversy and conflict, but the conference, with keynote speakers Molefi Asante, Joe Madison, Cheryl Dozier, Robert Hill and Toni Oliver, was a programming success. NABSW began discourse on a new item for its social agenda: the next 40 years.

Conclusion

The national and international communication network has been maintained by NABSW for more than 40 years. Presidential administrations, conference chairs and committee members fulfilled their responsibility in making certain that the network maintained stability during turbulent social times. The successful planning and implementation of national and international conferences provided the ongoing forum for Black social workers to discuss issues of social concern in the Black community. Moreover, the organization succeeded in establishing a safe haven for Black social workers and social activists whose highest priority was advocating for resources to support the social, cultural, economic and political empowerment of the Black community.

References:

Asante, Molefi Kete (1980). *Afrocentricity: A Theory of Social Change*, Trenton, NJ: Africa World Press.

_____ (1990). *Kemet, Afrocentricity and Knowledge*, Trenton, NJ: Africa World Press.

Baraka, Imamu Amiri (1972). *African Congress: A Documentary of the First Modern Pan-African Congress*, New York: William Morrow and Co.

Cruse, Harold (1967). *The Crisis of the Negro Intellectual*, New York: William Morrow.

Dellum, Ronald (1971). "Strategies for Freedom," *Third Annual Conference Proceedings National Association of Black Social Workers, Inc.*, pp. 1–22, New York: NABSW.

DuBois, W.E.B. (1968). *Black Reconstruction*, New Haven: Meridian Books.

_____ (1969). *The Souls of Black Folks*, New York: New American Library.

Farrakhan, Louis (1973). "Nation Building in the Black Community," *Fifth Annual Conference Proceedings*, National Association of Black Social Workers, Inc., pp. 1-14, New York: NABSW.

Franklin, John Hope and Alfred Moss, Jr. (2000). *From Slavery to Freedom*, New York: Alfred A. Knopf.

Karenga, Maulana. (2002). *An Introduction to Black Studies*, Los Angeles: University of Sankore Press.

_____ (1967). *The Quotable Karenga*, Inglewood, CA: Kawaida Publications.

Jackson, Judith (2009). Personal Interview, April.

Mandela, Nelson (1994). *A Long Walk to Freedom*, United States: QMB Publishing.

Mathis, Thaddeus P. (1972). "Social Work and Nation Building in the Black Community," *Proceedings of Fourth Annual Conference*, pp. 159–177, New York: NABSW.

Merritt, William T. (2009). Personal Interview, April.

Mitchell, Sandra (2009). Personal Interview, April.

National Association of Black Social Workers (1970-82). *Annual Conference Proceedings*, New York: NABSW.

_____ (1969-2009) *Annual Conference Brochures*.

Reid-Bookhart (1984). "Toward the Third Decade: The National Association of Black Social Workers," (Unpublished Report), New York: NABSW.

Rodney, Walter (1974). *How Europe Underdeveloped Africa*, Washington, D.C.: Howard University Press.

Sanders, Charles (1970). "Growth of the Association of Black Social Workers, *Social Casework*," (May), pp. 270 – 279.

St. Louis Dispatch Times (1979). "Black Social Workers Protest Hospital Segregation," April 8.

8

CRITICAL POLICY ACTIONS AND INITIATIVES

The National Association of Black Social Workers played a major role in highlighting critical needs in the Black community and developing position papers and policy initiatives to help influence the nation's social welfare policies. As indicated previously, a major concern by those involved in the BSWM was the impact of racism on the day-to-day lives of community members. As a membership association, NABSW utilized the expertise of its organizational members to investigate and document problem areas, and to help focus attention on social issues that impacted the quality of life for Black Americans. Throughout its 40-year history, the organization pushed its aggressive social agenda at conferences, steering committee meetings, policy institutes and workshops. It published *Position Papers* and newsletters, and held press conferences and protest rallies to inform the public of its positions. With varying degrees of success, the organization addressed problems associated with drug abuse and addiction, housing, elder services, public education, mental health, HIV/AIDS, crime, domestic violence, police brutality, political empowerment and environmental justice. Summaries of several of these policy initiatives are listed below.

However, one area in which the organization had its greatest impact was family and child welfare. The nation's ongoing child welfare crisis was a major challenge to the social work profession and to social service agencies entrusted with the responsibility to protect children at risk. Moreover, the struggle to determine which policy approaches and practices were in the best interest of the Black child was the focus of raging oppositional debate that pitted the principles of social integration against the belief in Black family preservation, self-determination and cultural survival. An examination of NABSW's positions on foster care, adoption, kinship care and family preservation provides greater insights on the complexity of these issues in American society.

Finally, Black social workers were equally passionate about state efforts to legalize the social work profession through licensing. Aggressive efforts by the National Association of Social Workers to grant states the right to legalize the profession through licensing was adamantly opposed by the organization. This section explores the intensity of efforts surrounding these critical policy initiatives and the organization's struggle to articulate its concerns to others.

Social Problems and the Black Community

A thorough analysis of the organization's official position statements on the plethora of social problems and social ills that impact the Black community is beyond the scope of this work. As indicated above, NABSW focused on a wide range of social concerns. The summaries below are intended to provide the reader with a glimpse of the diversity of issues addressed by NABSW over the past 40 years, and have been compiled from the organization's numerous position papers (NABSW, 1983, 1985, 1994, 2008). The irony here is that the organization's articulated positions on key public issues in the 1970s, 1980s and 1990s are still relevant today.

Equal Opportunity and Affirmative Action–NABSW supports the affirmative action concept as a necessary mechanism to help ensure equal access of opportunity for Blacks in a white-oriented society. Furthermore, NABSW maintains that policies and programs of affirmative action, and its philosophical underpinnings, should be viewed as legally sanctioned, morally justified approaches directed toward eliminating racial and sexual discrimination in employment and education.

158

Public Assistance-NABSW is committed to achieving full economic and social protection for impoverished and disadvantaged Black individuals and families. To this end, all resources — political, organizational, community and professional — must be marshaled in support of adequate payment levels and social services to Black families who are forced to depend on public income maintenance programs.

Employment–NABSW believes that employment policies must be implemented for the "structurally unemployed," i.e., those persons who are excluded from the job market due to inadequate educational opportunities, training and discrimination, in which Black people are disproportionately represented. Government employee policy must include quality job training, support services, job placement and effective enforcement of anti-discrimination laws. Sound employment policies must also include employment opportunities for the recently unemployed and for adolescents and young adults of poor families.

Housing–NABSW strongly believes that the federal government is responsible for providing opportunities for all of its citizens. The availability and accessibility of decent shelter at affordable prices is a basic provision any citizen of the United States should confidently expect its government to ensure. The denial of that assurance to Black and other poor Americans is an insult not only to this nation's largest racial minority, but an insult to democracy. NABSW is committed to the struggle for decent housing for all Black Americans. This message must be heard by the current administration and the Congress.

Political Empowerment–NABSW seeks to liberate the masses of Black people from dehumanizing conditions of racism, imperialism, sexual oppression and economic exploitation. We are committed to organizing the masses of Black people to force government and other forces of power to institute and implement policies designed to meet the fundamental needs of the majority of Black people in the United States in a manner that promotes and enhances human dignity. NABSW supports the right of Black and other Third World people for self-determination and the establishment of a more just and human social and economic order.

Preservation of the Black Family-NABSW advocates for the rights of families to keep and raise their children in loving, safe and supportive environments. We support the right of kinship to raise their relative child and demand fair and equitable treatment of families of African ancestry who wish to adopt. We remain forceful advocates for families of African ancestry to have equal rights and access to children of African ancestry who are free for adoption.

The Black Aged–NABSW is dedicated to the alleviation of problems that face the Black elderly. Practitioners who serve them should become more knowledgeable about the particular issues they face. As government policies are reviewed and considered for revisions NABSW will advocate for or against changes that impact the Black elderly either positively or negatively.

Black Youth–NABSW is committed to improving the quality of life for Black youth through innovative programming, strengthening community support systems, increased advocacy and responsible role-modeling. Through such efforts, NABSW seeks to reduce the probability of creating a permanent underclass in the Black community.

Teenage Pregnancy–NABSW actively supports teenage pregnancy prevention programs to address the dilemma of "children having children." NABSW also advocates programming for those teen parents and their children to avoid or lessen the adverse effects of teenage pregnancy, which includes higher infant anomalies and death, loss educational opportunities and career options, lower income levels and marriage and family disruption and dysfunction.

Energy–NABSW acknowledges the local, regional, national and global implications of America's energy policies. An unplanned approach to the energy question courts a disaster of monumental proportions on powerless groups and vulnerable populations. Moreover, we are alarmed by the number of hazardous waste sites located in or near Black communities and the failure to require responsible parties to bear the costs of cleanup. All signals indicate that our communities will become further dumping grounds for more deadly and unwanted materials. To combat these harmful energy policies, NABSW accepts the challenge of encouraging and mobilizing a truly "people-inspired" movement as a proactive strategy for positive economic, political and social change in Black and powerless communities.

Health Issues–NABSW recognizes that the physical and mental health needs of the Black community are not being met. Elected public officials have insisted on balancing budgets by risking the health of medically indigent and underserved populations, disproportionately represented by African Americans due to social factors beyond their immediate control. The maintenance of the "safety net" has been threatened by the transfer of federal programs to state control. NABSW is committed to advocacy to maintain support for vital health services and will lobby congressional representatives and elected state officials to support our just cause.

Domestic Violence–NABSW recognizes the violent nature of American society. Media images, movies, videos and print media glorify violence. NABSW denounces violence in all forms and stands firmly against violence toward women, both here and abroad. The collective survival of the race is threatened by domestic violence, and consequently is not a private concern but a public issue. Therefore, it is imperative that the problem be removed from private confines and placed squarely within the public arena. It is our collective responsibility to address this problem through words and deeds.

Black Students and Schools of Social Work–NABSW supports increased enrollment and retention of Black students in graduate schools of social work. The Black social worker's keen perspective on Black life is extremely valuable to the erstwhile white-dominated field of social welfare. As conduits for Black clients in need of services, and as field instructors for social work student interns, the need for Black social workers is unparalleled.

Cross-cultural Counseling–NABSW supports the development and the maintenance of quality, comprehensive cross-cultural counseling and research-oriented training programs at universities that encompass the socio-political and cultural realities of being Black in America. Furthermore, NABSW recognizes the paucity of relevant cross-cultural continuing education programs in community agencies and encourages practitioners and administrators to address this unmet need. NABSW encourages Black mental health practitioners to assume a leadership role in community-based research projects, and in the recruitment of culturally sensitive minority and non-minority practitioners. Finally, NABSW advocates for increased federal funding for community-based and community-controlled counseling services.

International Relations–NABSW advocates that United States foreign policy does not obstruct the legitimate struggles for majority rule, nor corrupt that majority rule in regard to African nations. We demand that United States foreign policy support the struggle of progressive Black nations and their people throughout the world.

The issuance of policy positions always included strategies to address the presenting problem. Education, research, public discourse, protest rallies, public awareness campaigns, petitioning legislators, coalition building and establishing new programs were often advocated as possible solutions, as well as emphasizing ways in which existing social problems could be prevented.

Family and Child Welfare Policy: Protecting
Our Children—The Adoption Initiative

There was no issue that Black social workers felt more passionately about than the protection of Black children and the preservation of the Black family. As experts in the field of family and child welfare, social workers have always been at the forefront of family and child welfare policy (NASW, 1977) and Black social workers proved that they were not an exception to the rule. The desire to create programs, policies, projects and initiatives to help preserve the Black family and keep Black children in the Black community remained a consistent theme from the very beginning of Movement activity.

At the very first national gathering of Black social workers, Audrey Russell, one of the organizers of the Philadelphia Alliance of Black Social Workers, presented her concerns about a burning issue that needed immediate attention: the placement and adoption of Black children. According to Russell, Black children, who had been forcibly removed from their homes and placed in the foster care system, were at risk of never being reunited with their families. Moreover, as the availability of young white infants decreased due to changing social conditions, the desire of white parents to adopt healthy Black children increased (Neal and Stumph, 2003). Sandra Mitchell, MSW, child and welfare service unit supervisor in Nashville, Tennessee, from 1966 to 1973, knew from her own personal experience that these predictions were true. According to Mitchell (2009):

> "White babies were no longer available. White families started looking, very specifically, for lighter skinned Black children. Their ignorance about the Black child as well as some of the questions that they raised was appalling. Having examined one Black infant with straight black hair, the mother asked: 'When does the child's hair fall out and come back in kinky?' We were witness to what was happening. That's one of the reasons why the Black social workers within the agency began to organize themselves."

According to Russell and others, if the current trend continued, potential Black adoptive parents would be forced to compete with more affluent white families for Black infants and children. Moreover, the removal of Black

162

children from their natural parents and the dismantling of Black families was too frequently related to poverty, poor housing, unemployment and other social conditions that had a disproportionate impact on the Black community. Black children were in dire need of social work advocates within the child welfare system, and Black social workers needed to assume greater responsibility for their care.

Child Welfare Services

The history of child welfare and adoption services in the United States reveals that Black children and Black families were never a system priority. Reinforced by a strong sense of personal values and cultural practices, Americans believed that the care of children was a parental responsibility. Intervention by the state occurred as a last resort. Since the early days of Charles Loring Brace (O'Conner, 2004; Brace, 2009), foster care was viewed as the best practice to provide for children without homes. In 1853, Brace, under the Children's Aid Society in New York, began a series of programs to help deal with the city's wayward youth, who were most often viewed as juvenile delinquents. Initial efforts to provide schooling and shelter for the city's burgeoning youth population met with limited success. As a result:

> "Brace soon became convinced that the only solution to the problems of the thousands of vagrant city children was to send them to the homes of farmers in the West. It is estimated that, during the society's first twenty-five years, over fifty thousand children were placed in private homes. Although Brace recognized that the success of the emigration program was in part due to the farmers' need for cheap agricultural labor, he was equally convinced that the children were receiving the care and individual attention it was impossible to give them in institutions" (NASW, 1977:87-88).

Brace's plan for foster care spread throughout the nation and became the model approach for social intervention in child welfare and protective services. However, like most of the early history of social services in the United States, this system was segregated by race and designed to meet the needs of white, mostly immigrant children who had begun to overwhelm the urban areas. Neal and Stumph (2003:1) have noted:

163

"Child welfare services in the United States show a history of exclusion of African American children. After slavery ended homeless black children were cared for by institutions and services set up by the Black community. The institutions run by Black people were concerned with the development of Black children as the future hope of the Black race and were based on the principles of self-help. These institutions were funded in a variety of ways. Some found their way to firm financial standing through private donations and/or the acquisition of public monies. Fraternal organizations such as the Masons and other Black organizations financed some of the Black orphanages while others came into existence through the endowments of Black philanthropists. Some of the larger institutions were quite formal with boards of trustees and hired directors."

From the period of Reconstruction to the mid-20th century, Blacks were underserved by public agencies, which based norms and standards of behaviors on white middle-class values and the need to maintain the system of white privilege in America. For example, during the 1940s and 1950s, Black families in the South, who received considerably less for public support, were regularly removed from local assistance during the planting and harvesting seasons (Trattner, 1989; Alston, 2007). This provided local farmers with a cheap, exploitable labor supply, thereby allowing the state to subsidize their businesses and expand the farmers' profit margins. In the North, inferior social service programs were designed specifically to serve the community's Black population. Examples include neighborhood YMCAs, mental health services, correctional institutions and public health programs (Trattner, 1989). However, it's also important to note that, given the oppressive societal conditions, Blacks discovered early on the need to develop their own forms of assistance — most notably, an informal foster care and adoption system within their extended families and community. Black Americans were among the first ethnic groups in America to develop social service agencies to fill the particular needs of the community, including homes for the aged, benevolent societies and Black adoption agencies (Carlton-Laney, 2001). As cries to integrate all of America's social systems became more audible in the mid-1960s, public agencies were forced to address the needs of its white as well as Black citizens. This marked the beginning of wide-scale intervention by state and local agencies into the Black community as they began to formally regulate the placement and adoption of Black children. And many (Ellis, 1983; Oliver, Neal and Oglesby, 1994) have argued that the state's disruption of these informal networks was not in the best needs of Black children or the Black community. As more and more Black children and workers entered the public systems, the clash between cultures became evident: Agencies designed to protect the interests of white children and families were poorly equipped to address the needs of America's new urban population (Kellogg, 1993; Neal and Stumph, 2003).

For the progressively informed Black social workers, the attack on the child welfare system was swift and immediate. In a society in which racism had impacted every area, it is no surprise that Black social workers found racist practices as a barrier to effective service in the Black community and in the child welfare system as well. And while racism in all social welfare agencies was a frequent target of attack, there was a particular concern about the nation's child protection agencies. Who would protect the rights of Black children? According to Sanders (1970), Black social workers' perceptions of the ability of the social work profession and social agencies to act in the best interests of Black people were overwhelmingly negative. Social service practices and decision making heavily favored the values of the majority community. At the peak of the Black Freedom Movement, and just as the BSWM continued to unfold, there was a sharp increase in the number of white families interested and willing to adopt Black children. This represented a policy shift in social agency practice that the organization and its members found untenable.

Transracial Adoption

NABSW's adamant opposition to transracial adoption is the most widely known and misunderstood of its official policy and position statements. The organization's position has been debated in hundreds of newspapers, articles, books and magazines, on televison, radio, and in the halls of Congress (Chestang, 1972; Jones, 1972; Vieni, 1075; Chimezie, 1975; Johnson, 1976; Howard, Royse, and Skerl, 1977; Simon and Roorda, 2000; Neal and Stumph, 2003). Even Hollywood joined the discourse, producing the emotionally charged film, *Losing Isaiah*, which portrayed the struggle of a single Black mother fighting to regain custody of her child from a white middle-class family (1995). And most recently, *ABC World News* (3/3/10) aired a segment that raised questions about the transfer of Black children, including the widespread dispersal of Haitian youth, to white families. The discourse on transracial adoption within the social work profession was explosive. Yet the issues surrounding transracial adoption were never considered a dominant theme in America's child welfare programming.

The history of foster care and adoptions reveals that both private and public adoption agencies preferred same-race and sometimes same-faith placements. In the late 19th century, one rationale used for the critical need for Catholic orphanages and adoption programs was to "save the Catholic souls" (Holloran, 1994) of children who were at risk of being placed outside of their known religion. Throughout the 20th century, race continued to be the most dominating social factor in considering placement of children in foster care. The placement of Black children in white homes, and vice versa, was rare. Prior to the 1960s, the majority of transracial placements were "transnational, from Asian countries like Korea, China and Japan. These fair-skinned 'yellow' children were preferable to Blacks. In addition, many white parents were willing to adopt Native American children, a practice that was, eventually, halted by the passage of the 1978 Indian Child Welfare Act" (Adoption Project, 2009). According to Johnson (1988), this act was modeled after NABSW's position on transracial adoption. While Americans have proven to be leaders in adopting children from other countries and cultures, the debate around transracial adoption in the United States pitted white parents against the Black community, where transracial adoption mostly involved the removal of Black and other children of color and placing them in white homes. A number of changing social conditions impacted adoption practices in the United States:

> *"After World War II, demographic pressures shaped this trend at least as powerfully as civil rights ideology. New contraceptive technology like the pill, legalized abortion after Roe v. Wade, and the sexual revolution all decreased the supply of healthy white infants, along with the stigma surrounding illegitimacy. The result was that some white parents reconsidered their preference for same-race adoptions" (Adoption Project, 2009).*

By the early 1970s, approximately 2,500 Black children were adopted by white families each year. However, in 1972, NABSW created a storm of controversy when they issued the official position statement (see Table IV), vehemently opposing all forms of transracial adoption (NABSW, 1972). This revolutionary statement called into question the altruistic claims of white

Table IV
Position Statement — National Association of Black Social Workers — 1972
Transracial Adoption

The National Association of Black Social Workers has taken a vehement stand against the placement of black children in white homes for any reason. We affirm the inviolable position of black children in black families where they belong physically, psychologically and culturally in order that they receive the total sense of themselves and develop a sound projection of their future.

Ethnicity is a way of life in these United States, and the world at large; a viable, sensitive, meaningful and legitimate societal construct. This is no less true nor legitimate for black people than for other ethnic groups. . . .

The socialization process for every child begins at birth and includes his cultural heritage as an important segment of the process. In our society, the developmental needs of Black children are significantly different from those of white children. Black children are taught, from an early age, highly sophisticated coping techniques to deal with racist practices perpetrated by individuals and institutions. These coping techniques become successfully integrated into ego functions and can be incorporated only through the process of developing positive identification with significant black others. Only a black family can transmit the emotional and sensitive subtleties of perception and reaction essential for a black child's survival in a racist society. Our society is distinctly black or white and characterized by white racism at every level. We repudiate the fallacious and fantasized reasoning of some that whites adopting black children will alter that basic character.

We fully recognize the phenomenon of transracial adoption as an expedient for white folk, not as an altruistic humane concern for black children. The supply of white children for adoption has all but vanished and adoption agencies, having always catered to middle class whites developed an answer to their desire for parenthood by motivating them to consider black children. This has brought about a re-definition of some black children. Those born of black-white alliances are no longer black as decreed by immutable law and social custom for centuries. They are now black-white, inter-racial, bi-racial, emphasizing the whiteness as the adoptable quality; a further subtle, but vicious design to further diminish black and accentuate white. We resent this high-handed arrogance and are insulted by this further assignment of chattel status to black people. . . .

White parents of black children seek out special help with their parenting; help with acquiring the normal and usually instinctual parental behaviors inherent in the cultural and psychological development of children. It is tantamount to having to be taught to do what comes naturally.

Special programming in learning to handle black children's hair, learning black culture, "trying to become black," puts normal family activities in the form of special family projects to accommodate the odd member of the family. This is accentuated by the white parents who had to *prepare* their neighbors for their forthcoming black child and those who hasten, even struggle, to make acquaintance with black persons. These actions highlight the unnatural character of trans racial adoption, giving rise to artificial conditions, logically lacking in substance. Superficialities convey nothing of worth and are more damaging than helpful.

Continued on next page

Table IV –Continued

We know there are numerous alternatives to the placement of black children with white families and challenge all agencies and organizations to commit themselves to the basic concept of black families for black children. With such commitment all else finds its way to successful realization of that concept. Black families can be found when agencies alter their requirements, methods of approach, definition of suitable family and tackle the legal machinery to facilitate inter-state placements. Additionally, the proposed commitment invokes the social work profession to a re-orientation to the black family permitting sight of the strengths therein. Exploration for resources within a child's biological family can reveal possibilities for permanent planning. The extended family of grandparents, aunts, cousins, etc. may well be viable resources if agencies will legitimize them; make them their area for initial exploration and work first to develop and cement their potential. This is valid and preferable even if financial assistance is necessary.

We denounce the assertions that blacks will not adopt; we affirm the fact that black people, in large numbers, can not maneuver the obstacle course of the traditional adoption process. This process has long been a screening out device. The emphasis on high income, educational achievement, residential status and other accoutrements of a white middle class life style eliminates black applicants by the score.

The National Association of Black Social Workers asserts the conviction that children should not remain in foster homes or institutions when adoption can be a reality. We stand firmly, though, on conviction that a white home is not a suitable placement for black children and contend it is totally unnecessary.

---

agencies and families who, rather suddenly, were interested in the adoption of a specific population of children: Black infants. The organization's position statement followed a carefully worded resolution that was presented by the Chicago chapter and passed by the National Steering Committee earlier in the year at the organization's annual conference (see Table V). It is important to note the relevance of the earlier resolution. The Chicago resolution clearly delineated the major areas of concern, including: the alarming increase in the number of Black children who had been removed from their homes and were now waiting adoption; the concern about the blatant forms of racism that existed in American society; and the questioning of the ability of white parents to rear racially and culturally secure Black children. Of significance is the organization's effort to put forth *solutions* to the problems generated by the transracial adoption controversy. These included: suggesting alternatives to the current system that too often overlooked single parents, extended parents and grandparents as potential adoptive parents; providing subsidies to families in the Black community who were willing to adopt but needed additional financial resources; and altering the

Table V
Trans-Racial Adoptions
Resolution of the Chicago Chapter of NABSW Concerning Trans-Racial Adoption in the United States

WHEREAS, The practice of trans-racial adoption has increased among adoptive agencies because of an alleged lack of potential Black parents,

WHEREAS, white adoptive agencies state that they have a tremendous number of Black children awaiting adoption,

WHEREAS, the practice of trans-racial adoption is detrimental to the Black adoptive child placed with a white family (because of the racism that exists in the present society),

WHEREAS, white parents do not have the ability to rear Black children in such a way, that the necessary emotional support and training is incorporated into the socialization process which will help the child survive in this racist society,

WHEREAS, the Black child must establish ties with his ethnic background at an early age so that he becomes identified with that group of people that accepts and understands him,

BE IT RESOLVED, there are a number of alternatives that can be utilized to produce Black adoptive parents, e.g. single parents, extended parents, grand-parent family, subsidies to families that qualify, but are financially unable to care for a child. This may be foster parents or potential adoptive parents,

BE IT RESOLVED, changes can be produced by hiring more Black staff and administrators. The Board of Directors should be representative of the community which it serves.

BE IT RESOLVED, it is imperative that the policies, and personnel practices of adoptive agencies need to revamped in order to produce changes that will meet the needs of the Black community.

BE IT RESOLVED, there should be a continuous program that will sensitize all workers, administrators, and Black parents (potential adoptive parents or not) to the necessity of locating Black adoptive homes.

BE IT RESOLVED, that local chapters devise and implement a program to bring about a positive change in the area of adoption. And be it resolved, that the program should meet the needs of the particular program it serves.

complexion of agency personnel and board of directors to reflect the communities the purported to serve, while concurrently providing education and training that would increase their cultural competency in the area of Black family service. Furthermore, it charged local chapters with the responsibility to "devise and implement a program to bring about a positive change in the area of adoption." In the years to come, state, local, private and nonprofit organizations would yield to these recommendations. (For example, Kinship Care is a major program initiative in state child welfare agencies in California, Georgia, Michigan, New Jersey, New York, Pennsylvania and Texas.)

NABSW's public militancy around the failure of the child welfare system brought transracial adoption to a screeching halt. Unfortunately, Black social workers had few vocal supporters as they continued to demand that Black children be placed in Black homes. NABSW also demanded that the child welfare system end its systematic discrimination against Black families who were willing to adopt Black children but oftentimes were denied the opportunity to do so by local child welfare agencies (NABSW, 1978). In the early 1970s, Cenie J. Williams, as NABSW's president or executive director, became the public face associated with the anti-transracial adoption movement. He was frequently vilified in the press, but his message reverberated around the nation. The Adoption History Project (2009) asserts that the release of NABSW's *Position Paper* coupled with Williams' persuasive arguments against transracial adoption "slowed black-white adoptions to a trickle." In its third year of existence, NABSW was having a major impact on national child welfare policy. Each subsequent president was destined to assume the same public role as Williams: defending the organization's policy position on transracial placements. As the pro-transracial adoption forces gained national momentum, NABSW would be forced to adjust its strategies to deal with legislation and new policy initiatives that granted the white community greater access to Black children. However, the organization never deviated from its basic beliefs and philosophy regarding the protection of Black children.

Changing Social Currents

Child and family welfare remained a major focus throughout the ensuing years and the organization kept abreast of changes in legislative policy. The passage of the Adoption Assistance and Child Welfare Act of 1980, (P.L. 96-272), supported NABSW's claim that more needed to be done to preserve African American and other families at risk. Local chapters developed programs, campaigns and partnerships to help inform the public about the need for Black homes for Black children. One strategy used was to lobby Congress to pass a National African American Heritage Child Welfare Act (NAAHCWA). NABSW solicited assistance from other national Black organizations to support the NAAHCWA and to aid in its fight to preserve Black families. For example, in 1981, the National Association for the Advancement of Colored People (NAACP) passed a resolution indicating that "...the National Association for the Advancement of Colored People support proposed legislation that would amend the current U.S. Indian and Child Welfare Act to include the National Association of Black Social Workers' proposed National African American Heritage Child Welfare Act..." The NAACP resolution cautioned that should transracial adoption become necessary, it should occur "only if all efforts for same race placement have been exhausted and only if 'monitoring bodies' of lay and professional persons from the African American community will be established for the purpose of ensuring agency compliance with the intent of the law..."

A National Child Welfare Act for the protection of African American children never materialized, and the NAACP's cautionary language about the possibility of "monitoring" future transracial placements proved to be a wake-up call for NABSW. Organizational members and leaders were cognizant of the shift in attitudes and the emerging reality of the increasing number of adoptions of Black children by white parents.

In its 1983 *Position Paper* on "Child Welfare Services for Black Children," NABSW further clarified its position on child welfare, noting that "the plight of Black children stranded in the child welfare system resulted in the published position in 1972 opposing trans-racial adoptive placements. Responses to the NABSW position drew widespread attention and were hotly debated. Seldom has a social welfare issue concerning Black children prompted such strident and sustained controversy" (NABSW, 1983:3). The organization noted the support for transracial adoption by past and present Black leaders, and the emerging literature that argued "Black children adopted by white families were doing well as measured by performance in school and as indicated by tests measuring self-esteem." The organization reemphasized its commitment to work toward the elimination of racism and discrimination in the child welfare system noting that "child welfare agencies fail to serve Black children as promptly and effectively as they do white children" and that the organization "sought to point the way to institutional change." Rejected were the myths that Black children were

171

hard to place Black adoptive families were hard to find and the superficiality of questions about having "a white family or no family at all." NABSW demanded change in adoption policy nationwide that would require agencies to engage in appropriate efforts to recruit Black homes for Black children. Its official position statement declared:

> *"NABSW supports a more pro-active and comprehensive position, and moves to address the continuum of child welfare services. A recognition that Black children, Black families, and Black communities have different strengths and different problems leads to the necessity to adopt these service programs to deal with the realities of the Black experience, with a special emphasis on <u>preventing entry into the child care system</u>" (Ibid).*

The organization pledged to mobilize its national resources and join forces with other child advocacy organizations to force full implementation of federal laws designed to support children and families by monitoring State activities to help ensure compliance.

Congressional activity around foster care and adoption focused on limiting the amount of time a child would spend in state care without the prospect of a permanent home as well as considering barriers to adoption (NACAC.org). The notion that race, (i.e., same-race placements), was in and of itself a barrier to adoption continued to gain support. Recognizing that the organization would not succeed in encouraging agencies to abandon their transracial adoption policies, NABSW issued a position paper on *Preserving African American Families* in in April 1994, which for the first time it offered guidelines for transracial placements. The organization was forced to modify its public position due to the increasing number of federal laws which supported transracial placements. The guidelines indicated that:

> *"Priority should be given to preserving families through the reunification or adoption of children with/by biological relatives. If that should fail, secondary priority should be given to the placement of a child within his own race. Trans-racial adoption of an African-American child should only be considered after documented evidence of unsuccessful same race placements have been reviewed and*

supported by appropriate representatives of the African American community. Under no circumstances should successful same race placements be impeded by obvious barriers (legal limits of states, state boundaries, fees, surrogate payments, intrusive applications, lethargic court systems, inadequate staffing patterns,etc.)" (NABSW, 1994).

Also in April 1994, NABSW held a series of policy institutes that focused on strengthening the African American family. At one of its sessions, "The Real Barriers to Same-Race Placements: Don't Believe the Hype," adoption and placement specialists Toni Oliver, Leora Neal and Zena Oglesby reemphasized the challenges that faced Black social workers in their efforts to preserve the Black family through the continued encouragement of same-race adoption placements. In their presentation they noted: (1) the strength of the Black community's heritage in providing for its own children prior to the push by government agencies to control foster care and adoption; (2) the failures of the bureaucratic system that produced foster care; (3) the inherent bias to reward agencies, through yearly payments, for managing the ineffective foster care system; and (4) a challenge to the notion that "cultural-free" environments existed in America, which would support and nurture the Black child. They also warned participants about the impact of the passage of Senator Howard Metzenbaum's bill, which would penalize states with the loss of funds for their failure to find permanent homes for children of color. According to this panel, "…the failure of the agencies to recruit Black and Latino adoptive parents" would result in these children being sent to white homes (NABSW, 1994:6).

In October 1994, Congress passed the Multi-Ethnic Placement Act (MEPA). The purpose of the act was to: (1) prevent discrimination in the placement of children on the basis of race, color or national origin; (2) facilitate the diligent recruitment of foster and adoptive parents; and (3) increase the number of children who are adopted. According to Neal and Al Stumph (2003:27):

"Some of the proponents of transracial adoption felt that MEPA did not go far enough to assure that race would not be a consideration in the placement of children and wanted a stronger law with monetary sanctions. Therefore, after extensive lobbying, on August 20, 1996 the

Inter-ethnic Adoption Provisions (PL104-188) was signed into law as part of the Small Business Job Protection Act."

And in 1997, the Adoption and Safe Families Act was added to the lengthening legislation that minimized the role race should play in the placement of children. Focused on foster care, this law aimed to: (1) shorten the length of time between permanency hearings and placement from ten to 12 months; (2) make reasonable efforts to reunify children with their parents; (3) enforce mandatory requirements for agencies to file termination of parental rights for most children in the system more than 15 months; and (4) utilize concurrent planning to shorten the length of time a child is in foster care.

In 1998, NABSW launched a new initiative, *A Fist Full of Families*. The organization refocused its efforts on highlighting structural inequities in the child welfare system, while at the same time pledging to inform and encourage members of the Black community to consider foster care and adoption. As the call went out across the nation, thousands of Black families and individuals responded. Furthermore, the organization's efforts in the new millennium included creating a national adoption and exchange program. Black family adoption and service agencies who benefitted from this new initiative, include: Another Choice for Black Children, North Carolina; Rejoice, Three Rivers Adoption Council, Pennsylvania; National One Church One Child, Virginia: Who If Not Us -Adoptions Together, Maryland; Black Adoption and Placement Resource Center, Institute for Black Parenting, California; ABSW Child Adoption and Research Center, New York; Institute for Black Parenting, Louisiana; ROOTS, Georgia; African American Adoption and Permanency Planning Agency, Minnesota; National Resource Center for Special Needs Adoption-Spaulding for Children, Homes for Black Children, Michigan; and, Mississippi Families for Kids. Black children continue to be disproportionately represented in the nation's foster care system. Of the estimated 500,000 children in foster care in 2006 (U.S. Census, 2006), many of whom are awaiting adoption, 32 percent were Black. These agencies have succeeded in the recruitment of Black families and in the placement of Black children in Black homes. (To repeat a frequently quoted adage in the Black community: "Where there is a will, there is a way!")

Licensure: The Legislating of Black Social Work Practice

Efforts by NASW to license the practice of social work in all 50 states had a tremendous impact on the growth and development of the Movement and NABSW. The perspectives of many who joined the BSWM were far more radical than those who were part of mainstream social work. Both individually and professionally, Black social workers had witnessed some of the negative effects of bureaucracy, government intervention, state control and exclusionary provisions as barriers to Black participation in the rich resources of American society. NASW's commitment to grant state control via licensing was viewed as suspicious by many. Social work, in its ideal form, is a profession pledged to upend unjust societal practices that privilege the needs of the few over the needs of the many. How could social work commit itself to social justice and social advocacy if it relinquished oversight of professional activities to the state? Moreover, NABSW rejected the argument that social work licensing would protect and/or improve the quality of services to the Black community.

The push for licensing of the social work profession was already under-way when advocates of the BSWM began to voice their concerns about restricting access to the profession through degree qualifications, examinations and state regulations. The need for licensing was initially linked to medical social workers who felt that advances in the field required stricter regulations for practitioners (NASW, 1977:623). It was believed that the advent of the third-party payment system in medical social services would eventually put the social worker at a disadvantage if they were prohibited from independent, autonomous practice. Following the merger of the six national professional social work organizations in 1955, the push for certification and licensing began in earnest as NASW proclaimed that licensing was in the best interest of the profession (NASW, 1977).

While the MSW degree was viewed as the level of education needed to practice professional social work, the term "social worker" was used loosely by many non-degreed persons. Many professional social workers felt that some form of title protection was needed and joined the movement for licensure in various states. Identifying who was a social worker was further complicated by the expansion of undergraduate social work in the late 1960s and early 1970s. Many of these graduates entered the workforce directly, without any further training or education (Ibid). This would lead to further discussions about what qualifications were needed to be called a social work professional.

When NABSW issued its first *Position Paper on Social Work Licensing*, which outlined its opposition, some form of legal protection already existed in 25 states (see Table VI). It argued that: (1) social work licensing was a quest for enhanced public status and access to third-party payments; (2) the practice of social work posed no threat to the public, and therefore government intervention was not necessary; (3) it supported the quality control standards for social work practice that were set by accredited schools of social work; and (4) there were no discernable benefits of social work licensing to the Black community.

For NABSW, the anti-licensing position was controversial and at times divisive. Even some of its most ardent supporters were troubled by the organization's position. Some feared the impact that it would have on their professional careers, especially those who were in states that required a social work license to retain professional positions. For others, it was denying oneself an added credential that spoke to a higher level of professional achievement. Zelma Smith joined the organization in the early 1970s as a graduate student at Hunter School of Social Work in New York. She has served the organization in numerous capacities, including national and international conference co-chair. Smith (2009) recalls:

> *"Refusing to get a license because of NABSW's position was a difficult decision to make. So many of us had fought our way through graduate schools and obtained social work positions that, potentially, would be of great assistance to Black folks. I don't think that everyone wanted to give up the benefits of all of that hard work. However, it was paramount that we publically support the position of the organization."*

The organization was vocal in its opposition and mounted aggressive campaigns in each state where licensing was under consideration. It succeeded in defeating, delaying and/or causing major modifications to licensing bills throughout the nation (e.g., New Jersey, New York, and Michigan.). And in states where the organization's opposition finally conceded to the inevitable, NABSW devised strategies to foster inclusion, fair representation and participation for members who were required by law to register with state licensing boards.

Table VI
NABSW 1983 Position Paper on Social Work Licensing

PROBLEM STATEMENT

The licensing of social work establishes an elitist hierarchy within the social work profession which has the long term implication of significantly changing the racial structure of the human service job market, the kind of quality of service available to the Black consumer, the number of Black service delivery agencies, and the allocation of resources.

In addition, licensing of social work is deceptive as it purports to protect the public and insure quality service, when in fact it merely serves to falsely legitimize professional status and assure qualification for third party reimbursement.

Social work licensure is worker's protection, not consumer protection.

POSITION STATEMENT

The National Association of Black Social Workers is opposed to any system to license social workers. While NABSW is in full support of standards and quality service and will advocate for such, it realizes the true motivation for licensure is not protection of the public and assurance of quality service. And, unless consumer protection is the issue, then government regulation of the profession is inappropriate.

BACKGROUND INFORMATION

A total of 25 states have some form of legal regulation of social work. Of these 25 states, 16 have acts licensing the practice of social work. A survey of these states reveal that "very little punitive action has been taken in response to complaints" filed against social work practitioners. According to data from the Complaint Analysis Division of the Department of Regulation of one state, only 52 complaints have been received in the seven years of regulations. Among the 52 complaints, only one (1) was for alleged incompetence, and the charge was dismissed.

Several explanations may be put forth to explain these findings. One explanation might be the complaint system available to the consumer is ineffective; a second explanation is little discernible abuse is occurring in the practice of social work. A more reasonable explanation is the efficacy of social work regulations to protect the consumer is highly questionable. A review of the literature provided substance to this latter explanation.

Literature which surveyed the outcomes of treatment by trained and untrained individuals revealed the following conclusion: No clear risk to the public from "unqualified" practitioners was identified; academic credentials are not in and of themselves a guarantee of competence. Interpersonal skills of empathy, ability to handle conflict and warmth are at least as critical as technical knowledge and skills.

In addition, leaders of many professions, social work included, admit that a real motivation for licensure is to enhance the status of the individual in the professions, such as: (1) assure receipt of third party reimbursement, and (2) enhance professional status of acquiring governmental sanction.

It is NABSW's position that the primary benefit of licensure has been to qualify for third party reimbursement for the less than 10% of social workers practicing in the private fee-for-service sector. However, this primary benefit is not in itself sufficient to warrant government regulations of the profession. The potential harm to the traditional social work constituency is far greater than the benefit licensure would bring to these few professionals in their new constituency, the private fee-for-service sector.

Continued on next page

Table VI-Continued

Finally, NABSW believes that social work is a helping profession that poses no danger to the public as accredited schools of social work are graduating competent, qualified social workers to provide social work service.

STRATEGIES

The National Association of Black Social Workers recommends several strategies to stop continued efforts to license social work: (1) conduct studies in states requiring regulation to further support NABSW's position; (2) take a visible stance on licensing (know what proponents of licensure are doing). Study the issue, develop factual data, publicly debate proponents of licensing. Remember the preamble of any licensure bill is protection of the public. This is pivotal in the challenge; destroy this deception and the weapon is destroyed; (3) contact all Black media (and white) and publicize the licensing issue; (4) establish political and social networks with elected officials and gain support and sentiment for NABSW's positions; (5) gather data on other licensed professions such as the medical profession, psychiatry, and psychology to demonstrate the minute success licensing has yielded in protecting the public; (6) study the cost of licensing in your state. Tackle the cost issue of a system that does not accomplish its purpose, consumer protection; (7) have NABSW members serve on the Board of Licensing and Regulations.

Conclusion

There were many critical social and policy issues addressed by NABSW, and they were part of the organization's ongoing social action agenda. NABSW targeted a wide range of social issues and concerns that plagued the Black community. While the organization was limited in its ability to have national impact on every major concern, its impact on child welfare policy is undeniable. Discussion surrounding the care, placement and adoption of Black children was elevated to the national level. The nation's child welfare policies have been amended to give consideration to single parents, grandparents and extended family members, creating a Kinship Care system that did not exist prior to the protests by Black social workers. Moreover, the organization's 30-year opposition to social work licensing forced the profession to pause and reconsider its quest for title protection and the lasting benefits that it would offer to the public. Finally, while the profession, in general, has succeeded in having some form of regulation passed in almost every state, according to one authoritarian source, "In some states, social work licensing regulations exclude just about everyone who is employed in public agencies as social workers and service providers!" And the anticipated benefit of licensing for the protection of the public remains unknown.

References:

ABC World News (2010). "Race and Reality," (March 3).

Adoption History Project (2009), University of Oregon, www.uoregon.edu/~adoption/topics/transracialadoption.htm.

Alston, Lee (2007). *Southern Paternalism and the American Welfare State: Economics, Politics, and Institutions in the South, 1865-1965 (Political Economy of Institutions and Decisions)*, Cambridge, MA: Cambridge University Press.

Brace, Charles Loring (2009). *The Life of Charles Loring Brace, Chiefly Told in His Own Letters* (original publication 1894), Ithaca, NY: Cornell University Library Print Collection.

Carlton-Laney, Iris (2001). *African American Leadership: An Empowerment Tradition in Social Welfare History*, Washington, D.C.: NASW Press.

Chestang, Leon ((1972). "The Dilemma of Biracial Adoption," *Social Work* 17 (May), pp. 100–105.

Chimezie, Amuzie (1975). "Transracial Adoption of Black Children," *Social Work*, 20 (July), pp. 296–301.

Ellis, Arthur (1983). "Metropolitan Family Councils: New Social Mechanisms for Empowering Inner City Families," *Black Caucus*, Vol.14, No. 1 Spring, pp. 4 – 9.

Holloran, Peter C. (1994). *Boston's Wayward Children: Social Services for Homeless Children*, 1830–1930, Boston: Northeastern University Press.

Howard, Alicia, David D. Royse and John Skerl (1977). "Transracial Adoption: The Black Community Perspective," *Social Work*, 22 (May), pp.184–189.

Inter-Ethnic Placement Act (1996). Public Law 104-188, August 20.

Johnson, Audreye (1988). *The National Association of Black Social Workers, Inc: A History for the Future*, New York: NABSW.

Johnson, Lincoln (1976). "Transracial Adoption: Victims or Ideology," *Social Work* 21 (May), pp. 241–242.

Jones, Edmond D. (1975). "On Transracial Adoption of Black Children," Child Welfare, 51 (March), pp.156–164.

Kellogg Foundation (1993). Families for Kids of Color: A Special Report on Challenges and Opportunities, Battle Creek, MI: W.K. Kellogg Foundation.

Losing Isaiah (1995). Hollywood: Paramount Pictures.

Mitchell, Sandra (2009). Personal Interview, April.

Multi-Ethnic Placement Act (1994). Public Law 103-382, October 20.

National Association for the Advancement of Colored People (undated). Suggested Revised Resolution, Unpublished Report.

National Association of Black Social Workers (1983). Position Papers, New York: NABSW.

_____(1983). "Child Welfare Services for Black Children," in Position Papers, pp. 3–4, New York: NABSW.

_____(1983). "Social Work Licensing," in Position Papers, pp. 1-2, New York: NABSW.

_____(1985). Position Papers, New York: NABSW.

_____(1994). Position Papers, Detroit: NABSW.

_____(1994). "Preserving African American Families," in Position Papers, Detroit: NABSW.

_____(2008). Position Papers, Washington, D.C.: NABSW National Association of Social Workers (1977). Encyclopedia of Social Work, 17th ed., Washington, D.C.: NASW Press.

_____(1977). "Professional Associations," Encyclopedia of Social Work, 17th ed., pp. 622–625, Washington, D.C.: NASW Press.

_____(1977). "Charles Loring Brace," Encyclopedia of Social Work, 17th ed., pp. 87–88, Washington, D.C.: NASW Press.

Neal, Leora and Al Stumph (2003). Transracial Adoptive Parenting: A Black/White Community Issue, New York: Haskett-Neal Publication.

O'Conner, Stephen (2004). Orphan Trains: *The Story of Charles Loring Brace and the Children He Saved and Failed*, Chicago: University of Chicago Press.

Sanders, Charles (1970). "Growth of the Association of Black Social Workers, *Social Casework*," (May) pp. 270–279.

Simon, Rita and Rhonda Roorda (2000). In their Own Voices: Transracial Adoptees Tell Their Stories, New York: Columbia University Press.

Smith, Zelma (2009). Personal Interview, April.

Trattner, Walter (1989). *From Poor Law to Welfare State* (6th ed.), New York: The Free Press.

U.S. Department of Health and Human Services. (2006). *The AFCARS Report: Final Estimate for FY 1998 Through FY 2002* (12),www.acf.hhs.gov/programs/cb/stats_ research/afcars/tar/report12.htm.

Vieni, Miriam (1975). "Transracial Adoption Is a Solution Now," Social Work, 20 (September), pp. 419–421.

Website:

www.NACAC.org

9

EMERGING PARADIGMS OF BLACK SOCIAL WORK PRACTICE

D eveloping a theory of social work based on liberation rather than adjustment was the rallying call for the founders of the BSWM. There was near unanimous agreement that social work practice in the Black community was inadequate, failing to meet the needs of the most vulnerable members of society. Moreover, while schools of social work began to recognize the need for a more ethnically and racially diverse educational foundation, scholarly research on the multifaceted dimensions of Black life had not been fully integrated into school curricula.

For Black social work activists, identifying a new educational foundation and value base reflective of the hopes and aspirations of the Black community proved to be a daunting task. The challenges were many and required the support of Black social work scholars and intellectuals. These professionals needed to engage in research, test new applications and publish and disseminate their findings among the larger professional community. Within the Movement and NABSW, practice, social programming and social activism were highly valued activities. The need to alleviate oppressive social conditions like poverty, poor housing, joblessness and social violence was immediate. Thus, encouraging Black social workers to engage in scholarship and theoretical development often took a back seat to social action. Yet many Black social workers accepted the challenge and pursued research and scholarly activities that would contribute to the development of new approaches to social work intervention in African American communities.

Social Work with "Minority" Groups

Following the Civil Rights and Black Power movements, discourse around the needs of "minority populations" emerged in the social work literature. Scholars, both Black and white, produced literature that focused on understanding the special needs of minority groups (Chunn, Dunston and Rose-Sheriff, 1983; Akins, Morten and Sue, 1983). The goal of social work was to be informed about the unique characteristics of America's racial and ethnic populations. In this approach, the basic foundation and tenets of social work remained unaltered as the profession sought ways to include information about these groups in graduate and undergraduate curricula. Mainstream social work texts (Goodman, 1973; Brieland, Costin and Atherton, 1975; Vargus, 1975; Compton and Galaway, 1975) also utilized this approach, often including a chapter on Black Americans and other minority group members but not necessarily integrating the Black experience in the full body of the work. Most of the literature provided descriptive analyses on the unique cultural aspects of the Black community.

CSWE's creation of the Commission on Minority Groups (1970) and the establishment of Policy Curriculum Statements mandating the inclusion of culturally diverse educational materials in all teaching and practice areas (Dieppa, 1984) helped to induce change at schools of social work. Discourse advanced from an emphasis on minority inclusion to concepts suggesting "ethnic-sensitivity," "cultural diversity," "cultural sensitivity," "cultural responsiveness" and "cultural competence" (Lum, 1992; Devore and Schlesinger, 1996; Miley, O'Melia and Dubois, 2001). Much of this discourse was viewed from the prism of Eurocentric perspectives. The dominance of the European worldview was as much a reflection of the profession's history as well as a firm belief in the righteousness of its approach to the alleviation of human suffering. However, many of those involved in the BSWM questioned the applicability and universality of traditional social work knowledge, values and skills, and continued to explore the possibility of developing racially specific approaches to practice. Within mainstream social work texts, literature that focused on racially specific actions, including discussions of the BSWM and the emergence of an alternative professional organization, was extremely limited if it existed at all. Black social workers, challenged by the obstacles and limitations within the profession, pressed forward, ultimately contributing to the expansion of knowledge of social work practice in Black America.

Black Social Work Practice

The desire to engage in an effective and meaningful form of professional social work practice in the Black community was the goal of many. But how did one define Black social work practice? Shirley Better (1972) was among the first of a long list of scholars (Sanders, 1971; Gilbert, 1974; Mathis and Leonard, 1978; Washington, 1978; Blackburne, 1978) to address this question. In "The Black Social Worker's Role in the Black Community," Better attempted to delineate the role that the new Black social work professional would play in support of the liberation movement. According to Better (1972:5), Black social workers were presented with the unprecedented "opportunity for challenging and vigorous roles as effective community planners rather than continuing our despised function as social controllers." Social workers in the Black community needed to take a comprehensive approach to practice. Narrow definitions of social work as casework, group work or community organizing restricted the new Black social worker's vision for social change. Black social workers should:

> "...initiate periodic seminars focusing on an interdisciplinary training program in social planning, along with other joint vehicles to encourage interchange between Black professionals. We must remember that we are Black people with special skills, but first of all we are Black people" (Ibid:8).

Moreover, Black social workers needed to close ranks with all members of the Black community for the purpose of survival. They needed to be active participants in the political arena by: (1) providing review of legislation to determine its value to the Black community; (2) offering testimony regarding the social ramifications of proposed legislation; and (3) engaging Black legislators, holding them accountable for their actions. Finally, Black social workers needed to ensure the equal participation of "community people" in decision making. This would be an essential component in rebuilding trust between the community,

Black social workers and the social welfare institutions they represent.

Gilbert (1974) advocated for a new role for Black social workers as liberators of the community. She (Ibid:20) argued that the Black social worker needed to utilize "relevant concepts from black psychology, sociology and other disciplines" as their knowledge base. Furthermore, Black social workers needed to create an innovative system for service and intervention strategies within the community. She notes:

> "This system must initiate, encourage and support programs for the elimination of racism, programs of cultural and revolutionary nationalism, reform, the development of independent black social service agencies and institutions, provision of basic survival needs and projection of the black perspective in white-controlled agencies. The system must enhance economic and political empowerment" (Ibid:20-21).

Gilbert argued for a generalist approach that would encourage Black social workers to integrate all available practice modalities as they sought solutions to problems.

In Solomon's *Black Empowerment: Social Work in Oppressed Communities* (1978), emphasis was placed on enhancing existing social work models and approaches by providing Black and white social workers with information on the Black experience. According to Solomon, members of the Black community expressed feelings of powerlessness when addressing their problems. The need to understand, negotiate and leverage power for the benefit of the community was a key component of effective social work practice. This empowerment model, which infused new knowledge about the life experiences of the Black community, would result in the preparation of more competent social workers engaged in the helping process.

There was a proliferation of literature that followed the early discussions on Black social work practice that focused on specific populations or specialized practice settings. For example, Martin and Martin (1985) focused on the needs of the Black family; Chunn, Dunston and Rose-Sheriff (1983) on mental health; Anderson (1983) on health care; Trader (1975) on drug abuse and addiction; and Dunmore (1970), Mathis and Leonard (1978) on social work education. While racially specific models of social work practice were slow to materialize, articulating the need for culturally specific approaches gained acceptance. Logan, Freedman and McCoy's *Social Work Practice with Black Families: A Culturally-Specific Perspective* (1990) offered a collection of essays that emphasized the importance of diversifying traditional social work knowledge and perspectives by including information on ethnic and minority populations. More specifically, they emphasized the importance of training social workers as culturally competent practitioners in the Black community.

As the BSWM progressed, Black social workers produced few theoretical models of their own and relied rather heavily on social and behavioral scientists (Hill, 1972; Ladner, 1973; Hare, 1976; Staples, 1976, 1978; Wilson, 1978; Cross, 1980; Rodgers-Rose, 1980; Sudarkasa, 1980, 1981; Akbar, 1981; McAdoo, 1981; Nobles and Goddard, 1984; Aldridge, 1989; Wilson, 1990; Billingsley, 1992) who produced volumes of research on the Black community. This aided Black social workers in their quest to equip themselves with knowledge of the history, culture and experiences of Black people in America, and hopefully contribute to the development of innovative modes of practice.

Afrocentric Social Work

By the early 1990s, Black social workers began to argue for the inclusion of an Afrocentric perspective in social work practice (Schiele, 1990; Mathis, 1994; Thompson, 1995). This approach challenged the dominance of European values and worldview as the basis for social work intervention in all communities. The new generation of Black social work scholars, educators and practitioners expressed some of the same concerns as those in the past: Current models and approaches to social work intervention in the Black community seemed inadequate. While the profession had shown marked improvement in diversifying the literature to include concerns about unique ethnic and cultural groups, traditional approaches, values, skills and philosophical views prevailed. However, the language and terminology utilized by the profession had been altered. The discourse around the needs of caseworkers, group workers, community organizers and policy planners had been replaced with the term "generalist" social work practitioner. The new, contemporary social worker was capable of integrating multilevel methods, skills and approaches to achieve the purpose and objectives of social work (Miley, O'Melia and Dubois, 1995). The generalist approach discussed the requirements of "cultural competency," suggesting that a "base of cultural knowledge" (Ibid:65), i.e., additional study and readings on ethnic groups, would lead to culturally competent practice. Many Black social workers disagreed. These practitioners, seeking culturally and racially specific knowledge that detailed the intersection of social work and the Black experience, turned to the concept of Afrocentricity.

As discussed in Chapter Six, the theory of Afrocentricity was popularized by Asante (1980, 1987, 1988) in the 1980s. In part, Afrocentricity is defined as "the belief in the centrality of Africans in post modern history. It is our history, our mythology, our creative motif, and our ethos exemplifying our collective will" (Ibid,1988:6). As noted previously, Asante argues:

> *"...that African descendant peoples experience of 'disorientation'*
> *and 'dislocation' in the contemporary world results from a process of*
> *'de-centering' emanating from European domination and colonization*
> *of Africa and the Holocaust of Enslavement that followed in the*
> *Americas. In an effort to gain a positive social and cultural identity,*
> *individuals seek to reclaim their African identities by centering*
> *themselves in their own values, history and culture and embracing*
> *that which is a reflection of their true heritage, i.e. locating themselves*
> *in an 'Afrocentric reality'" (Reid-Merritt, 2008:98).*

Afrocentricity requires the placement of African ideals at the center of any analysis of African behavior, granting the community members control or "agency" over their own life experiences and destiny.

Scholars, particularly those in Black studies, expanded on the Afrocentric idea. For Myers (1988), "Afrocentric" is that which originates in the African world. Karenga (1993:35) notes that while there is no singular conception of Afrocentricity, there is a "general conceptual agreement that Afrocentric means essentially viewing social and human reality from an African perspective or standpoint." In *An Africa Centered- Perspective of History,* Keto (1989) further clarifies the concept of an African center by stating that:

> *"...there is profound intellectual merit in treating the continent*
> *of Africa as a geo-cultural starting point, a 'center' so to speak, that*
> *serves as an axiological reference point for the purpose of gathering,*
> *ordering and interpreting information about African people at home*
> *on the continent and throughout those parts of the world where African*
> *people have formed culturally significant communities. African people*

become subjects and makers of their own history when we employ the Afrocentric paradigm as our primary foundation for creating theoretical tools of analysis" (1989:12).

Still others (Harvey and Rauch, 1997; Clegg, 1997; Roberts, 2000) preferred to use the term "Africentric" or "African-centered" to describe the concepts of "center," "location" and "agency."

Afrocentricity was scrutinized, criticized and interrogated in contemporary scholarly discourse (Oyabede, 1990; Hall, 1992; Lemelle, 1994; Lefkowitz, 1996; Walker, 2000), but gained acceptance in popular culture (Reid-Merritt, 2008). Moreover, it is important to note that while Asante is given credit for introducing the contemporary conceptual framework, the desire to be authentically African in one's view of self and the world, to develop a theoretical analysis from an African perspective, to give voice to the African American experience and to contribute to the development of Black intellectual thought, can be traced back to African and African American intellectuals of the past who used a different language to put forth similar concepts (Cooper, 1892; DuBois, 1969; Woodson, 1969; Frazier, 1973; Garvey, 1996; Stewart, 1996; May, 2007).

As the discourse on Black social work evolved, the use of the terms "Black social work," "the Black experience," "culturally competent social work in the Black community," "Afrocentric," "Africentric" and "African-centered social work" were frequently cited in the literature, used interchangeably and often unintentionally implying that all social work with Black people constituted a fundamentally new form of social work practice. This added confusion rather than clarity to the variety of emerging paradigms that attempted to address the need for innovations in social work. For example, Black social workers first adapted Karenga's (2002) Nguzo Saba principles as the basis for a new value foundation in Black social work (Mathis, 1972; Gilbert, 1974). However, the Nguzo Saba is also used to describe Black family strengths (Logan, 2001), culturally competent social work (Boyd-Franklin, 2006), Afrocentric social work (King, 1994), Africentric social work (Harvey and Hill, 2004) and African-centered social work (Crawley, 2001). One might question: What were the distinguishing characteristics of these different conceptualizations of Black social work practice?

Alternative Views of Social Work

Mathis (1994) offered a topology that describes various alternative approaches to social work practice. He delineates two major perspectives, one Eurocentric and the other Afrocentric, each offering two different but related orientations to practice (see Table VII). The Eurocentric approach reflects a European worldview and incorporates the history, values and beliefs of Western culture. It has been a dominant theme in social work practice both here and abroad (Graham, 1999). The Eurocentric approach offers the practitioner two possible orientations: Orthodox Social Work and Culturally Sensitive or Ethnic Social Work. On the other hand, the Afrocentric approach emerged from challenges to the hegemony of European culture as universally applicable to all humankind (Asante, 1988, 1990). The two possible orientations are: Black or African American Social Work and African-Centered Social Work. Each orientation utilizes a different philosophical and value base to achieve social work objectives.

According to Mathis (1994:4), the traditional or orthodox orientation to social work:

> "... holds that African culture was completely destroyed by the removal of Africans from the continent of Africa and their subsequent enslavement. Thus, African Americans share a universal American culture. The differences which manifest themselves among the African American population are based on poverty and the legacy of enslavement. Thus, no special knowledge of Black culture or special skills are required for successful social work intervention. The universally applicable social work knowledge and skills are sufficient. The objectives of social work intervention are to restore the individual, family, or group to some specified level of social functioning. In this perspective, the focus is upon personal improvement and the expansion of opportunities. There are no distinctions between social work with African Americans and social work with any other individual or group. This orientation challenges the assumption that there are any significant racial or cultural differences that must be recognized in the social work transaction... Social work intervention proceeds on the basis of a presumed universality of relevance. The dominant values expressed by this orientation are individualism, independence / dependency, competition, and materialism."

188

This traditional form of social work practice dominated the profession from its beginning until the mid 20th century. In the midst of the modern-day Civil Rights Movement, it became evident that the history and culture of unique ethnic and racial populations were not included in mainstream social work literature. Thus, the profession sought corrective measures that would mirror the diversity that existed in American culture (Dieppa, 1984).

Table VII
Mathis Topology: Alternative Views of Social Work Practice

Eurocentric Approaches	Afrocentric Approaches
------------------(Values)------------------------	---------------------(Values)---------------------
Orthodox Social Work	**Black/African American Social Work**
Individualism, Competition,	Nguzo Saba — Umoja, Kugichagulia
Independence/Dependence, Materialism	Ujima, Ujamaa, Nia, Kuumba, Imani
------------------(Values)------------------------	---------------------(Values)--------------------
Culturally/Ethnic-Sensitive Social Work	**African-Centered Social Work**
Primacy of Family, Education	Ma'at — Truth, Justice, Propriety
Individual Enterprise, Hard Work	Balance, Harmony, Reciprocity, Order

Mathis (1994:5) describes the second orientation within the Eurocentric paradigm as Culturally Sensitive or Ethnic Social Work. Here the practitioner:

"...recognizes cultural differences between African Americans and others, but does not link these differences to any African derivation. These differences are generated by the adaptation of an African people to the 'American' experience of enslavement, social degradation and disproportionate impoverishment. African Americans are viewed as a sub-culture of American culture (their original African culture having been destroyed by the experience of enslavement). Any observed differences are assumed to be the products of African American adaptation to poverty and discrimination. General social work knowledge is modified by adding information about African American attitudes and customs and specific information regarding reactions to impoverishment. The dominant values espoused in this orientation are: primacy of family, importance of education, necessity for individual enterprise, and hard work."

189

This approach was popularized in the 1980s (Norton, 1978; Devore and Schlesinger, 1981) and remains the dominant perspective for schools of social work (Miley, O'Melia and Dubois, 1995; Saleebey, 1997; Hepworth, Rooney, Rooney, Strom-Gottfried and Larsen, 2010).

The emergence of the Afrocentric paradigm challenged the fundamental base of social work practice in the Black community, or what Mathis (1994:6) describes as the "beginning breach within the organized profession of social work." Once introduced, Black social workers reconsidered the effectiveness of traditional Eurocentric approaches to social work with African Americans and African diasporic populations and attempted to apply a new worldview to practice (Reid-Merritt, 1995; Schiele, 1996; Harvey and Rauch, 1997; Graham, 1999; Crawley, 2001; Bent-Goodley, 2005). Mathis (1994:2) notes that the practice of Afrocentric social work requires "the self-conscious practice of social responsibility" on the part of those providing services. He explains that the first of two possible orientations, Black or African American Social Work:

> "...postulates the uniqueness of African American culture and attributes this uniqueness, to some extent, to African origins, but stresses the experiences generated in America. It is a culturally-specific approach to practice rooted in the synthesis of African and African American cultural experiences...According to this view, African Americans have a dual perspective (Norton, 1978). They are, in fact, hyphenated-Americans. African culture is fused with American culture to produce an historically unique pattern of values and perspectives. However, enslavement and continuing racial domination are the primary shaping forces in the development of African people in the U.S.

Practitioners who adopt this orientation must expand their general social work knowledge base to include African American history, political economy, and ideology. Understanding the history and dynamics of racial oppression and institutional domination is paramount...The primary values espoused in this model are typified by the Nguzo Saba or Seven Principles of Kawaida (Karenga, 1982). Similarly, practitioners who adopt this orientation must expand their social work skills to include political activity and systems change work. The objective of social work practice is the continued resistance to racial domination and social and economic inequality. The primary focus of social work intervention is on personal and collective transformation and social change" (Mathis, 1994;6).

Harvey's (1997) model of intervention with Black youth provides one such example of the Afrocentric orientation in social work. He describes a psychosocial Africentric approach in the development of rites of passage programs, which utilize the Nguzo Saba as its value base. However, he expands upon the Nguzo Saba by adding the principles of Africentricism (RIPSO). He identifies these principles as: responsibility, reciprocity, respect, restraint, reason, reconciliation, interconnectedness, interdependence, inclusivity, participation, patience, perseverance, sharing, sacrifice, spirituality, cooperation, discipline and unconditional love. Harvey concludes that social workers could increase their level of cultural competency if they are capable of incorporating this approach to practice.

Finally, Mathis (1994:7) argues that African-centered orientation insists practice be derived from the African experience as the primary point of departure and "represents the greatest challenge to the existing social work knowledge base." African-centered social work:

> "...contends that African culture survived the Maafa of enslavement and is reproduced and enhanced through the continuous resistance to and struggle against white supremacy and racial domination. Thus, though Africans were systematically separated from their original cultural, spiritual, and physical contexts, the core of African culture remained intact and became the basis for subsequent development...Since the core component of African American culture is held to be African, a thorough understanding of African history and culture is required, particularly knowledge of African classical cultures. As in the previous orientation, this view is rooted in a new system of values. In addition to the Nguzo Saba, principles of Ma'at are employed to guide understanding and action. These principles are: truth, justice, propriety, harmony, balance, reciprocity, and order. Principles of Ma'at are drawn from the sacred texts of the ancient Egyptians (Karenga, 1989). The primary focus of social work activity, within this orientation, is on the unity of all African people in their struggle against racial domination and social oppression. This view is rooted in the premise that despite the physical

separation and cultural disruption between Africans on the continent and Africans in the Diaspora, there remain strong cultural, spiritual, and ideological bonds between them" (Black Diaspora Committee, 1989) (Mathis,1994:8-9).

Graham (1999:117) concurs, further noting that the African-centered worldview "promotes humanitarian values that are in accord with the core principles of social work." She further states:

"The African-centered worldview offers the opportunity to develop social work designs that are proactive rather than being reactively bound by the limitations of an ethnocentric knowledge base. This approach generates empowerment, growth, transformation, and developments, as the African is placed at the center of analysis in the context of his or her authenticity" (Ibid).

Developing theories and models of practice that incorporate Afrocentric orientations is an ongoing challenge for Black social workers. The effort to capture the essence of Africana Social Work, an emerging paradigm within the discipline of Africana studies and the profession of social work, served as the foundation for curriculum building for NABSW's Academy for the Certification of African-Centered Social Work and led to the development of numerous innovative approaches. An African-Centered Approach to Social Work (AFCENA)—first introduced by me at the NABSW Policy Institute in 1995—is another example of the expanding body of literature in Africana Social Work that seeks to explore new possibilities for social work intervention in African-based communities.

AFCENA: An African-Centered Approach to Social Work Practice

As described by Mathis (1994), AFCENA is derived from the Afrocentric perspective (Asante, 1988; Myers, 1988; Keto, 1989; Gray, 2001; Karenga, 2002; Mazama, 2002). It is grounded in the belief that African knowledge, philosophy, values and worldview must be at the center (i.e., the starting point) of any analysis of African descendant people. According to Graham (2005:71), the Afrocentric approach to social work "embraces an African-centered worldview as the basis for theories and models of practice." For Schiele (1996:285), it offers the opportunity to apply "traditional African philosophical concepts as a foundation for a new social work practice model," and for Crawley (2001:127) it's "a framework that allows clients to connect to a vital sphere of their identity—that is, being of African descent."

While many scholars and practitioners have incorporated the Afrocentric perspective, African-centered models for practice are still in the early stages of development. AFCENA fused African-centered contemporary intellectual thought with the fundamental principles, goals and purposes of social work and recognized the significant contribution that good social work practice could have on the African American community. More specifically, social work, in its ideal form, emerged as an organized method of social intervention designed to eliminate social suffering, promote social justice and improve the quality of life for society's most vulnerable populations NASW, 1977). On a day-to-day basis, social workers continue to work toward the achievement of these objectives. As previously noted, there has been and continues to be many deficiencies in the profession's efforts to successfully intervene in the Black community. Progressive Black social workers sought models that contributed to the transformation of professional practice in ways that justified their continued existence in the Black community as the best representatives and advocates for those in need. The AFCENA model for practice helped to fulfill that goal. It offered a comprehensive approach, applicable to the African American community as a whole, not its fragmented parts.

Conceptualization of Practice

Historically, the conceptualization of good social work practice required three essential components: knowledge, values and skills. These three components were prominently identified in standard introductory social work texts (Zastrow, 1984; Macht and Quam, 1986; Morales, Sheafor and Scott, 1990) and provided the social worker with a framework for understanding human intervention and interaction.

The usefulness of the knowledge, values and skills configuration for effective social work practice in the Black community proved problematic. First, as previously documented, the knowledge base of social work was skewed to reflect the assumed hegemonic superiority of European history and culture. In America, the analysis of human functioning was based on mainstream populations that often excluded African Americans and other people of color. Moreover, the purported "knowledge" of racial and ethnic populations was often marginalized and disproportionately represented the people as "deviant," "dysfunctional," "underprivileged" and "culturally deprived" (Karpas, 1964; Moynihan, 1965; Lewis, 1966). Second, traditional social work approaches also reflected the preference for a Western-based value system that intuitively ran counter to African values and beliefs. For example, the emphasis on "individualism" versus "communalism" pitted two diametrically opposing positions at the very starting point of social service intervention. Social work's value on the primacy of individual needs above all others ran counter to the traditional African value of "community first" and the African American heritage of caring for all members of the community (Billingsley, 1992). Third, basic social work skills, i.e., listening, communication, observation, etc., appeared to be ineffective and attributed largely to the dissonance between the client and the professional. While the knowledge, values and skills configuration were essential components of traditional social work practice, this configuration lacked two important elements deemed necessary for effective social work intervention in African-based communities: the spirit/life force and the Afrocentric perspective. In addition, the epistemology, implementation and practical application of the educational foundation for professional social work were brought into question. AFCENA discarded the traditional configuration of practice, as well as assumptions about the universally applicable knowledge, values and skills base of social work, and reformulated a model of practice appropriate for intervention in African descendant communities.

Preparation for Practice: The Communal Framework

In articulating and understanding the critical link between the Black social work professional and the community, the practitioner is often confronted with an important question: What is the depth of understanding self as a member of the community? What specific training and/or educational processes helped to transform the social work practitioner into a professional cognizant of their own history, culture and heritage? Pioneers in social work understood the importance of self as one of the most effective tools in social work practice (Brill, 1973). However, the concept of self has a different meaning in the African world. The African worldview recognizes the importance of self in relationship to the community. Mbiti's (1970) frequently quoted phrase, "I am because we are, we are therefore I am," emphasizes the importance of the relationship between the individual and the community. Within a contemporary context, this sense of "connectedness" serves as the foundation in the establishment of a relationship between the African American social worker and members of the community (i.e., client population). The African American social worker requires a framework for practice that is inclusive of the social, cultural and historical experiences of African people in America and throughout the diaspora. In essence, African American social workers must be prepared to bring to the arena an understanding of their own cultural strengths, or collective inheritance, as a communal framework for practice. There are four major components of this collective inheritance: ancestral wisdom, epic memory, cultural legacy and victorious visions.

Collective Inheritance

The "collective inheritance" belongs to all members of the community, although many are not consciously aware of its enormous bounty. Transmission of this knowledge occurs within families, churches and community-based institutions and organizations (Karenga, 1967; Sudarkasa, 1981; Gay and Baber, 1997). The institutionalization of this information is likely to occur in institutions where people of African descent control the design, resources and implementation of the educational programs (The New Concept School, started in 1972 by the Institute of Positive Education in Chicago; the Clara Mohammad School established in 1970 in Philadelphia; and Afro-One Dance, Drama and Drum Theatre, Inc., started in 1974 in Willingboro, New Jersey, are examples of such institutions.) In the United States, most elementary and secondary school curricula are seriously flawed with respect to the accuracy of the African diasporic experience, and some would deny the contributions of Africans and African Americans to world history (Lefkowitz, 1996; Asante, 1999; Ginwright, 2004).

Nor is this first level of cultural awareness and appreciation likely to be gained at institutions of higher education or in schools of social work. Indeed, any expectation that professional schools of social work would help to bring clarity to one's ethnic and cultural identity is unrealistic. Unless the undergraduate has been exposed to a curriculum in Africana studies, gaps in general knowledge about the African world experience persist. To overcome this level of ignorance, students must engage in a process of self-education. They must seek out the truths about their own heritage and they must be prepared to come to the table with a clear, definitive sense of self. Understanding, embracing and accepting your identity

195

as a person of African descent remains a prerequisite for effective social work practice in the African American community.

Ancestral Wisdom

"Ancestral wisdom" provides the Black community with an historical understanding of their identity as an African people (Karenga and Carruthers, 1986; Richards, 1989). It is the collective knowledge and the practical use of information gathered and passed on from one generation to the next. The African ancestors were scholars, scientists, physicians, philosophers, warriors, teachers, mothers, fathers, builders and survivors. They assumed every role imaginable. They built villages, cities, nations and empires. They waged wars and made peace. They were triumphant. They were defeated. They made a unique contribution to the development of civilization and left a record of their accomplishments (Williams, 1974; Diop, 1991). As members of the community, African Americans are exposed to the depths of ancestral wisdom when searching for truths about their history and culture. They further develop an understanding and appreciation for these truths by respecting the wisdom of the elders, current representatives of the living history, building on the strengths of those who preceded them and learning to avoid the errors of poor judgment. The present is linked to the future, and the future is linked to an understanding of the past.

Epic Memory

"Epic memory" is defined as "a deep remembrance of habits, styles, mannerisms, and behaviors which reflects itself in language, music, and people customs" (Asante, 1988:65). It is the epic memories that continue to give expression to the Black community's identity as an African people. The physical movement from one continent to another did not eradicate memories of an African past. Efforts to destroy the language and cultural practices of the people have not succeeded in eliminating behavioral patterns. African retentions are present in the transformed and adaptive cultural patterns of African Americans in the United States and African-based cultures throughout the diaspora. This commonality of feeling and expression reflects the traits and elements of a deeply rooted collective consciousness. It helps to preserve the memories of the African past and provides a uniquely textured expression to contemporary existence. It is the manner in which "blacks color life, a colorfulness propelled by a deep and rich feeling capacity that vividly shades every phase, every manifestation, every thought, every endeavor of life, with movement" that cannot be forgotten (Pastuer and Toldson, 1982:237).

Cultural Legacy

African Americans have also inherited a rich "cultural legacy." Culture reflects the ways in which people live and celebrate life. It is inclusive of values, beliefs, philosophies and world views (Stuckey, 1987; Levine, 2007). The ability to organize and structure the environment around the needs of the people and the requirements of nature is a unique aspect of the African American cultural legacy. The mastery of survival skills in social adaptability, environmental reconciliation and psychological manipulation has strengthened this legacy (Hill, 1972). It is a legacy rich in creativity. It has given birth to rhythm, blues, syncopation, scatilization and rap (Maultsby, 1992). And it has given voice and movement to the spirit (Murphy, 1994). The cultural legacy makes sacred the values, practices and beliefs that embrace the Black community, as each generation discovers new ways to preserve and enhance these unique social traditions.

Victorious Vision

Finally, faith (Imani), briefly defined as the belief in the survivability of the community and its inherent capacity to "rise to greatness," is an important aspect of "victorious vision" (Karenga, 1980, 2002). Faith is the belief that "we will be able to work together, to pray together, to struggle together, to go to jail together, to stand up for freedom together, knowing that we will be free one day" (King, 1996:676). It is "the measure of our progress as a race in precise relation to the depth of the faith in our people...and our leaders" (Bethune, 1996:672). It is the anticipation of a strong family, a viable community and the good life. According to Asante (1988:52), the "consciousness of victory is the awareness that all attitudes and behaviors are achievable. Such a will overpowers any obstacle in your way and restores the Afrocentrists to strength."

Individual transformation to a Black, Afrocentric or African-centered consciousness is a lifelong process. Whether one is a Black social worker or member of the Black community, all must be guided by a desire to embrace the wisdom of the ancestors, celebrate and preserve the traditions of the past, contribute to the strengthening of the cultural legacy and envision a future of social, cultural, intellectual and spiritual excellence.

A Model for Practice

There are five basic components to the AFCENA model (Figure 1) : an Afrocentric perspective, knowledge/experience, values/ethics, skills/behaviors and spirit/life force. Note that these are nonlinear, circular components, fluid in application and fully accessible throughout all stages of the helping process. They are constant, flowing and interchangeable. The beginning is the end and the end is the beginning of the process.

Afrocentricity

Afrocentricity provides a common framework for understanding and analyzing the history, philosophies, religious beliefs and cultural practices of African people. An Afrocentric perspective allows the social worker to enter into the helping arena, firmly grounded in an understanding of the African and African American historical and cultural heritage. The Afrocentric perspective requires the social worker to start analysis of client need from the client's cultural center. The practitioner can assess the cultural currency of the existing view of the community and determine how one utilizes traditional wisdom, practices and beliefs to aid in the development of the African world community.

Knowledge and Experience

The social and behavioral sciences provide the foundation for social work practice. Traditional theories in psychology, sociology, political science and economics have provided the foundation for understanding social and human interaction. While these theoretical perspectives, most often grounded in a European worldview, offer some general insights about human need, they may prove inadequate and/or inaccurate when addressing the African or African American experience. AFCENA calls for the expansion of the social work knowledge base and, when dictated, the replacement of distorted or inaccurate information that is inapplicable to the African experience. Africana studies is the liberal arts base needed for African-centered practice; Afrocentric theories of growth, development and social interaction are needed for specialized knowledge. For example, since the early 1920s, traditional social work has been "informed predominantly by psychodynamic perspectives derived from Freudian and neo-Freudian theories of human behavior and society" (NASW, 1987). While there

198

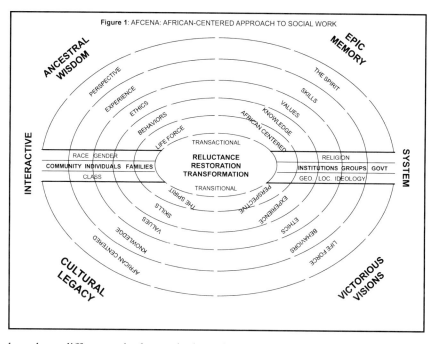

Figure 1: AFCENA: AFRICAN-CENTERED APPROACH TO SOCIAL WORK

have been differences in the particular point of view from the various schools of thought, there is little disagreement on the fundamental assumptions about human growth and behavior. The psychological theories aggressively embraced by social work are based on the study of European people and culture. The tremendous emphasis on individualism, a starting point for understanding human functioning for many of these theories, runs counter to the prevailing meaning of self in the African worldview. Linda James Myers' (1988) theory of optimal psychology, Kambon's (1992) Afrocentric theory of Black personality, Nobles' (1986) theory of the Black conscious and Akbar's (1981) specificity on the needs of the Black psyche provide a far greater understanding of the psychological needs of African Americans than Sigmund Freud, Erik Erikson, Otto Rank or Carl Jung (Beckett, 2002).

The same arguments are made for the accuracy and relevance of other disciplines as well. Social and behavioral science theories on culture, social organization, family formation, gender, status, roles, religion, etc., must be weighed against the contributions of Hill (1997), Collins (2000), Billingsley (1992), Ladner (1973), Martin and Martin (1978), Sudarkasa (1980, 1981), Cone (1970) and others who speak specifically to the African and African American

199

experience. At this juncture, it is important to note that the basic requirement for the development of an African-centered paradigm is not restricted by race. All Black scholars are not Afrocentric, nor is all African-centered scholarship produced by those of African descent. Rather, the basis for the incorporation of scholarship that contributes to the expansion of the African-centered paradigm is measured against criteria that conforms to the fundamental assumption of the African-centered approach, i.e., that Africa and her descendants are viewed as equals in the development of human history and are placed at the "center" of any analysis that portends to explain their existence.

It is critically important to emphasize that social workers must assume the primary responsibility for the development of practice knowledge specific to the discipline. Contributions by Better (1972), Gilbert (1974), Mathis (1972), Ross (1978) and Solomon (1978) were part of the early efforts to articulate Black social work practice and to explore African American helping traditions. Culturally sensitive or ethnic social work approaches have been developed by Logan, Freeman and McRoy (1990); Norton (1978) and Chung (1983). And a plethora of literature has been produced on social work in the African American community. The benefits of utilizing an Afrocentric perspective has been argued by Schiele (1996), Harvey and Rauch (1997), Harvey (2001), Graham (2005), Crawley (2001) and others. However, the African-centered link remains weak and needs to be the focus of intense scholarly development in the forth coming decade.

Finally, African American social workers must make greater use of practice wisdom. Knowledge is tested and strengthened through real life experiences as social work professionals. Black social workers must continue to test their theoretical understandings against the day-to-day social realities faced by clientele and other members of the African diasporic community and assume greater responsibility in the gathering, documentation and reporting of their findings to the professional community.

Values and Ethics

Karenga (1965), through his development of Kawaida philosophy, offered the Nguzo Saba principles as a guide to socially responsible behavior in the Black community. These include: Umoja (Unity), Kujichagulia (Self-Determination), Ujima (Collective Work and Responsibility), Ujamaa, (Cooperative Economics), Nia (Purpose), Kuumba (Creativity) and Imani (Faith). The Nguzo Saba has

200

been described as the principles of nationhood, the principles of Blackness and the Kwanzaa principles. These principles represent a statement of values, a view on how things ought to be in the African American community. The ongoing search for historical accuracy and relevance resulted in a return to ancient Egypt (Kemet) and the unveiling of the sacred values of Ma'at. These include: truth, justice, propriety, harmony, balance, reciprocity and order. The principles of Ma'at can serve as a moral code, reminiscent of the wisdom and creativity of the African ancestors. They offer a perspective on life that speaks to the "inherent good" by showing "the way to truth, justice and righteousness" (Karenga, 1993:86). It is these seven value principles that the racially conscious African American or African-centered social worker seeks to operationalize in practice.

The NABSW code of ethics (see Table I) provides guidelines for professional practice and personal conduct. Created at the very beginning of the organization's existence, the code of ethics speaks to the linkages between the Black social worker and the African American community; elevates the needs of the community over personal and professional interests; acknowledges the oppressive social conditions for both the worker and community members; and calls to action the Black social workers' conscious struggle for the freedom and liberation of the African American community.

Skills and Behaviors

There are basic skills in social work that serve all members of the profession: listening, communication, observation, engagement, assessment and a litany of others. A skillful social worker is one who seeks appropriate methods and techniques that will facilitate client movement toward their ultimate goals and objectives. While the profession has not been remiss in acknowledging the existence of some cultural differences among various populations (Lum, 1992; Devore and Schlesinger, 1996; Miley, O'Melia, Dubois, 2001), the ability to develop effective intervention skills for practice with culturally unique groups has been lacking.

Changes in language, attitudes and nonverbal posturing are superficial responses to skill development for culturally distinct populations. The use of an African expression is hollow without some depth of understanding about its meaning. For example, "It takes a whole village to raise a child," is one the most overused and misunderstood African proverbs in contemporary America. While it provides "communication-friendly" access to the African American community, one should respond, perhaps, with the questions: "Do you know where the village is?" or "Can you recreate the village in urban America?"

AFCENA requires the social worker to gain proficiency in helping skills that are valued, appreciated and understood in African-based communities. For example, the rhythm and tones in which we communicate the message are as important as the words we use. Goodley (1997) discusses the need to perfect our communication skills by sharpening our "call and response" techniques. Preparation to meet with clients gains greater acceptance when ritualistic behaviors are incorporated into the setting—candle-lighting, meditation, libations (Monges, 1990). Style, form, function and consistency are essential elements in establishing a bond with members of the African American community. "Stage setting" takes on a new meaning when visual representations from the past—art, images, materials, etc.—are present in the meeting room. Creativity, establishing social rituals and the initiation of new rites of passage are some of the skills needed for an African-centered approach.

The intuitive senses—the third ear, the sixth sense, the "vibe"—have greater meaning in African-based communities (Pasteur and Toldson, 1982). The African worldview accounts for the influence of things that cannot be seen or heard. Traditional social work's demand for objectivity is likely to prove dysfunctional with some Black folks. A skillful social worker is one who can translate these feelings into action. Social workers must possess the ability to "work their mojo" for the good of the people. The African American community is quick to dismiss those who give the appearance of detachment and aloofness. Like most African-based cultures, the African American community does not promote a spectator culture. It demands involvement. Every experience is potentially a group experience. Higher education, degree attainment and professional titles do not lessen the requirements for an active, expressive involvement in the helping process.

Professional conduct is the ultimate measure of one's commitment to the community and to an African-centered approach. Black social workers must possess the ability to negotiate two distinctly different cultural worlds, decipher the subtleties of oppression, traverse the racial divide and still return home as authentic African people. The continuous presence and visibility among the people is a fundamental requirement for effective practice. Social action and social advocacy must be elevated as professional priorities and Black social workers must engage in community-based activities that permit their knowledge and values to become fully actualized in both the professional arena and in the community.

The Spirit/Life Force

In the past two decades, there have been calls to transform social work practice by acknowledging the significance of spirituality in clients' lives and encouraging practitioners to develop spiritually sensitive approaches to social work practice (Bellis, 1995; Derezotes 2006; Matthews, 2009; Canda and Furman, 2009). This movement is consistent with an African-centered approach. Historically, the social work profession recognized the importance of spiritual and religious beliefs but discouraged active involvement in the spiritual realm. The nature of this work fell within the purview of religious leaders engaged in various forms of pastoral counseling. While social work acknowledges religious and spiritual beliefs, it does not claim the use of the spiritual life force as part of the helping process. Practice is segmented rather than holistic, and a client's desire to pray, meditate or call on ancestors is likely to be referred first to the minister and second to the mental health professional. The desire to maintain currency with one's spiritual life force should be viewed as a positive development. And client revelations that they are engaging in discussions with ancestors should not be viewed as paranoid hallucinations of the type II psychotic variation. The belief in the eternal life of the spirit in African communities is real.

In *Let the Circle be Unbroken,* Dona Richards (1989:1-8) informs us about the power of the "spirit" and its relationship to our understanding of who we are as an African people. Richards argues that the spirit provides a continual manifestation of our African "beingness" and "that diasporic Africans are a spiritual people living in a profane society." The spirit must be viewed as an essential element of the life force. It should be viewed as the very essence of life, providing meaning to our physical being and relationship with the wider universe. It is the spirit that reaffirms our humanity and "gives meaning to our positive human development."

The belief in the spirit is most often manifested, but not limited to, religious beliefs and practices. Opoku (1978:1) further explains that religion is at the very root of African culture. "It is no exaggeration, therefore, to say that in traditional Africa, religion is life and life, religion." The spirit is present in the living, in the dead, in objects and in abstractions in the universe, and the spirit is always powerful enough to exert influence. The spirit is all encompassing. Its presence is everywhere. The individual is driven by this powerful life force. It provides a direct link with the Supreme Being and contributes to our ability to do good and positive things in life. Ultimately, clients and community members are strengthened when they can locate themselves on the life force continuum.

The social worker who encounters troubled, depressed, addicted and dispossessed client populations must be reminded that these are the dispirited members of the community who are temporarily disconnected from their own nurturing life force.

The Work That Must Be Done:
The Interactive System

The interactive system is, hopefully, the place where good deeds are done. It is the workplace, the agency, the field setting or the practice environment. It is where the official transaction takes place, assigning a temporary, transitional status to those seeking help, support and constructive avenues to change. It is at the moment of "first contact" that the social worker begins the process of professional assessment. It is where all knowledge manifests into action. AFCENA requires expertise and proficiency in understanding the African worldview, as well as the history, culture, social practices, values, customs and beliefs of the African American community. However, that information alone is not enough. The social worker cannot operate in a vacuum. One cannot embrace an African-centered approach and deny the social conditions which shape the distribution of valuable resources in our society. What are the boundaries that constrict and/or impede the flow of social services to the African American community?

There are six major external factors that impinge upon the interactive system and influence the delivery of social services : race, gender, class, religion, geographic location and ideology. These factors carry both positive and negative connotations. They play a decisive role in determining who are the powerful and the powerless. They also help to shape social character and individual personalities. They are not inherently malignant or benign, but are given meaning and assigned value by the dominant members of society and are reflective of the current social order. These six factors have profound influence on the interactive system. They should be viewed as part of a permanent border that provides the system information, both accurate and inaccurate, about the needs and distribution of service. They impact every aspect and every constituent component of the helping relationship. Here, the African-centered social worker is reminded of some of the more valuable aspects of professional training and must make use of the person and community in environment configuration, the ecological perspective and the systems approach that provide explanations of the reciprocal relationship that may exist between the clients and the socially constructed communities in which they reside (Miley, O'Melia and DuBois, 2001) Finally, in a racially dominated, socially oppressive society, one must be mindful of the need to challenge social injustices anywhere and everywhere, and work toward fair and equitable distribution of societal resources.

Reluctance, Restoration and Transformation

There are three evolving levels in the interactive system that move clientele from the initial transaction to final transition out of the systems: reluctance, restoration and transformation. Reluctance describes the level of ambivalence many members of the African American community experience when seeking public or nonprofit social services. As repeatedly emphasized, the African American community has viewed social service agencies with suspicion and concern. Social workers, embracing the basic principle of starting where the client is, must recognize this reluctance as an obstacle and barrier to service that can only be overcome through demonstrated success in the provision of promised services and resources. Black social workers must change the community's perceptions of their roles as social control agents and advocate and serve the client and community in ways that elevate the role of the social worker to partner, collaborator and extended community member.

Social workers embrace the concept of restoration as a first step in returning clients to a level of social functioning that will allow them to regain a sense of balance that may have been lost prior to their need for service intervention. Restoration is an important step, but the intervention remains incomplete if a significant altering of the client's situation has not occurred.

AFCENA is grounded in the belief that given the continued racial dominance and social oppression that exists in America, transformation becomes the ultimate goal of African-centered practice. Transformation is the ability to help clients "locate" themselves within the cultural context of the African community; connect clients with the internal and external existing community strengths; heighten their sense of "belongingness"; articulate a vision for success; and actively engage in plans for future endeavors.

Conclusion

There have been numerous attempts to articulate liberating forms of Black social work practice. The significance of this work cannot be underestimated. Afrocentric approaches to social work offer the greatest potential for the development of racially and culturally specific models of social work practice intervention in the Black community. It is the role and responsibility of the Black social worker to expand the theoretical and practice base of Africana social work. The African American community faces constant challenges, and the forces of oppression will not pass quietly and silently into the night. In order to move our agenda forward, we must remain vigilant in our struggle for human rights and human dignity. It is the passion of this position that must be applied to social work.

References:

Akbar, Na'im (1981). "Mental Disorders Among African Americans," *Black Books Bulletin*, 5, 2, pp.18 – 25.

Akins, D. R., G. Morten and D. W. Sue (1983). *Counseling American Minorities: A Cross Cultural Perspective*, (2nd ed.), Dubuque, IA: William C. Brown.

Aldridge, Delores (ed.) (1989). *Black Male—Female Relationships: A Resource Book of Selected Materials*, Dubuque, IA: Kendall/Hunt Publishing.

Anderson, J. R. Jr. (1983). "The Black Experience with the Health Care Delivery System," in A.E. Johnson (ed.), *The Black Experience: Considerations for Health and Human Services*, 99, 149 – 150, Davis, CA: International Dialogue Press.

Asante, Molefi Kete (1980) *Afrocentricity: The Theory of Social Change*, 2nd ed.,Chicago: African American Images.

_____(1988). *Afrocentric Idea*, Trenton, NJ: Africa World Press.

_____ (1990). *Kemet, Afrocentricity and Knowledge,* Trenton, NJ: Africa World Press.

_____(1999). *The Painful Demise of Eurocentrism: An Afrocentric Response to Critics,* Trenton, NJ: Africa World Press.

Beckett, Chris (2002). *Human Growth and Development,* Thousand Oaks, CA: Sage Publishing Co.

Bellis, Ronald (1996). *Spirituality and Social Work Practice*, Washington, D.C.: Taylor and Francis.

Bent-Goodley, T.B. (2005). *"An African Centered Approach to Domestic Violence,"* Families in Society, 86, 197 – 206.

Bethune, Mary McLeod (1996). "My Last Will and Testament," in Molefi Kete Asante and Abu S. Abarry (eds.), *African Intellectual Heritage: A Book of Sources*, Philadelphia: Temple University Press.

Better, Shirley (1972). "The Black Social Worker's Role in the Black Community," *Black World*, November, pp. 4 – 14.

Billingsley, Andrew (1992). *Climbing Jacob's Ladder: The Enduring Legacy of African American Families*, New York: Simon and Schuster.

Blackburne, Elmer H. (1978). "Toward Expanding the Role of the Social Work Practitioner and Social and community Service Agencies in the Delivery of Mental Health Services in the Black Community," in *Tenth Anniversary Conference Proceedings*, New York: NABSW.

Boyd-Franklin, Nancy (2006). Black Families in Therapy, *Understanding the African American Experience*, New York: Gilford Publications.

Brieland, Donald, Lela B. Costin and Charles R. Atherton (eds.) (1975). *Contemporary Social Work: An Introduction to Social Work and Social Welfare*, New York McGraw-Hill Book Company.

Canda, Edward and Leola Dyrud Furman (2009). *Spiritual Diversity in Social Work Practice: The Heart of Helping*, New York: Oxford University Press.

Chunn, Jay, Patricia Dunston and Fariyal Rose-Sheriff (eds.) (1983). *Mental Health and People of Color: Curriculum Development and Change*, Washington, D.C.: Howard University Press.

Clegg, Legrand (1997). "A Brief History of Africentric Scholarship," *MAAT News*, Vol 1, No. 2, www.melanet.com.

Compton, Beulah and Burt Galaway (1975). *Social Work Processes*, Homewood, IL: The Dorsey Press.

Cone, James (1970). *A Theology of Black Liberation*, Philadelphia: Lippincott Co.

Cooper, Anna Julia (1892). *A Voice From the South,* Xenia, OH: Aldine Printing House.

Crawley, Brenda (2001). "Effective Programs and Services for African American Families and Children: An African-Centered Perspective," in Sadye L. M. Logan (ed.), The Black Family: *Strengths, Self-Help and Positive Change*, Boulder, CO: Westview Press.

Cross, William E., Jr. (1980). "Models of Psychological Negrescence: A Literature Review," in Reginald L. Jones (ed.), *Black Psychology*, New York: Harper and Row.

Derezotes, David (2006. *Spirituality Oriented Social Work Practice,* Boston: Allyn and Bacon.

Devore, Wynetta and Elfriede G. Schlesinger (1996). *Ethnic-Sensitive Social Work Practice*, Boston: Allyn and Bacon.

Diop, Cheikh Anta (1991). Civilization or Barbarism: *An Authentic Anthropology,* New York: Lawrence Hill Books.

Dunmore, Charlotte (ed.) (1970). *Black Americans: A Selected Bibliography for Use in Social Work Education*, New York: Council on Social Work Education.

Frazier, E. Franklin (1973). "The Failure of the Negro Intellectual," *in The Death of White Sociology*, Joyce Ladner (ed.), New York: Vintage Books, pp. 52 – 66.

Garvey, Marcus (1996). "Philosophy and Opinions," in Molefi Kete Asante and Abu S. Abarry (eds.), *African Intellectual Heritage: A Book of Sources,* Philadelphia: Temple University Press.

Gay, Geneva and Willie L. Baber (eds.) (1997). *Expressively Black: The Cultural Basis of Black Identity,* Westport, CT: Greenwood Press.

Gilbert, Gwendolyn C. (1974). "The Role of Social Work in Black Liberation," *The Black Scholar*, December, Vol. 6, No. 4, pp. 16 – 23.

Ginwright, Shawn (2004). *Black in School: Afrocentric Reform, Urban Youth and the Promise of Hip Hop Culture*, New York: Teachers College Press.

Goodman, James (ed.) (1973). *Dynamics of Racism in Social Work Practice*, Washington, D.C.: NASW Press.

Graham, Mekada J. (1999). "The African-Centered Worldview: Toward a Paradigm for Social Work," *Journal of Black Studies*, 30 Spring, pp. 103 – 121.

_____(2005). "Afrocentric Social Work," in *Encyclopedia of Black Studies*, Molefi Kete Asante and Ama Mazama (eds.), Thousand Oaks, CA: Sage Publications.

Gray, Cecil (2001). *Afrocentric Thought and Praxis: An Intellectual History*, Trenton, NJ: Africa World Press.

Hare, Nathan (1976). "What Black Intellectuals Misunderstand About the Black Family," *Black World*, March, pp. 5 – 14.

Harvey, Aminifu and J. B. Rauch (1997). "A Comprehensive Afrocentric Rites of Passage Program for Black Male Adolescents," *Health & Social Work,* 22, pp. 30 – 37.

Hepworth, Dean H., Ronald H. Rooney, Glenda Dewberry Rooney, Kimberly Strom-Gottfired and JoAnn Larsen (8th ed.) (2010). *Direct Social Work Practice: Theory and Skills*, Belmont, CA: Brook/Cole.

Hill, Robert (1972). *Strengths of Black Families*, New York: Emerson Hall.

_____(1997). *Strengths of Black Families Twenty Five Years Later*, Washington, D.C.: R and B Publishers.

Kambon, Kobi (1992). *The African Personality in America: An African-Centered Framework*, Tallahassee, FL: Nubian Nation Publications.

Karenga, Maulana (1980). Kawaida Theory: *An Introductory Outline*, Inglewood, CA: Kawaida Publications.

_____ (1967). *The Quotable Karenga,* Inglewood, CA: Kawaida Publications.

_____(2002). *An Introduction to Black Studies*, (3rd ed.), Los Angeles: University of Sankore Press.

_____(1993). *An Introduction to Black Studies*, (2nd ed.), Los Angeles: University of Sankore Press.

_____(2008). *Kawaida and Questions of Life and Struggle: Africa American, Pan-African and Global Issues*, Los Angeles: University of Sankore Press.

Karenga, Maulana and Jacob Carruthers (1986). *Kemet and the African Worldview: Research, Rescue and Restoration*, Los Angeles: University of Sankore Press.

Karpas, Melvin Ronald (1964). *Readings in Cultural Deprivation*, Chicago: Juvenile Delinquency Research Projects.

Keto, C. Tsehloane (1989). *An Introduction to the Africa-Centered Perspective of History*, London: Research Association School Times Publication.

King, A. (1994). "An Afrocentric Cultural Awareness Program for Incarcerated African American Males," *Journal of Multicultural Social Work*, 3 (4), pp. 17 – 28.

King, Martin Luther, Jr. (1996). "I Have a Dream," in Molefi Kete Asante and Abu S. Abarry (eds.), *African Intellectual Heritage: A Book of Sources*, Philadelphia: Temple University Press.

Ladner, Joyce (1973). *The Death of White Sociology*, New York: Vintage Books.

Lefkowitz, Mary R. (1996). *Not Out of Africa: How Afrocentrism Became an Excuse to Teach Myth as History*, New York: Free Press.

Lemelle, Sydney J. (1994). "The Politics of Cultural Existence: Pan Africanism, Historical Materialism, and Afrocentricity," in *Imagining Home: Class, Culture and Nationalism in the African Diaspora*, Sidney J. Lemelle and Robin D. G. Kelley (eds.). New York: Verso, 1994.

Levin, Lawrence (2007). Black Culture and Black Consciousness: *Afro-American Folk Thought from Slavery to Freedom, 30th Anniversary Edition*, New York: Oxford Press.

Lewis, Oscar (1966). "The Culture of Poverty," *Scientific America*, October 1966.

Logan, Sadye, Edith M. Freeman and Ruth G. McRoy (1990). Social Work Practice with Black Families: *A Culturally Specific Perspective*, New York: Longman Press.

Lum, D. (1992). *Social Work Practice with People of Color*, Monterey, CA: Brooks/Cole.

Macht, Mary and Jean Quam (1986). *Social Work: An Introduction*, New York: Merrill Publishing Company.

Martin J. M. and M. P. Martin (1985). *The Helping Tradition in the Black Family and Community*, Washington, D.C.: NASW Press.

_____(1978). *The Black Extended Family*, Chicago: University of Chicago Press.

Mathis, Thaddeus P. and Curtis Leonard (1978). "Race, Class and Bureaucracy: Role Orientation for Black Social Workers," *Black Caucus*, 9, 1 Spring, pp. 23 – 27.

Matthews, Ian (2009). *Social Work and Spirituality: Transforming Social Work Practice*, Exeter, UK: Learning Matters

May, Vivian (2007). *Anna Julia Cooper, Visionary Black Feminist: A Critical Introduction*, New York: Routledge.

Mazama, Ama (2002). *The Afrocentric Paradigm*, Trenton, NJ: Africa World Press.

Mbiti, John (1970). *African Religions and Philosophy,* Garden City, NY: Anchor Books.

McAdoo, Harriette (ed.) (1981). *Black Families*, Beverly Hills, CA: Sage Publications.

Miley, Karla Krogsrud, Michael O'Melia and Brenda DuBois (1995). *Generalist Social Work Practice: An Empowering Approach* (2nd ed.), Boston:Allyn and Bacon.

_____(2001). *Generalist Social Work Practice: An Empowering Approach* (3rd ed.), Boston: Allyn and Bacon.

Monges, Miriam (1990). "Engaging Community: The North Philadelphia Initiative," Professional Development Workshop, April, Temple University, Philadelphia, PA.

Morales, Armando, Bradford Sheafor and Malcolm Scott (1990). *Social Work: A Profession of Many Faces,* Boston: Allyn and Bacon.

Moynihan, Daniel (1965). *The Negro Family*, Washington, D.C.: Office of Planning and Research, U.S. Department of Labor.

Myers, Linda James (1988). *Understanding an Afrocentric World View: Introduction to an Optimal Psychology*, Dubuque, IA: Kendall/Hunt.

National Association of Social Workers (1977). *Encyclopedia of Social Work*, 17th ed., Washington, D.C.: NASW Press.

Nobles, Wade (1986). *African Psychology: Toward Its Reclamation, Reascension and Revitalization*, Oakland: Black Family Institute Publishers.

Nobles, Wade and L.L. Goddard (1984). *Understanding the Black Family: A Guide for Scholarship and Research*, Oakland: Black Family Institute Publishers.

Norton, Delores (1978). *The Dual Perspective: Inclusion of Ethnic MinorityContent in the Social Work Curriculum*, New York: Council on Social Work Education.

Opoku, Kofi Asare (1978). *West African Traditional Religions*, FEP International.

Pasteur, Alfred and Ivory L. Toldson (1982), *The Roots of Soul*, New York: Anchor/ Doubleday Press.

Reid-Merritt, Patricia (2008). "The Spread of Afrocentricity Among the People, in Mazama, Mambo Ama (ed.) *Essays in Honor of an Intellectual Warrior· Molefi Kete Asante*, Paris: Menaibuc.

_____(1995). "An African-Centered Approach to Social Work Practice," (Unpublished), October.

Richards, Dona Marimba (1989). *Let the Circle Be Unbroken, Implications for African Spirituality in the Diaspora,* New York: Self-Published.

Roberts, J. Deotis (2000). *Africentric Christianity: A Theological Appraisal for Ministry,* Valley Forge: Judson Press.

Rodgers-Rose, La Frances (ed.) (1980). *The Black Woman*, Beverly Hills, CA: Sage Publications.

Saleebey, Dennis (ed.) (1997). *The Strengths Perspective in Social Work Practice*, New York: Longman.

Sanders, Charles (ed.) (1971). *Black Agenda for Social Work in the Seventies*, Atlanta, GA: Atlanta University School of Social Work.

Schiele, Jerome (1990). "Organizational Theory From an Afrocentric Perspective, *Journal of Black Studies*, 21, pp. 145 – 161.

_____(1996). "Afrocentricity: An Emerging Paradigm in Social Work Practice," *Social Work*, (May), 41 (3) pp.284 – 294.

Staples, Robert (1976). *Introduction to Black Sociology*, New York: McGraw Hill.

_____(ed.) (1978). *The Black Family: Essays and Studies*, Belmont, CA: Wadsworth Publishing Company.

Stewart, Maria (1996). "On African Rights and Liberty," in Molefi Kete Asante and Abu S. Abarry (eds.), *African Intellectual Heritage: A Book of Sources*, Philadelphia: Temple University Press.

Stuckey, Sterling (1987). *Slave Culture: Nationalist Theory and the Foundations of Black America*, New York: Oxford Press.

Sudarkasa, Niara (1980). *"African and Afro-American Family Structure: A Comparison,"* Black Scholar, 11 November/December, pp. 37 – 60.

_____(1981). "Interpreting the African Heritage in Afro-American Family Organization," in *Black Families*, Harriette P. McAdoo, (ed.), Beverly Hills: Sage Publications.

Trader, Harriet P. (1975). "Black Families and Their Black Adolescent Addicts," *Black Caucus,* Spring, Vol. 6, No.1, pp. 18 – 29.

Vargus, Ione (1975). "The Minority Practitioner," in *Contemporary Social Work: An Introduction to Social Work and Social Welfare*, Donald Brieland, Lela B. Costin, Charles R. Atherton (eds.), New York: McGraw-Hill Book Company.

Walker, Clarence E. (2000). *We Can't Go Home Again: An Argument about Afrocentrism*, New York: Oxford University Press.

Washington, R.O. (1978). "Toward a Theory of Ethnicity and Social Competence: Implications for Black Social Work Practice," in *Tenth Anniversary Conference Proceedings*, New York: NABSW.

Williams, Chancellor (1974). *The Destruction of Black Civilization*, Chicago: Third World Press.

Wilson, Amos N. (1990). *Black-on-Black Violence: The Psychodynamics of Black Self Annihilation in Service of White Domination*, New York: Afrikan World Infosystems.

Wilson, Williams J. (1978). *The Declining Significance of Race,* Chicago: University of Chicago Press.

Woodson, Carter G. (1969). *The Mis-education of the Negro*, Washington, D.C.: Associated Publishers.

Zastrow, Charles (1984). *Introduction to Social Work and Social Welfare*, Monterey, CA: Brooks/Cole.

10

THE ONGOING CHALLENGE OF BLACKNESS: A LOOK BACK AND A LOOK FORWARD

Conclusion

How does one measure the magnitude of the BSWM? As indicated previously, there were five major Movement objectives: to create a national forum for Black human service workers; to attack racist practices in social welfare; to assume an advocacy role and remain accountable to the Black community; to contribute to the transformation of mainstream social work; and to develop liberating models for social work practice. Based on a review of historical events, one could only conclude that the magnitude of the Movement was substantial, impacting upon Black human service workers, their clientele, the profession of social work and the larger community. However, there were peaks and valleys in the Movement's activity, with some target areas experiencing greater impact than others.

From the very beginning, the organized protests and subsequent establishment of a national Black social work organization could not be ignored. These actions were too massive. The profession of social work was forced to respond. Ironically, the wide-scale separation of Black professionals from the mainstream presented a major quandary for social work. The separatist action contradicted the basic philosophical and value positions purportedly held by the profession. Social work, a profession that espoused a belief in the worth and dignity of all individuals and historically had championed the cause of the disadvantaged, was being charged with racism—and justifiably so. In the mid-1960s, professional social work mirrored some of the same negative values, hostile actions and forms of institutionalized racism of the larger society. These issues required extensive examination and, eventually, a purging from personal and professional practices. When one examines the current standing of professional social work, substantial changes in the level of participation of African Americans must be noted. The BSWM, which was part and parcel to the larger Black Freedom Movement, was responsible for initiating this process. To suggest that benign professional altruism generated the movement toward equality, acceptance and ethnic and racial integration of its professional ranks is totally indefensible. The aggressive posture and sharp verbalization of demands by Black social work professionals and students forced the profession into action.

The BSWM was born during the turbulence of the 1960s and sustained by calls to Black consciousness. The Movement was successful because it: (1) organized a collectivity of politically ineffective Black social welfare practitioners into action; (2) existed within and outside the formal organization; (3) established goals and objectives for Black social work activists; and (4) influenced the direction of the social work profession. Its major accomplishments included establishing and maintaining a national organization(NABSW); institutionalizing a national communication network for Black social workers; sensitizing social work/social welfare schools, organizations and agencies to unfair, discriminatory practices; legitimizing social advocacy as a primary role for Black social work practitioners; and, to a lesser degree, transforming mainstream social work. The inclusion of African-American students, practitioners and educators into the profession and the expansion of content on the African American experience into educational curricula produced tremendous ramifications. More specifically, student enrollment and activism surged, faculty participation peaked, social agency staff became diversified and local, state and federal officials heeded the call for change made by Black social workers.

Black social workers challenged and engaged every aspect of professional social work. For more than 40 years, they aggressively pushed for radical social change. However, the mere presence of African American faces did not transform the fundamental philosophical and value orientation of the profession. Psychotherapeutic clinical approaches to productive citizenship still remain at the core of professional social work training and practice. The brevity of popularity of other approaches to practice—community organization, planning and social action—suggests that professional social work was unable to maintain and promote social transformation, structural readjustment or any form of radical social change as its primary objective. This, albeit covertly, was an implicit objective of the BSWM.

The BSWM experienced some difficulty in translating the passion of the Black Freedom Movement into the knowledge and skills needed for Black social work practice. The activities of the Movement were all encompassing and included a frontal attack on issues related to welfare, housing, health care, employment, economics, politics, criminal justice, child care, family services, social policy and international relations. And although social activism was the BSWM's strongest suit, it was not an area that could be claimed exclusively as its own. As indicated by Sanders (1970), there were many social activist, anti-racist efforts unfolding in the field of social welfare in particular and society in general. Black social workers needed to prioritize their efforts and lay claim to an area of expertise. In many ways, this was an impossible task. The expansiveness of racism required that Black social workers address all areas affecting the client and the community. What was needed and within the realm of Black social work capability were models of social work practice that would make a difference, models that aided in the social transformation of the African American community.

One must remain mindful that the problems that plagued the BSWM were not isolated from issues that faced both the Black Freedom Movement and the social work profession, i.e., that of purpose and identity. Social work sought to ameliorate societal problems that impacted poor and vulnerable populations. A 20th century phenomenon, social work struggled to define its area of expertise, enhance its public image and foster its acceptance as a full-fledged profession. Social work has suffered from an identity crisis that stemmed, in part, from its

217

inability to achieve professional respect, social status and compensation congruent with other professions.

Seeking a stronger sense of racial identity for African Americans here at home and those in the diaspora, the Black Freedom Movement demanded a higher level of consciousness from members of the community. Such awareness often resulted in the desire to commit oneself to action to help alleviate the harmful effects of racial domination and social oppression in the Black community. Some, but not all, members of the community would accept this challenge.

The BSWM sought to create a safe haven for the racially conscious Black social work professionals who were struggling with these issues. Perhaps those who have been involved in the BSWM can best be described as generic freedom fighters and human service advocates. In all probability, what initially attracted many Black social workers to the profession of social work and the BSWM was the opportunity to advance the cause of social justice through the fair distribution of social resources and social supports. Social work provided the opportunity to fight for the rights of the oppressed and disadvantaged as a paid social advocate, and to do so while simultaneously committed to the cause of Black freedom. The efforts of all who attempted to do so have been duly noted.

NABSW served as the focal point for Black social work organizing and activism. However, much like a reflection of the many issues and ideological positions that dominated the larger Black Freedom Movement, Black social work activists were not a monolithic group. Rather, they could be classified into three major categories: nationalists, social integrationists and pragmatists.

The nationalists represented the same wide spectrum of ideological beliefs and philosophies that permeated the larger movement. There were varying combinations of Pan-Africanists, cultural-nationalists and social separatists, and they shared a common ground: Blackness. Their desire to belong to the organization and labor to implement its goals and objectives appeared inexplicably linked to the primacy of their identity as a Black person. Perhaps they can best be described as those who possessed an Afrocentric orientation or worldview.

Social integrationists, on the other hand, saw little need for the separation of Black social work practitioners from the professional mainstream. They were likely to express the view that working within the traditional structure was the best strategy to achieve the desired change. Social integrationists tended to identify themselves as professional social workers first, then as activist members of the Black community.

And for a variety of reasons, pragmatists attempted to create a presence in both camps. For example, many Black social workers felt the need to possess professional credentials that they believed could only be acquired as a member of NASW. Some Black social workers argued that since many social service agencies advertised for social work positions that required a social work license, they were compelled to join NASW and participate in continuing education training and workshops. Others pointed to the inherent contradiction in attempting to belong to both NABSW and NASW. These organizations were diametrically opposed on at least one major issue: the licensing of the profession.

None of these above-listed categories existed in pure form. Rather, aggregates of Black social workers could be located along varying points of the continuum. And although these various orientations existed within the organized Movement, the compelling desire to present a unified front sometimes resulted in the inability to reconcile differences and resolve minor conflicts. Finally, NABSW was both a professional and social activist organization. Its broad-based social agenda was difficult to maintain and implement. This proved to be an ongoing dilemma for the organization.

Future Directions

More than 40 years have passed since the initiation of the BSWM and the creation of NABSW. While the popular Movement has all but faded away, members of the NABSW confirm that the Movement to uplift and improve the quality of life for African Americans is far from over. There is a spirit and resiliency that cannot be dampened. Within the formal organization, there is a core, diehard membership, recently strengthened by a younger generation who are diligently preparing for the next surge of social activism. By its very definition, social movements are emergent phenomenon in a constant state of flux. Internal and external forces continually shape the character, direction and context of movement activity. There are periods of extreme activism, tempered by temporary resting periods.

One of the larger questions regarding the continuation of NABSW and other Black organizations is simply this: Just how "Black" does the community want to be? This "challenge to Blackness," as first articulated by Bennett (1972), asked Black Americans to clarify and add meaning to their cultural values, attitudes, beliefs and orientations, all of which provided the community with a sense of "peoplehood." Today, one might question: Does race still matter, and if so, who will champion the cause of the Black community? The BSWM and NABSW emerged as the result of visible disparities that existed in American society in general and the social welfare system in particular. Social advocates joined forces to attack racist and discriminatory practices that impeded social progress in the Black community. As indicated previously, a plethora of Black organizations were founded or strengthened during this peak period of social activism as members of the Black community targeted specific areas of need. While much has been accomplished, the larger goal of freedom, liberation, full equality and equitable distribution of societal resources has not yet been fully achieved. As former NABSW president Judith Jackson (2009) notes:

> *"One only needs to look at the current conditions in the Black community to realize that our job is not over. The persistence of social disparities and social despair that exist within the younger generation of Black folks may very well lead to the resurgence and revitalization of NABSW. The problems of our people are too great to ignore."*

Following the election of Barack Obama as the 44th president of the United States, discussions about postracial America emerged. This may have given some the false impression that race matters were a thing of the past, that we now live in a colorblind nation where opportunities and outcomes have been equalized. However, as we approach the 2010 Census, members of the Black social work community anticipate some of the same negative findings that were evident at the turn of the century (U.S. Census, 2004). The major social indicators will demonstrate continued racial disparities in housing, education, employment, health, wealth, wages, violence, incarceration and premature death. Attention to these areas remains the primary focus of NABSW and other social work activists.

In the 20th anniversary reflection on the growth of NABSW, Johnson stated that "Through its organization structure and function NABSW sought to improve or change service delivery and conceptual framework of service as practiced in the African American community" (1988:12). This goal, while not yet fully realized, remains within reach of Black social work activists. The challenge is still upon us.

References:

Bennett, Lerone (1972). *The Challenge of Blackness*, Chicago: Johnson Publishing Co.

Johnson, Audreye (1988). *Reflections on the History and Growth of the National Association of Black Social Workers*, New York: NABSW.

Sanders, Charles (1970). "Growth of the Association of Black Social Workers," *Social Casework*, (May), pp. 270 – 279.

U.S. Census (2004). "The Black Population in the United States," March, (PPL-186).

Past Presidents

Cenie Williams
(Ancestor) 1970-1974

Jay Carrington Chunn
1974-1978

Howard V. Brabson
1978-1982

William T. Merritt
1982-1986

Morris F.X. Jeff Jr.
(Ancestor) 1986-1990

Gerald K. Smith
(Ancestor) 1990-1994

Leonard G. Dunston
1994-1998

Rudolph C. Smith
1998-2002

Judith D. Jackson
2002-2006

Gloria Batiste-Roberts
2006-2010

223

Building an Organization requires commitment, dedication and self-sacrifice. The men and women in NABSW demonstrate all these qualities as they work to build an effective organization. The above picture was taken at NABSW Steering Committee meeting held in Washington, D.C. Left to Right, Jay Chun, National Vice President, Cenie J. Williams, Jr., National President, Jim Madry, National Secretary, Janice Thomas, Washington Chapter representative, Jerry Hubbard, President Detroit Chapter, and Jim Ryan, President Richmond Chapter.

NABSW Steering Committee Meeting, Washington, DC

ABSW Newspaper frontpage, March 1972

ABSW Newspaper frontpage, March 1972

Howard Brabson, Audrey Johnson

225

Twelfth Annual Conference Statement from
Howard Brabson, National President

It is a great pleasure, as your National President, to welcome our chapters and each of you individually to the Twelfth Annual Conference. The theme for the Conference is "Developing an Action Plan: Social, Economic and Political Directions for the Black Community." The theme charges us to develop plans of action which are applicable at the local, state, regional and national level. These plans must be inter-related and directed toward improving the social, political and economic conditions of Black people.

The focus of our attack should be consistent with our social welfare agenda. This means we must continue to fight the oppression of Black people. We must fight the battle of resource distribution with both public and private organizations. It is also important that we address the problem of providing our own resources, thereby gaining more control over resources usage. Plans to achieve this goal must include Black people in general and our Association's units in particular. The focus of such plans must be economic and political development in the Black community.

It is important that we as people gain control over our own resources to enhance the economic conditions of our people. We must develop plans to provide more jobs. We must socialize our people to use the resources that they develop within their community; thereby enhancing the community economically. Such goals are within our grasp, we need only to make the first move.

The purpose of this conference is to develop plans to enable us to make the first moves. As you examine the critical issues and problems which serve as barriers to the achievement of these goals, it is important that you: (1) examine education as a tool of liberation; (2) study various political and social actions necessary for goal achievement; (3) design plans of actions to be used in the political, social and economic arenas for goal attainment; and (4) dedicate yourselves and your chapters and the national organization to the accomplishment of these goals.

We owe such an effort to our Black community. Time is of essence. Hard work and follow-through are necessary to goal achievement. The question is: Will you commit yourselves to the task at hand? I am sure the answer is yes to the question. Therefore, the time to start is now in each of the workshops.

Your Brother in the Struggle.

Howard V. Brabson, D.S.W.
National President

7

YOUR QUARTERLY CONNECTION TO THE AFRICAN DIASPORA

NABSW

National Association of Black Social Workers, Inc.

October 2002

JUDITH JACKSON MAKES NABSW HISTORY

A new page was written into the history of the **National Association of Black Social Workers** on April 5, 2001, in Albuquerque, New Mexico, when *Judith D. Jackson* of Detroit, Michigan, was elected the "first woman president" of the 34-year old organization. Mrs. Jackson is no stranger to NABSW. She began her involvement as a graduate student while attending Washington University over 20 years ago. Since that time, she has been actively involved on both the National and local levels, serving as National Conference Chair, National Treasurer, and most recently as National Vice President. She has also served as President of the Detroit Chapter (the largest chapter in our organization), and has worked on numerous task forces and committees, both locally and nationally. Choosing as her theme, "The Right Leader at the Right Time for All the Right Reasons", Mrs. Jackson plans to embark on an aggressive campaign to make NABSW the major social welfare organization of the new millennium advocating for the needs of African Americans. Also on her agenda is making NABSW visible on the national scene, influencing those who make public policy and advocating for innovative programs and new approaches to service delivery. She states, "Priority attention in this decade must be given to dealing with social issues affecting people of African descent and to insure that NABSW thrives and grows as an independent, cohesive force in this country. . .and to continue NABSW's collaborative initiatives including health education, AIDS, juvenile justice, and reparations."

In a most impressive and spiritual Installation Ceremony marking this historic NABSW occasion, Mrs. Jackson was embraced with words of wisdom and encouragement from past presidents, Dr. Howard V. Brabson, Dr. Morris F. X. Jeff, Jr., Dr. Gerald K. Smith, Leonard G. Dunston, and outgoing president, Rudolph C. Smith. They also presented the "Queen" with gifts and expressions of love.

President Jackson is the Vice President/COO of the Detroit Youth Foundation (DYF), an outgrowth of W. K. Kellogg's long-standing commitment to youth development in Detroit's northern high school area. She is the former Executive Director of Franklin-Wright Settlement, Inc., Michigan's oldest settlement house. In addition to her NABSW involvement, Mrs. Jackson is active in many civic and community organizations.

A graduate of Indiana University, where she earned a Bachelor of Arts Degree, Mrs. Jackson received a Master of Social Work in Policy and Planning from Washington University in St. Louis, Missouri. She has also taken course-work towards an MBA from Lawrence Technological Institute, as well as pursuing continuing education from the American Management Association. President Jackson comes to us well qualified to lead NABSW to higher heights!!

L.A. Conference A Big Success – 5,000 Attend

Left to right: Jim Madry, Paul Hubbard, member, Howard Brabson and Dewey Lawrence.   Sisters relaxing at L.A. National Conference.

NABSW Newspaper image, September 1974

NABSW Newspaper frontpage, April 1981

National Association of Black Social Workers News

Vol. 1, No. 7   NABSW, 1969 Madison Ave., New York, N.Y. 10035   APRIL 1981

Joan Coleman, NABSW co-founder (left)
with NABSW officers, 2009

Dr. Dorothy Height (seated) with NABSW members
at 2009 annual conference in Washington

NABSW Headquarters in Washington, DC

AMANDALAbelize (Belizean newspaper)
story highlighting NABSW July 31, 2005

Sunday, July 31, 2005   *AMANDALABelize*   Page 18

Expanding linkages among the African Diaspora
African-American social workers hold conference in Belize

Dr. Sandra Mitchell (left), chair, international conference; Judith Jackson, president

Participants in the 31st International Education Conference visit KREMANDALA

NABSW Fall 2006 Newsletter annoucing transition
of founding mother Audreye E. Johnson

Roots adoption agency poster

231

Congressman Walter Fauntroy and William Merritt

International Conference in Kenya. Betty Shabazz, far left,
Coretta Scott King, far right,1985

Maulana Karenga

Shirley Better,
NABSW co-founder

Thaddeus Mathis

Molefi Kete Asante

Tricia Bent Goodley

Index

Symbols

100 Black Men and Women 91

A

Abarry, Abu S. 81, 135, 207, 208, 210, 212
ABSW Child Adoption and Research Center 174
Adoption
  Transracial
    Black Family Adoption Agencies 93
Academy for the Certification of African-Centered Social Work xiii, xv, 80, 109, 192, 223
Action Beyond the Rhetoric xiii, xv, 80, 93, 109, 223
Adams, John Hurst xiii, xv, 80, 109, 152, 223
Addams, Jane xiii, xv, 15, 39, 80, 109, 223
Adler, Alfred xiii, xv, 80, 109, 124, 223
Adoption xiii, xv, 80, 109, 223
Adoption and Safe Families Act xiii, xv, 80, 109, 174, 223
Adoption Assistance and Child Welfare Act of 1980 170
Adoption History Project 170, 179
Affirmative Action xiii, xv, 80, 109, 158, 223
A Fist Full of Families xiii, xv, 80, 109, 174, 223
African American Adoption and Permanency Planning Agency 174
Africana Social Work 102, 192
African-centered 101, 102, 103, 126, 133, 134, 153, 187, 191, 192, 193, 197, 198, 200, 201, 202, 203, 204, 205
African National Congress 152
Africentric 133, 139, 187, 191, 208, 211
Afro-American Day Parade 54
Afrocentricity 56, 101, 131, 132, 133, 134, 135, 137, 138, 152, 155, 186, 187, 198, 207, 210, 211, 212
Afrocentrists 197
Afro-One Dance 195
Agencies
  Adoption
    Black Adoption and Placement Resource Center 174
AHSA 128
Aid to Families with Dependent Children (AFDC) xiii, xv, 80, 109, 223
Akbar, Na'im 126, 149
Allen, Richard xiii, xv, 60, 80, 109, 223
Alliance of Black Social Workers 36, 40, 130, 162
Alston, Horace xiii, xv, 40, 80, 109, 223
American Association of Group Workers (AAGW) 45
American Association of Medical Social Workers (AAMSW) 45
American Association of Psychiatric Social Workers (AAPSW) 45
American Association of Social Workers (AASW) 45
American Social Science Association 44
Ancestral wisdom 196
Anderson, Marva xiii, xv, 80, 101, 109, 223
Another Choice for Black Children 174
Appelrouth, Scott xiii, xv, 80, 109, 136, 223
Armstrong, Charles B. xiii, xv, 79, 80, 109, 223

DR. PATRICIA REID-MERRITT — best-selling author, educator, scholar and performing artist — is Professor of Social Work and Africana Studies at the Richard Stockton College in Pomona, New Jersey. She is a regular contributor to scholarly journals and magazines. Dr. Reid-Merritt served as founding president of the National Association of Black Social Workers, South Jersey Chapter. Her many accomplishments include the New Jersey State Council of Black Social Workers selection as Social Worker of the Year. A community-oriented activist scholar, she currently serves on the Board of Directors for the National Council for Black Studies. She is married to William T. Merritt, President/CEO National Black United Fund. They have four children